THIS RECRUIT

THIS RECRUIT

A FIRSTHAND ACCOUNT OF MARINE CORPS BOOT CAMP,
WRITTEN WHILE KNEE-DEEP IN THE MAYHEM OF PARRIS ISLAND

KIERAN MICHAEL LALOR

iUniverse, Inc.

New York   Bloomington

This Recruit
A Firsthand Account of Marine Corps Boot Camp, Written While Knee-Deep in the Mayhem of Parris Island

iUniverse books may be ordered through booksellers or by contacting:

iUniverse
1663 Liberty Drive
Bloomington, IN 47403
www.iuniverse.com
1-800-Authors (1-800-288-4677)

ISBN: 978-1-4502-6458-7 (sc)
ISBN: 978-1-4502-6457-0 (dj)
ISBN: 978-1-4502-6456-3 (ebk)

Library of Congress Control Number: 2010915048

Printed in the United States of America

iUniverse rev. date: 11/03/2010

This book is dedicated to the memory of
Lance Corporal Michael D. Glover
KIA Fallujah, Iraq
16 August 2006

Contents

Contents

AUTHOR'S NOTE

What you are about to read is the true story of my enlistment in the United States Marine Corps and subsequent three months as a recruit aboard Marine Corps Recruit Training Depot Parris Island. Because I knew Marine Corps boot camp would be the ultimate trial by fire, I wanted to document my experiences as they happened rather than through the haze of retrospect. Beginning with the trip to the recruiting office, through the day I marched across the parade deck as a newly minted Marine, I kept this journal. Most of it was written at night in the barracks under my blanket using a flashlight. Whenever possible I mailed home my journal entries because getting caught chronicling the events of each day would have brought upon me the merciless fury of the Drill Instructors.

***

Before I shipped to Parris Island a family friend correctly predicted that in boot camp I would see men at their best and worst. As a result I have changed certain names, biographical information, and dates.

***

For most of boot camp the Drill Instructor is the mortal enemy of the recruit. Because of this dynamic I am harshly critical of the Drill Instructors throughout this book. However, removed from the misery of boot camp, I have realized that the training those impeccable Marines provided over twelve grueling weeks on Parris Island has had a positive impact on me as a Marine and as a civilian and will forever be a great source of strength and discipline.

PROLOGUE

Saturday, August 12, 2000

Until today, I'd been a pretty good recruit. In nearly six weeks on Parris Island I've rarely ever been singled-out for punishment by the Drill Instructors (DIs). When I went to sleep last night I was still on-track to follow in my brother's footsteps and graduate as the platoon "Honor Man." But from almost the moment I woke up, things went wrong. What is called "gear accountability" (knowing where your stuff is at all times), is the key to being a good recruit. The guys who can never find what they need when they need it are invariably the same guys who can't march, stand-still, or PT (physical training). Up until today, I had a pretty good track record of accounting for my gear. Now I have become one of the "shit birds."

Early this morning, when it was time to "step off" and head outside and down the ladder well (stairway) to formation, I realized I didn't have my cover (hat) and began panicking. First I frantically checked my cargo pockets. Nothing. Then I searched the area around my rack. No luck. I quietly whispered to some nearby recruits but they hadn't seen it. My last resort, as the entire company was forming up, was to hold up all six platoons and tell Drill Instructor Staff Sergeant Erickson that I didn't have my cover. As the platoon filed out of the squad bay, I bellowed, "Sir, Recruit Lalor requests permission to speak with Drill Instructor Staff Sergeant Erickson." When he gave me the okay to proceed I shouted, "Sir, this recruit lost his cover, Sir." He berated me briefly and then sent me outside to formation with the rest of the company. I stood out in formation with one hand on my head, the standard procedure for recruits who lose their cover. The ridiculous sight of a coverless recruit with his paw plopped on top of his noggin inevitably attracts the DIs from other platoons to come and mock him. After a few minutes of humiliation, Drill Instructor Staff Sergeant Erickson appeared with an old cover he found in the back of the big gear locker. This crisis was over but the bad day was only beginning.

The hump (forced march) out to the rifle range was unremarkable except for some trouble with my boot laces constantly coming untied. After the hump, the platoons competed in a single-elimination tug-of-war tournament. The DIs selected the guys they thought were the strongest. I wasn't one of them. This pissed me off a lot because my whole life I had been chosen for, and excelled in, tug-of-war competitions and sports in general. This was a cruel reminder that at twenty four years old I was quickly moving past my prime and that after more than a month, the DIs didn't view me as one of the twelve strongest guys in the platoon.

As if the lost cover and the tug-of-war disappointment weren't enough, I also had an unpleasant encounter with Drill Instructor Sergeant Willis today. After we moved all our belongings into our new squad bay, it was time to change over into PT gear and begin cleaning our home in the rifle range barracks. We got undressed "by the numbers," and Drill Instructor Sergeant Willis's first order was to remove our right boot. During the hump that very boot came untied and rather than fall behind and be viewed a straggler, I hastily tied a bunch of knots in the laces. Now those knots were haunting me. When the knotted laces prevented me from untying my boot on Willis's count, he bent down, reached around the back of my leg, grabbed the heel of my boot and completely upended me. As I lay on my back, with my foot in the hands of this madman, he pulled and tugged on the boot, indifferent to the fact that he was literally swabbing the floor with my flailing body. When somehow the tied boot came free of my aching-foot, Willis hurled it toward me as I lay in stunned disbelief on the squad bay floor. The size eleven combat boot drilled me in the chest and, although adrenaline prevented it from hurting, it knocked the wind out of me. This was undoubtedly the most furious and frustrated I had been in my life. Defeated, I rose and returned to my spot in front of my footlocker. As I stood online, with one boot on and the other still cradled in my arms, I began shaking violently, consumed by rage, despair, and regret.

God I hate this fucking place.

CHAPTER 1: The Decision

Monday, March 20, 2000

I had been setting deadlines for myself to decide whether or not to go to the recruiter's office for weeks now, but I kept breaking them. My latest deadline came and went Friday. But this morning I was going out to my car before work and I saw a neighbor wearing a Marine Corps bulldog t-shirt identical to one that I got for Christmas when I was eight years old. When I saw this, I knew it was a sign and I finally decided that today would be the day I would go to the recruiter and begin the process of enlisting.

After work, I went to the Poughkeepsie recruiting station and spoke with Sergeant Hackert, a short but solid guy with a small, blond, military-style mustache. Sergeant Hackert, who appeared to be in his mid-twenties, gave me the whole ooh-rah, gung-ho pep-talk. I sat impatiently in his neatly organized office adorned with recruiting posters extolling the virtues of Marine Corps service. There I read brochures about the Marine Corps and fielded questions from Sergeant Hackert about my background to determine whether I was qualified to enlist. Then I watched a video about boot camp and spoke with Gunnery Sergeant Collins, a wiry guy, well over six feet tall who I estimate is in his early thirties. He is the man in charge of this particular recruiting station and used to fly aboard Marine Corps One, the helicopter that flies the President. He flew with both Presidents Bush and Clinton. This bullet on his resume impressed the hell out of me and was a reminder that it is a Marine that salutes the President when he lands at the White House. I am sure the subconscious correlation that the Commander-in-Chief surrounds himself with Marines is why he mentioned it.

I have been seriously considering enlisting in the Reserves for months. I decided once and for all to do it after I saw the guy with the t-shirt this morning, but there was something that gave me an uneasy feeling while I was visiting the recruiters and especially after I left. You know that feeling you get in the middle of your gut when you hear really bad news, like someone you know has died? I've had that queasiness non-stop since I left the recruiters at 6:30 PM. Just before I left, all of these recruiters dressed in their khaki uniform shirts and bright blue pants with the distinctive red stripe were congratulating me for making this decision. I guess all of the handshakes and back slapping left me feeling a little trapped. I went in there looking for information, not necessarily to finalize my commitment to go to boot camp this summer. But here these guys are, praising me for enlisting, which I'm sure is designed to do just what it has and make me feel locked in. I am scheduled to take the physical and the ASVAB (Armed Services Vocational Aptitude Battery) test in Albany on Friday.

I am concerned that my students at the high school where I teach might find out about my plans because two of my seniors have already enlisted with these same recruiters. I don't want any students or other teachers asking me questions or wondering why a guy with a college degree in his second year of teaching high school is enlisting in the Marine Corps. I have not even told the school that I am not coming back to teach next year.

Not too many men stick around for long in Catholic education because it doesn't pay well. Most of the young men teach a couple of years and then either go work at public schools or move on to other careers. Plus, Karl Luther, one of the few men who has taught at the school for a long time, has made it his mission to make my life miserable for most of the two years I've been here. He tried to bully me out of participating in a union-organized "sick-out" my first week of school because he was an administrator trying to quash the union. Despite his unlawful union busting tactics, I participated in the sick-out and my name has been on his shit list ever since. Because of all these dynamics I don't think anyone at the school will be shocked that I'm leaving. That I'm enlisting in the Marine Corps will undoubtedly come as a surprise.

In case you're wondering, the reason I chose the Marine Corps is a simple one. On and off since I was five years old, I've wanted to be a Marine. My dad was in the Marine Reserves and my brother was an active duty Marine. I went to the Virginia Military Institute (VMI) six years ago thinking I was going to be a Marine officer and flirting with the idea of enlisting in the Reserves after my freshman year. My dad wasn't crazy about me enlisting in the Reserves back then, and I was eighteen years old and in military school. Now I am twenty-four, I've been a high school teacher in the two years since graduating from college, and he probably will think it is really ridiculous. I know I'm going to feel that I have to defend this decision to everyone I know and they are all going to think its weird or a bad idea or that I have low self-esteem or some bullshit like that.

Anyway, there are a lot of reasons why I am doing this. The primary reason I enlisted is a patriotic desire to serve this great country that I have had for as long as I can remember. Serious thoughts about enlisting began again in January when I went to Washington DC over the long Martin Luther King Jr. holiday weekend. While in D.C., I saw the new Korean War Memorial. Etched in dark black marble beside large silver statues of soldiers dutifully slogging through a cold Korean winter, are the words "FREEDOM IS NOT FREE." These four words made me start to wonder if I had been freeloading and enjoying the prosperity of America without meaningfully contributing to it. This rekindled the desire I've had since I was a kid to pick up a rifle and serve my country.

At parades and on the Fourth of July I always feel like I can't be patriotic because I never served my country. It sounds ridiculous even to me but I can't help feeling this way. It's not that you have to have been in the military to be a patriot; it's just that I have always wanted to do it, so I feel like I have some unfinished business.

Another reason for enlisting is the fact that there is still a big part of me that regrets leaving VMI. VMI is a military college in Lexington, Virginia. When I was there for two semesters from 1994–95 it was the last all-male military college in the country. About a year after I left, the Supreme Court ruled that an all-male, state-run college was unconstitutional. I went there for my freshman year and endured what is called the "Rat Line" where the upper-classmen who run the Corps of Cadets dominate your life. I left, frankly, because I didn't care to live such a regimented lifestyle with classes Monday through Saturday and lights out at 11:00 PM. I was doing push-ups and getting screamed at by upperclassmen while my high school buddies were doing keg stands and chasing girls.

Adding to my decision to transfer from VMI to a normal college was finding out at Christmas that my dad had cancer.

I hated being in Virginia at a school where you couldn't have a car until you were a senior and needed formal permission from a Colonel to go home to see your sick dad. While I was at VMI, my dad had a couple of big chunks of his lungs removed and went through chemo and radiation treatment. Eventually he got better and his cancer is a distant memory. Even though it was a very close call it always seemed inevitable that he'd beat it. Old Marines are hard to kill.

I also have some practical reasons for enlisting, such as the boost military service might give my application when I apply to law school. On the less practical side, I still hold the unrealistic and very immature dream that I might be able to play college football in law school and enlisting will help me achieve that. A twenty-five-year-old walk-on who hasn't played organized football in almost seven years is a little less ridiculous if he is a Marine who recently graduated from Marine Corps Recruit Training. Plus, the Reserve G.I. Bill will provide me with a little income to make it easier to pursue my law degree. Although I don't talk about it, in twenty years I might want to run for Congress or something. If I do, I don't want to be one of those guys criticized for never having "worn the uniform." He might be exaggerating or flat out bullshitting me, but Sergeant Hackert told me today that one-third of Congress served in the Marines, or maybe he said a third of Congress served in the military; I can't remember.

Maybe it was because I had four or five cups of coffee, but I left the recruiter with a weird sense that I had just made I huge mistake that I am going to deeply regret. In the four hours since I exited the recruiting station I have continued to have this feeling that I did the wrong thing. I need to talk to my parents to get my birth certificate and high school diploma to complete my enlistment package but I am embarrassed that they will think this is a foolish decision.

I keep trying to remember if I had these same thoughts when I was deciding on VMI. I don't think I had these reservations then because I was too naive or young or dumb or all of the above. I actually thought my year at VMI would make this decision a lot less of a big deal but I am worried about a lot of things. Will I be homesick like I was at VMI? Am I still in good enough shape to do this? Am I going to be absolutely miserable for the twelve weeks of basic training and the ten weeks of infantry school? Is it going to suck spending one weekend a month and two weeks a year drilling over the next six years of my life? Is there a chance I could be activated and sent to war? Should I become an officer even though I would have to be on active duty for four years? If you said to me this morning, "You are going to be very unsure that this is what you want to do after you go to the recruiter," I would have thought you were nuts. But before VMI, I would never have thought I would get homesick down in Virginia and I was more homesick than anyone there.

I am supposed to check in at the recruiter's office tomorrow to see if everything is "good to go" but I'm dreading doing it because I am afraid taking that next step will bring more doubt. I also know if I don't do this I'll regret it forever. At every parade when I hear the Marine Corps hymn I'll feel like more of a pansy than I already do. Every July Fourth I will feel more unworthy to be patriotic than now. Every time I see a war movie I'll hate myself for wussing out twice, at VMI and now. Actually three times, because four years ago when I was a sophomore at Providence College I went to the recruiters and took a practice ASVAB test. I never went any further than that because I didn't want to give up my summer of hanging out with my friends.

I'm hoping that a night's sleep will remove all the nagging pessimism. However, I know when the lights go off and I am all alone in my bed, today's decision will consume me. This feels like the biggest decision of my life but it shouldn't. It's only six months active and then one weekend a month. I still can't get over the fact that I'm this worked up about it. I feel like it's a done deal and there's something bad that they are not telling me and there is nothing I can do about it.

I'm also afraid that if I back out, the recruiters will tell the kids in my class who are enlisting. Having my students find out I signed up then backed out would be a hundred times worse than having them find out I was joining. I'm probably just overreacting and I'm going to read this tomorrow or down the road and be embarrassed by what a drama queen I am being.

Friday, March 24, 2000

I went up to the Albany, New York MEPS (Military Entrance Processing) last night with my recruiter and took the ASVAB Exam. It was a pretty easy test. There were some weird questions like "name that tool" with a picture of a screw and you had to pick which tool went with it. No problem. But some of the questions were very technical about mechanical things that I knew nothing about. This type of question pretty much kicked my ass because I am the least handy person alive. Overall, I'm sure I did pretty well: the test is designed to see if you are smart enough to get into the USMC not M.I.T.

After the test, the other enlistees and I were shuttled to a hotel in Troy, NY, which is about fifteen minutes outside of Albany. We had dinner on the government's dime in the hotel restaurant and then went to bed. At 4:30 this morning we got up, ate, and took a van back to MEPS for the physical. This had to be the most boring day of my life. "Hurry up and wait" is often used to describe military life and it perfectly describes my day at MEPS.

Basically, you wait online to get blood drawn then rush to a never-ending line to take a piss test, then a flexibility test, and so on. This goes on all morning and half the afternoon.

Eventually we got to the only bright spot in the day. They put us all in a fancy mahogany room with an American flag and the flags of all of the military branches and we swore to uphold the Constitution and all that good All-American, apple pie stuff that I love. Pledging to serve my country, surrounded by pictures of Elvis Presley, Ted Williams and other icons swearing into the military, made this horribly tedious day worth it. At around 4:00 PM my recruiter picked me up and drove me home.

Thursday, March 30, 2000

When he was in the Marine Corps, my brother Patrick sustained a horrible broken leg while working on the flight deck of a ship in the Mediterranean Sea. He and some other Marines were unloading a cannon off of a helicopter and Pat's leg got pinched between a forklift and a trailer hitch. When he stumbled, the weight of the cannon shifted and came crashing down on his leg. He had to have a series of surgeries and had metal rods inserted into his legs and eventually got medically discharged. His leg has healed and he still plays tackle football on Thanksgiving and works a physically demanding job. However, I think my mother associates enlisting in the Marine Corps with my brother's injury. This is one reason why I have put off informing my parents about enlisting.

Another thing that makes me hesitant to tell my parents about joining is the fact that my decision to go to VMI after high school was sort of an unspoken compromise between my mother and me. I was thinking of enlisting right after high school but somehow ended up on the path toward a military college. I only applied to two colleges: VMI and the Citadel, which is a military school in South Carolina comparable to VMI. By selecting VMI as my college choice, my mother got what she wanted in that I was going to college and earning a degree. I got what I wanted because I was working toward a commission in the Marine Corps.

My decision to leave VMI and chart the course I have taken in the intervening five years, in effect erased any worries my mom had about me joining the military; until now. It is not that she is anti-military. In fact she is a great patriot and was extremely proud of my brother's Marine Corps service. It is just that she is a mother who is worried about her son. I know my mother well and I'm sure when she gets used to the idea she will be extremely supportive. Still I'm not in looking forward to making the announcement.

Saturday, April 1, 2000

It took me almost two weeks, but today I finally told my parents about my decision to leave my teaching job and enlist in the Marine Corps. As I unveiled my plans, tears welled in my mother's eyes. While my mom tried to convince herself that it was an April Fool's joke, my dad, after quietly absorbing the initial shock, was very supportive. He enthusiastically asked questions about when I'd be shipping to Parris Island, what changes there were to boot camp since he was a recruit in 1962, and what he could do to help me get my affairs in order before I go. My little sister Meghan, a junior in college, happened to be home when I dropped the bombshell and asked if I was "having a mid-life crisis at age twenty-four?"

On the surface my decision appears to be immature and irrational but I know it is something I have to do. I have only told my parents some of the more practical reasons for my decision, like the G.I. Bill for law school and stuff like that. The core of my decision is the desire to fulfill a boyhood dream, follow in the footsteps of the generations of American men who have served in the Marine Corps and exorcise the demons of VMI.

Anyway, I feel good that I have broken the news and have gotten it over with.

Tuesday, July 4, 2000

I came up to Albany this evening because tomorrow I leave for Recruit Training. I was actually supposed to come to Albany tomorrow afternoon, but the recruiters moved up the time for some unknown reason. The recruiters ship guys to boot camp all the time so it is not a big deal whether I leave Tuesday night or early Wednesday morning. To them it's just an insignificant number of hours. To me, the difference between Tuesday night and Wednesday morning is everything because I want to enjoy my last night of freedom before I spend the next three months at boot camp away everyone I know. At one point they were trying to get me to head up to Albany on Monday night but I had to tell them no because I still needed to move everything I own out of my apartment into my parents' house.

I spent all of last night and this morning moving with the help of my buddies Dave and Goober. Goob flew home unexpectedly from Chicago, where he is working this summer, to hang out one last time before I left. I had dinner with my parents and then we said our goodbyes. Thankfully the goodbye wasn't as teary as I had anticipated. My mom stood her ground, shedding no tears at all, which shocked the hell out of me. When my parents dropped me off at VMI six years ago and it was time to say goodbye my mother was balling so badly the chaplain came over to comfort her. I was eighteen then and now I'm twenty-four so I guess that explains why Mom was able to keep her composure. As I expected, my dad offered a couple of words of encouragement telling me to "do your best," to obey the DIs and to try to have fun. As I left to be third member of our immediate family to claim the title United States Marine he beamed with pride and gave me a hug. Then, at 7:30 PM, my buddy Dave drove me to the recruiter's office so the recruiter could drive me to Albany to begin the adventure.

I rode up with two recruiters and a couple of guys who just graduated high school a few weeks earlier. One of these characters was supposed to leave for boot camp a week ago but got arrested for a pulling a senior prank. He and "his boys" let the air out of the tires of the school district's entire fleet of buses and forced the district to cancel school. I remember reading about it in the paper a few weeks back. From what I can tell, recruiters are good at getting guys out of trouble and judges and district attorneys are usually agreeable to let a guy off lightly if he is enlisting.

The other kid with us had to drive all the way up to Albany, stay overnight in a hotel, and spend all day at MEPS because they spilt his original piss test. Essentially, this kid, who had a week left before leaving all of his friends and family for boot camp, had to waste a day and a half just to take a wiz.

As we drove north on the New York State Thruway to Albany, passing a local Independence Day fireworks display every few minutes, I couldn't help but think how appropriate it was to be leaving for Marine Corps Boot Camp on the 224th birthday of the country. Last year, I spent the Fourth playing in a baseball tournament at Doubleday Field at the Baseball Hall of Fame in Cooperstown thinking that was the most patriotic thing you could do on the Fourth of July. But this definitely tops that.

I've been worried for the past week that I'm going to weigh more than 216 pounds, which is the maximum weight for a guy five feet eleven inches. If I'm over the weight I'm not sure what will happen but I don't want to be sent home because I'm too fat. I sort of dieted the past few days but it is almost impossible to lose weight on Fourth of July weekend. I might even go on a run through the streets of Troy early tomorrow to lose some water weight and burn off the Sam Adams I had with dinner.

As I sit in my hotel room I still have a few things to take care of. I have to decline an invitation to the wedding of an old high school friend because I will be at Parris Island. Believe it or not, I still have a few bills to pay and I wanted to write my parents to thank them for their support and tell them all the things I avoided telling them in person when we said goodbye because I was afraid it would be awkward and lead to a lot of tears.

I watched TV in my hotel room hoping like hell that there'd be something good on because this will be my last time in front of the boob tube for a long time. Ironically, the Discovery Channel just ran a documentary on what else? Marine Corps boot camp at Parris Island. Of course I couldn't resist and I watched the whole show intently.

Even after watching the documentary, I'm really not nervous at all. I thought for sure I would be very anxious but I'm actually quite relaxed. I know at some point in the next twenty four hours it's going to hit me that my life for the next three months will be unlike anything I have ever experienced. I guess the reason I'm not nervous is because tomorrow is going to be so long and boring because of all the administrative bullshit and obligatory sitting around and waiting.

Wednesday, July 5, 2000

The phone rings at 4:30 AM. It's my very early wake up call but I really don't mind because I'm anxious to get started and get this adventure underway. My roommate in the hotel was a guy who is joining the Navy tomorrow. It was kind of uncomfortable though because he had his girlfriend spend the night in the hotel room. I'm not sure if this annoyed me because it made my last night of civilian life socially awkward or because I was jealous that he was smarter than me and arranged to have a girl meet up with him in Troy.

After showering and shaving, I bought the newspaper because I love to read the paper every day, but also because I know from past experiences at MEPS that there will be a ton of sitting around with nothing to do but read.

A couple of vans took me and the other "new joins," representing every branch of the Armed Forces from our motel in Troy to the federal building in downtown Albany which houses MEPS. Of course, in classic military style the vans arrive at the federal building at 5:45 AM and the damned building doesn't even open until 6:00 AM. Before the day even really begins we are already standing around with nothing to do. Luckily, I had my trusty newspaper to read.

After filling out some paperwork, I get a ridiculously brief physical from the doctor who basically looked at me for a half second and asked if anything had changed since my comprehensive physical in March. Nothing had changed, and even if it had there was no way I would have volunteered any of that information to this guy and risk delaying my departure or, worse, stop me from going.

Finally, at around 7:00 AM it was time for the big weigh-in. I have been on a half-ass diet for the past week. I don't know what the consequences are for being overweight but my brother Patrick, who went to boot camp in 1989, told me about "Pork Chop Platoon" where the fat guys go in boot camp to train and get ridiculed by their instructors and by their fellow recruits until they are fit enough to start regular boot camp. I don't know if my ego could endure that horrible fate.

When I stepped on the old fashion scale, the doctor set the first knob to 150 pounds and I was thinking "is this guy freakin' crazy?" There is no way I'm under two hundred pounds. Eventually he realized his mistake and set the first dial at two hundred pounds and the second one wound up at twenty-six pounds. Oh Shit! I was 226 pounds, ten pounds over the max for my height. I looked at the doctor's face to try to interpret his expression but his face was blank. What does this mean? "Pork Chop Platoon?" Getting shipped at a later date? I was going to lose my mind if I didn't find out soon.

I spent the next two hours in the MEPS waiting room reading my paper and a book I had brought about the one thousand most influential people of the past two thousand years. I tried to sleep but there was no way that was happening with my future hanging in the balance. After what seemed like forever, the Marine Corps liaison officer told me and another hefty guy that we had to drive over to the Marine headquarters for a body fat test. Why they couldn't do the test here at MEPS was a mystery to me. But what was I gonna do?

We got to the Albany Marine Corps Headquarters and sat there doing nothing for an hour. Like a jackass, I left my book and newspaper back at MEPS and had nothing to do but sit and stare at nothing and worry if I was going to make weight. I tried to strike up a conversation with the other body fat testee, a guy named Kruder from near Binghamton. Other than his name and hometown, I got little else out of this big farm-boy-looking kid who was at least 6 foot 2, 240 pounds and looked like he should be playing defensive end for Nebraska.

After an eternity, a Marine came and gave me a form to fill out. I had to write a statement explaining why I thought

I was physically able to endure boot camp despite my girth. I wrote something about playing sports and about how I'm a good distance runner. Next they measured my neck, waist and thighs and somehow deduced that I had 17% body fat and was okay to ship to Parris Island. Of course it was another hour of sitting around doing nothing at all until the van returned to take us back over to MEPS.

When I got back upstairs to MEPS, the thirty or so kids who had stayed at the hotel last night were gone. The Marine liaison told me that they went to the airport to fly to wherever it was that their branch of the service was going to train them. Unfortunately, my body fat test took too long and I could not fly to Parris Island until the next day. The Marine liaison assured me that I would still graduate on the same date and that I was actually lucky because that is one less day I'll spend on Parris Island. He explained that the first few days of boot camp aren't really training days. The first couple of days are a matriculation period called "Forming" where everybody is processed. He said recruits arrive all week and that training would not start until the following Monday or Tuesday.

At around 3:00 PM I found myself down on the sidewalk in front of the federal building waiting for a government van to drive me back to Troy to spend my last afternoon and night of freedom with two strangers in a motel room. The other two guys waiting for the van were Kruder, the no-talker from Binghamton, and another little guy named Bilderband who couldn't stop talking about how many scholarships he had to college and what a big wrestling star he was in high school. I knew I would lose my mind if I had to sit around, bored stiff in godforsaken Troy, New York with these two clowns on my last night before boot camp. One of my best friends, Mike

Rooney, works at a bar somewhere in downtown Albany. I decided I'd go on a pre-boot camp reconnaissance mission to find Rooney and suck down a few beers with him and live it up a little before I left.

When I told Kruder and Bilderband I was not going to take the shuttle back with them they looked at me as if I were insane and probably were thinking to themselves, "This fat old bastard is pussing out already." Anyway, I started walking the streets of Albany looking for the Big House Brewing Company, a place I'd been to a couple of times but not recently and never during the daytime. After only a couple of wrong turns, at around 3:30 PM, I found my friend's place of employment. Rooney was shocked to see me. I explained the situation, and we made plans for after he got out of work that night. He gave me the keys and directions to his apartment so I could go and sleep and do whatever I had to do until 10:00 PM when he got off work.

When Rooney got home we met up with his roommate Mike Glover and went to the bar across the street and I ate what I considered my "Last Supper." I managed to shove just about every appetizer on the menu down my throat and chased it with a bacon cheeseburger and a few icy cold pints of Sam Adams. I consciously savored every gluttonous bite and each tasty sip. I had been watching what I ate for a week in preparation for the weigh-in, which we now know I sort-of failed. Now, however, I was reasonably certain that I was not going to be weighed again any time soon and that I was going to make up for all of the good eating I had missed over the Fourth of July weekend and all of the grub I was going to miss over the next three months. As I gorged myself and watched the Yankees on TV, I fielded questions from Rooney and Glover about whether or not I was nervous and what I expected boot camp to be like. I was so glad I didn't get on that shuttle back to the hotel and I enjoyed this extra night of freedom. I guess being a fat ass has its advantages.

Thursday, July 6, 2000

I got up at 5:30 AM and Rooney drove me down to the federal building. I underwent some more administrative things, filled out about a million forms and had to swear that I had not made a fraudulent enlistment. A fraudulent enlistment is when you lie about past drug use or about some injury or illness you once had. The Marine liaison told us it's better to get it out now because if you get down to Parris Island and they find out you lied about something it is a crime and you can go to jail for eighteen months and get a $25,000 fine. Incredibly, some guys had a sudden urge to come clean on what they lied about earlier. The way it works, the recruiter wants you to tell him everything so he can get the waivers for any problems and get credit for signing you up. If you get to MEPS and then tell the liaison that you smoked weed a few times in high school but didn't tell the recruiter, the recruiter looks bad because he was unable to get it out of you. The liaison's job is to get you to come clean at the last minute. From what the liaison said, the guys who do the "Moment of Truth" on Parris Island must be the final line of defense against fraudulent enlistments.

I have nothing to hide and I'm heading to the airport in an hour or so. The guys who came clean about a fraudulent enlistment to the liaison were escorted out of the waiting room. I'm not sure what happened to them but I think they get their balls busted and so long as the indiscretion is not too outrageous, they eventually ship to boot camp.

I'm flying out of Albany Airport with a stopover at Reagan National in D.C. I'm thrilled that my trek to Parris Island will pass through Reagan National because Ronald Reagan was President when I was growing up and because he is my second favorite President of all-time behind the Rough Rider, Teddy Roosevelt.

They gave us each a $16 voucher for dinner but for some reason we're not allowed to use it until we stop in Washington. The Marine liaison told us that the voucher is only good for one purchase. If you go to McDonald's and get a $5 value meal they don't give you the government's $11 bucks back; it's just gone. As a good Reagan Republican, I was hell bent on getting the government's $16 dollars worth, but trying to get the biggest bang for the government's buck lead me to embarrass myself during my layover. I miscalculated and my bill at the airport terminal pizza stand came to a whopping $17.50. I didn't have any cash to pay the difference because I was told not to bring money to boot camp. Red faced, I had to tell the pizza clerk to take away one of my eight slices. I stopped being hungry after the fourth slice but I was determined to finish every last piece because this is definitely the last thing I'm going to eat as a civilian.

I was told that it was best to arrive at Parris Island empty-handed so I just threw out the book I had been reading. I know this will make the last leg of the journey from D.C. to South Carolina unbearably boring, but I want to conceal the fact that I'm a college grad and a social studies teacher. So showing up with a history book is not a great idea. VMI taught me that in these intense military training situations it is in your best interest to remain as anonymous as possible. I'm already five years above the average boot camp age so I don't want to also become known as the platoon geek. Plus, I don't want the DIs expecting me to know a lot of Marine Corps and military history, because I don't.

There were seven other guys entering the Marine Corps at the airport with me. My initial guess is that six of them are absolute pussies. The guy Kruder from Binghamton is the only guy that seems somewhat tough and he actually looks like a Marine. I guess the coming weeks will test the accuracy of my assessment.

In my pocket, I have two Ripped Fuels which are basically over the counter caffeine pills. I hear you don't get to sleep the first twenty-four hours you are there and I don't want to get a reputation for being tired or lazy or sluggish on the first day. When I get off the bus I'll pop one Ripped Fuel and hold on to the other until I really need it.

I'm starting to ramble now and a few butterflies are whirling around in my stomach. I guess with boot camp looming only a few hours away I'm getting very anxious.

I hear that the Marines pretty much escort you off the plane and onto the bus to Parris Island so this will have to be my last entry for I don't know how long. I plan to mail these journal entries home for safe keeping just as soon as I've written the last word. That is my plan for keeping this journal. I know you get to write letters because I remember corresponding with my brother when he was in boot camp eleven years ago. I want to get the entries home because there is no way I'm going to leave a written record of my experiences, thoughts, and opinions lying around for the Drill Instructors to find.

My connecting flight to Charleston, South Carolina leaves in about a half hour. I just found a mailbox in the airport and in seconds I will drop this journal entry in an envelope and send it home for safekeeping. I'm not sure when my next entry will be but I'm determined to memorize all important events and jot them down the first time I get a chance.

CHAPTER 2: Forming and Picking Up

Thursday, July 13, 2000 (I think)

I've been here one full week and I already feel as if I have been here a year. So far the first day was without a doubt the longest and worst simply because I was so tired, nervous and completely disoriented. After getting up at 4:00 AM on Thursday, July 6, 2000 in Troy, we arrived on Parris Island in the wee hours of Friday, July 7, 2000 and didn't sleep until late Friday night. It had to be close to forty hours without any sleep. I remember sitting on the bus from the Charleston Airport tired and wanting to rest but unable to fall asleep due to anxiety.

The signs advertising hotels near Parris Island tormented me for the last hour of the approximately two-hour bus ride. At the bottom of every billboard advertising a hotel it read *"Only Two Miles From Parris Island."* I fell for this at least a dozen times before realizing the billboard meant that the hotel itself was only two miles from Parris Island and not that we were currently two miles away from the start of boot camp.

When finally we reached the gate at Parris Island, the bus stopped at the guard post and the bus driver told the Marine on duty that she had a bus full of recruits. The Marine came on the bus and yelled at us for no apparent reason. One of the other new joins at the airport had told me that they drive you around in circles once on Parris Island so that you get confused and don't know how to get off the island should you try and escape at some point. I don't know if that's true or an old recruit's tale but it does make sense and it did seem to take a while to get to our first stop on the island.

Just before the bus stopped we drove under a sign that arched the road which read *"Where The Difference Begins."* I wondered whether, at my age, a truly fundamental difference would occur. At VMI they told our parents that when we came home for Thanksgiving break we would be folding our socks and making our bed with hospital corners but that turned out to be a load of crap. If anything I returned from VMI a bigger slob than when I left. We'll have to wait and see what the Marines can do.

As it happens, I sat in the front seat behind the driver with some guy who had to be the dumbest person I have ever met. He was a white kid but he was all decked out in thug gear as if he was a member if the Crips. I could not understand a word this kid said and couldn't help thinking that boot camp is going to eat this stupid sonovabitch alive.

Because my seat was on the aisle right behind the bus driver and nearest the door, I happened to be the first one off. As I was getting off the bus, I panicked and tossed the energy pills I'd been carrying under my seat. I was terrified of what they would do to me if I got caught because I was sure they would think the pills were something a lot worse than caffeine pills.

As a result of being the first to touch down on Parris Island, I was the first to line up on the famous "yellow footprints." The yellow footprints were explained in the documentary I saw on

TV in the hotel in Troy. Everybody stands on a set of footprints, which are lined up in four columns in a marching formation. Of course, I was so disoriented and confused that I jumped off the bus and stood on the footprints facing the wrong way. The Drill Instructor was kind enough to show me the error of my ways, referring to me as a "moron." After they got me facing the proper direction and everybody lined up on the yellow footprints, they marched us through these big, huge, shiny metal doors. Above the doors it said, "*Through These Portals Pass Prospects For America's Finest Fighting Force.*" Reading these words reminded me of why I was here and calmed me down at the same time as it filled me with unprecedented sense of purpose and motivation.

The very first thing we did was get our hair shaved bald, down to the scalp. Some of the guys with pretty locks took it hard but it was not a traumatic experience for me because I'm losing my hair and because I pretty much already had a crew cut anyway. Then we filled out a ton of paperwork, which I swear I already filled out at the recruiter's office and again while at MEPS. I must have signed my name one thousand times that night at these huge steel desks in this big classroom that I remember being so cold it hurt. The next thing they did was let us make a thirty second, collect phone call home to let someone know that we had made it down here safely.

A woman Marine issued us our clothes. She had to be the most obnoxious and miserable person on Earth. She would screech every instruction she gave us at the top of her lungs and you could tell she relished exercising absolute power over seventy or so men. After the wicked witch of Parris Island gave us our uniforms and sneakers, we changed into an olive green t-shirt and matching pair of shorts that serve as underwear. Then we donned our crisp new camouflage trousers and "blouse," which is the unfortunate name for the long-sleeved camouflage uniform shirt. Then we put all of our "civies" in a brown paper shopping bag, put our names and addresses on it and turned in our last connection to the civilian world.

After we got issued our "cammies," toothbrushes, deodorant, boots and assorted other things, which have I since learned we get billed for, they took us to the "chow hall" as the sun was rising. Without exaggeration, it took all seventy of us less than five minutes to get our food, sit down, eat, and turn in our trays. We were literally sprinting through the line as what I think were other recruits in a more advanced stage of training, threw food on our plates. Even the veteran recruits handing out the food screamed at us. "TrayOverChowRecruit!" which means, put your tray over the bin where the slop originates so you don't get any on the floor or on the counter. I was hesitant to look around too much but what I did see were other recruits who have been around a while smirking at us because we are so disoriented by our new surroundings and terrified by the Drill Instructors. The Drill Instructor in charge of us is a tiny little guy named Staff Sergeant Oscar. He is a pissed-off little fellow and you just know he's got the worst Napoleon complex since Napoleon.

After breakfast we got our eyes, ears and teeth checked. Then we got a bunch of shots by Navy medical personnel who seemed to hate us as much as everybody else around here. Even the female Navy personnel screamed at us and belittled us when we made a mistake. The Albany MEPS physical I took back in March was hurry up and wait. This physical can best be described as hurry up, wait and get screamed at for no reason.

***

In Albany they told us not to drink alcohol at the airports because we would be getting a breathalyzer and a urinalysis upon arriving on Parris Island. The urinalysis part was true but there was no breathalyzer, although the threat of it deterred me and I'm sure most others from boozing on the way down.

While on line to get my eyes checked, I dozed off standing up and fell over and felt like a real idiot. I also hallucinated a lot. I would see other recruits or Marines and really believed they were people I knew from home until I regained consciousness and realized how ridiculous that was. Maybe it was the similarity of the situations, but I kept seeing other recruits that I thought were guys I knew at VMI, which blew my mind. For years my subconscious has been warning me not to do this. Pretty regularly since I left VMI I've had a vivid recurring dream that I am back there, doing push-ups, homesick, getting yelled by jackasses, and downright miserable. During the dream I am thinking aloud, "Why the hell did I do this to myself?" Now I'm actually down here on Parris Island, in that same horrible environment, half-unconscious due to fatigue and my mind is saying to me, "I told you so, asshole."

As advertised, we had the "Moment of Truth" Friday afternoon. Some Marine came and asked to see anyone who had lied to their recruiter or the liaisons at MEPS. Sure enough, a few guys who managed to keep their conscience in-check with their recruiters and at their respective MEPS had a sudden change of heart and told the Marine about their fraudulent enlistment. As with the guys who spilled the beans in Albany, I'm not sure what happened to these guys either.

Friday afternoon we also got issued our weapons. While on line at the armory to get our rifles, a DI came up to me and asked if I was going to pass the IST (Initial Strength Test) which was scheduled for the next day. The IST consists of a 1.5 mile run plus pull-ups and crunches. Passing is relatively easy because you only need to complete the run in 13:30 and do two pull ups and thirty-five crunches. The questioning of my athletic ability pissed me off a lot because despite packing on a few pounds in the two years since I graduated from college, I was still athletic and could run very well and had been practicing crunches and pull-ups for a couple of months before I left.

It was around this time on Friday I got my second wind, so I volunteered to shuttle canteens of water back and forth from the spigot behind the armory to my platoon on the other side of the building. I hate to admit it, but I volunteered for this task solely for the purpose of impressing the DIs, thinking that it was possible to get on their good side and make the next three months run a little smoother. I'm pretty sure that they didn't even notice.

Eventually, my first day on Parris Island came to an end. We were assigned "racks" (bunk beds) based on alphabetical order. Just before he turned out the lights, Staff Sergeant Oscar said that whoever was first alphabetically in the platoon should remain dressed because he had the first hour of something called "Fire Watch," which is another way of saying guard duty. When Staff Sergeant Oscar announced this, Recruit Abate's face completely dropped as if the life was somehow sucked out of him. I felt bad for the guy. I really did. As much as I pitied the poor bastard, I was so glad it wasn't me who had to stay up. Abate would be awake for an extra hour until being relieved by another recruit unfortunate enough to have been born into a family whose name begins with a letter that falls early in the alphabet.

The seventy guys in my platoon live in a huge "squad bay," which is a big room about one hundred feet long and thirty feet wide. There are twenty or so bunk beds on each side of the squad bay. We all have a footlocker, which is basically a Marine Corps name for a trunk. The most common command we get around here is "Get on-line" which basically means that we stand at attention in front of our footlocker with our heels on a line that surrounds the squad bay.

Right now it is late evening. Before we hit the rack we get a few minutes to write letters and shine our boots. We are all lined up in two long rows sitting on the back edge of the footlocker, leaning over and writing on the front edge of the footlocker. We sit pretty much shoulder to shoulder and my knees and feet actually touch the guys on either side of me if I move around too much.

***

On Saturday, July 8, we took the IST. I heard if you fail it you get banished to "Pork Chop Platoon," which I have learned is officially called "Physical Conditioning Platoon" or PCP. Obviously most of the guys in PCP are fat and out of shape, hence the derogatory moniker. I knew I would pass the test fairly easily but for some reason I was worried that maybe I'd been practicing the pull-ups all wrong and wouldn't be able to do them the proper way. Even when I was young and in fantastic shape, I still had problems with sit-ups. At VMI, I actually failed the first time we were tested. Running I knew, despite being a little bit on the portly side these days, was not going to be a problem. I beat my recruiter in a 1.5 mile run back in June and my time was like 10:30. Like Forrest Gump said, "You wouldn't know it to look at me but I can run like the wind blows." Unlike Forrest, my speed only applies to distances. Put me in a sprint and I'm slow as shit. Fortunately for me this was a distance race.

All I could think about leading up to the IST was how awful it would be to come down here and fail the IST and get banished to PCP. I'd have to write my family and tell them that I was too out-of-shape even to start boot camp and I didn't know when I'd officially begin training, let alone when I would graduate.

As it turns out I did okay on the IST. And while I wasn't thrilled with my 5 pull-ups, 66 crunches, and 10:29 run time, I was relieved that I wasn't dropped to PCP as four guys in my platoon were.

After the IST, we met our Drill Instructors. That guy, Staff Sergeant Oscar, who had been in charge of us really had nothing to do with us after we met our real Drill Instructors. I guess I wasted my time and energy trying to impress him. Since we "picked-up" on Saturday we have had the same three DIs. Our Senior Drill Instructor is Staff Sergeant Jefferson. He is a white guy, pretty tall, 6 foot 1 maybe 6 foot 2. He is actually very skinny and not all that impressive physically. You might even say he seems a little geeky. Like one of those guys who has never driven even one mile over the speed limit in his life.

The other two drill instructors are Staff Sergeant Erickson and Sergeant Willis. Staff Sergeant Erickson is a blond-haired guy who seems like a pretty-boy. He's not particularly tall, 5 foot 10 if he's lucky, but built pretty well. Sergeant Willis is black guy, stocky but not fat, and when he yells at you his eyes kind of pop out of his head. Willis is a mean mother too and he kind of freaks you out because his tongue and lips are as red as fire. Of the three, Willis is the only one that truly scares me.

***

We pretty much spent the whole day Sunday, July 9, 2000 marking all of our gear with our names, platoon number and our laundry number. By the way, my platoon is #1377, which is very important because we do everything as a platoon and so far we don't really associate with recruits or Drill Instructors outside our platoon. All we ever hear about is how we are the worst platoon the Drill Instructors have ever seen. Maybe the younger guys buy that crap but I know that's all part of the game.

Just so you know, the reason I always write out each Drill Instructor's full title is habit. We have learned the hard way that we must always refer to the Drill Instructors by their full titles. God forbid if you ever say, "Drill Sergeant" to one of them, they'll bite your head off because apparently that term is reserved for the lowly Army boot camp instructors.

It's a huge deal just to take a wiz around here. First you must ask for permission by saying, "Sir, Recruit Schmukatelli requests permission to speak to Drill Instructor Sergeant Willis." If he is gracious enough to give you permission to speak to him you then say, "Sir, Recruit Schmukatelli requests permission to make a head call." These requests must be recited verbatim because you won't be able to go until you get it right, which can take a nervous recruit seven or eight attempts. In case you're wondering, the "head" is the Marines word for the bathroom, although the DIs will from time to time refer to it as the "shitter," "crapper," or "pisser." Incidentally, toilet paper is colorfully known as "shit paper" around here.

By the way, "Recruit Schmukatelli" is the Parris Island way of saying John Doe. When a DI or medical personnel, or just about anyone else, is explaining how to do something they always refer to the generic Recruit Schmukatelli. For example, the night we got here the receiving DIs were explaining how to fill out the forms. They would say "Then sign your name, Recruit Schmukatelli, using your "payroll signature." I have yet to discover what the payroll signature is versus a regular signature. If I figure it out, you'll be the first to know.

***

I estimate that after my $16 government subsidized pizza at the airport, I set foot on Parris Island at a robust 230 pounds. I've been on Parris Island drinking nothing but water and eating about 25% of my normal intake for almost four days. When I got weighed in on Monday, July 10, 2000 for the first time since MEPS, I tipped the scales at 224 pounds. The reason I am crazy about my weight is because a guy my height (seventy-one inches) has to weigh 197 pounds or less to graduate. Along with a dozen or so other recruits in my platoon, I am on what is officially called "diet tray," but known colloquially as being a "fat body." Diet tray basically means we eat chicken and rice every day rather than red meat. We don't get dressing or Bacos on our salad, or peanut butter and jelly on our bread. Nearly four decades ago when my dad was here they left him on diet tray too long and he dropped too much weight. To fix this, they had to put him on the diet they put the really skinny guys on so he could bulk back up. We have a guy who needs to pack on some pounds in our platoon named Daniels who looks just like "Beaker" from the Muppets. That lucky bastard gets to eat "double rations" or "double rats" at every meal, including cookies and a cold glass of milk. In the interest of full disclosure, regular milk is known as "white cow" and chocolate milk is known as "brown cow." Because according to Drill Instructor Sergeant Willis I am "a great big, disgusting fat body," I get no cow.

***

Although it seems like we've been "training" since we got off the bus, Tuesday, July 11, 2000 was technically the first day of training. We got up, ate, cleaned up the squad bay and then went to PT. PT was basically a lot of calisthenics and a mile or so run. One innovation that the Marine Corps has pioneered that I was not familiar with was the dive-bomber push-up. For a dive-bomber you get in a modified push-up position with your legs spread and your ass way up in the air so your body resembles a pyramid. Then you simultaneously swoop down and forward lowering your butt until your back is arched and most of your torso is in front of your hands. Finally, you swing backward and return up at your original position. As with traditional push-ups, two dive-bomber push-ups are equal to only one Marine Corps push-up. Basically, you start in the up position, go down and yell "one." Then back up and yell "two." Down again and yell "three." Back up and yell "one" and that only counts as one damned push-up. So it sounds like this "one-two-three-one, one two three-two, one-two-three-four, one-two-three-five."

After PT, we take what is known as a "PT shower." Everybody strips down except for their shower shoes and towel. To give you an idea of what a fatty I am, I have to hold on to the towel at all times because it's too small to even fit around my waist and tuck in like most of the other guys. To prepare of the PT shower, we line up single file. Then the first guy to get to the shower drops his towel on the bench outside the shower and runs under each of the dozen or so showerheads shooting out freezing cold water. To expedite the process even further, Drill Instructor Sergeant Willis is kind enough scream at us to *"MOVE! MOVE! MOVE!"* Although we don't get all that clean, this method is quite effective. Seventy of us managed to get in and out in just under ninety seconds.

Even though the letter is dated Sunday, July 9 it wasn't until July 11th that we got to send our first letter home. It wasn't even a real letter though. It was a form letter to let our parents know that we were alive. The letter reads:

Dear _____ Date: July 9 2000
I have arrived safely to Parris Island and have been assigned to Platoon 1377, which is comprised of 72 recruits from various parts of the country. Our Senior Drill instructor is Senior Drill Instructor Staff Sergeant Jefferson. He is the one who is responsible for our training here. We will live and train together for the next three months until our graduation on September 29, 2000. There are two other Drill Instructors' assigned to my platoon and I am told there will be at least one with the platoon each day we are here. I will send you their names later. Because of the balanced diet we will be on, it is recommended that you not send packages containing food items. I am enclosing my address to be sure you have the information needed to write me. Be sure you address all mail to me as I have it below.

Recruit Lalor, KM 226-83-9144
Platoon 1377 Alpha Co, 2nd RTBN MCRD
Parris Island, South Carolina 29905-1004

I managed to scrawl a quick note to my parents on the form letter even though I don't think we were supposed to. I thought that if I didn't write anything my parents would think something was wrong, like when you see POWs in movies and they are talking like robots claiming that things are just swell in the concentration camp. I also underlined the part about not sending food because my brother Patrick told me you get tormented if you get food in the mail. According to Pat, they make you stand in front of everyone and eat all of what you are sent in one mouthful in front of everyone. Pat actually threatened to send nasty stuff like pickled eggs and Vienna sausages so I would have to down that nastiness in one bite. I pray to God he was just kidding, but honestly I don't think he was.

It was either Tuesday or Wednesday that we learned some hand-to-hand combat skills. Our platoon and two others spent three or four hours learning how to fall to the ground properly when fighting. Earlier this week we also had our first "Pit Call." Outside each barracks there is a huge sandpit. When the platoon screws up, we go there and do a variety of exercises. In "the Pit" we do push-ups, sit-ups, side straddle hops, up/downs, mountain climbers and the like. Mountain-climbers are probably the worst thing we do in the pit. A mountain climber involves running in place while on all fours on the Senior Drill Instructors command. They suck because the guy in front of you is chugging away kicking tons of sand in your face. Up/downs are also common in the pit. With up/downs, you run in place until the DI tells you to "hit it" and then you dive into the sand and do push-ups until he says "up" at which point you get to your feet and run in place some more. The thing that makes the pit so miserable is that the sand stays in your scalp, on your skin, on your clothes, and even in your ass crack for the rest of the day.

We'll be in the pit going at it for like ten minutes in the blazing South Carolina sun and the Senior Drill Instructor will tell us to stop. On the command "stop" we are all supposed to stand there motionless and listen to the Senior Drill Instructor tell us how worthless we are. Of course, some dumbass always has to scratch or wipe the sweat from his face with his sandy hand and this pisses the Senior Drill Instructor off and we go right back to rolling around in the sand box.

Today we got a close range combat lesson. This time we learned how to strike with our knees and elbows. They make it so clinical and basic that it's pretty unrealistic. You stand there like a boxer in a "warrior's stance" and the instructor says "A-TTACK" and you elbow your partner. In real life, the guy would not be standing there letting you clobber him with a perfectly clean shot. Regardless, it was still pretty fun stuff to learn although I hated just standing there and getting kicked and elbowed when it was my partner's turn to go. It's not actually all that painful but it is the anticipation of pain that kills me and the fact that I have to mute my natural reaction to being hit. We haven't done pugil sticks yet, but I know we will. You have probably seen pugil sticks in movies and old military photos. They are giant Q-tip looking things that you fight with to simulate the movements of close combat with a rifle and bayonet. I'm looking forward to it because at VMI I had a lot of success in the pugil stick department.

We also learned the basics of fighting with a bayonet at the end of your rifle. After learning the fundamental strokes, you run along this course screaming your head off, stopping every twenty yards to hit a dummy with your bayonet or rifle butt. It is the kind of stuff that you see in boot camp movies and I loved it.

Everyday here on Parris Island we do what is called drill. Basically drill is the same thing as the marching and rifle manual we did at VMI but it seems like there are a lot more movements and those movements are more complicated than they were at VMI. I had heard that boot camp was 90% drill and so far that has turned out to be true. I also mistakenly thought that my VMI days would benefit me in this apparently all-important area, but my VMI experience really hasn't helped. In fact, I think in some ways it has hurt me because there are subtle differences between the Marine Corps drill and VMI drill so I have some bad habits that the Drill Instructors were kind enough to help me break.

We drill sometimes for three or four hours at a time. I think it's three or four hours but I can't be sure because we can't have watches and I'm afraid to glance too long at the Drill Instructor's watch to get an idea of what time it is. Besides, I'm pretty sure the Drill Instructor's put their watches on upside down or on the wrong time just to mess with us and to keep us clueless.

Drill is so miserable because it is depressing and painfully redundant. There is so much time to stand there executing the commands with nothing to do but think about how unhappy you are and about all of the fun things you could be doing on a July day if you weren't at boot camp. Then there is the tediousness. "Forward march!" And we all step off with the left foot and everyone's foot is supposed to hit the ground at the same time. "Platoon Halt!" And we take one more step and in theory we all stop at the same moment. "Right Shoulder Arms!" And we all move our rifles to our right shoulder supposedly at the exact same time. "Left shoulder arms!" And we mechanically maneuver our rifles to the left shoulder in the prescribed manner. Of course, a couple of guys mess up left and right and we get bitched at and have to do push-ups.

Drill also gives the Drill Instructors all of the ammunition they need to make our lives hell. When drilling you can't scratch or squirm. When not executing a command you have to stand perfectly still even if a bead of sweat is tickling the end of your nose or if a swarm of sand fleas (nasty little flies that like to bite) are gnawing away at your flesh. If you try to be smart and scratch when the Drill Instructor's back is turned and you get caught, the Drill Instructor will bitch at you to "stop digging your face." He will then make a mental note to "reserve some one-on-one time later," at which point he will host a personal exercise session. Also, if your hands are not perfectly clenched at your sides, Drill Instructor Sergeant Willis will come by and slap the hell out of your hand. We have learned quickly to keep our hands "cupped, thumb along the trouser seam" or suffer the stinging consequences.

If we are not performing up to the Drill Instructor's impossible expectations, we often hold our rifles straight out in front of our faces for like a half hour. This seems pretty easy for the first minute or so until you start to feel a sharp pain shooting all the way from your finger tips, through your shoulder, and into your chest. When you think you are about done with this particular installment of torture, some jackass drops his weapon and the unimaginable hell continues for ten more minutes. When I was very small, I remember watching a movie about boot camp where this guy was teaching everybody to think about pleasant things while they were doing really painful exercises. I usually think of girls or ice cream or the Yankees and, although it didn't work quite as well for me as it did for the guy in that old movie, it does take my mind off of things for a moment or two.

Another facet of boot camp that I loathe is polishing boots and shining brass. Every night while half of the platoon is in the shower, the other half shines their boots and polishes their brass belt buckles. The left side of the squad bay is called the port side while the right is called starboard side, just like a boat. The Drill Instructor baby-sitting us will call, "Port side, Shine 'em up. Starboard side, shave 'em up." This is the cue for half of us to "shine our shit" and for the other half to march into the head like good little toy soldiers to "hygiene." After a few minutes the DI will yell, "Change Over." We in unison respond, "Change Over, aye, aye sir."

The reason I hate "shining my shit" so much is because I know that ten minutes after we wake up the next morning my boots are going to be all sandy from marching to morning chow and just putting my belt on is going to smudge the brass buckle.

***

Today was the first opportunity that we've had to write letters, except for that stupid form letter. I jotted a quick note to my parents and now I'm doing my best to remember all of the important events since my last correspondence exactly a week ago at the airport in Washington DC. I hope in the future I will get to write on a more regular basis even if I have to stay up at night and write it under my blanket with my flashlight.

***

Comparison of VMI and Boot Camp Experiences

I am surprised at a lot of the similarities between VMI and boot camp. Shining boots and drill are the obvious similarities but there are so many others. At VMI, we had what was called a "Rat Bible," which was a small book of all of the rules and regulations, important cadets, and VMI history. Similarly, the Marine Corps has "knowledge" contained in a book with an olive cover called the "Green Monster" which is basically the same stuff; rules, rank structure, our chain of command, and of course Marine Corps history.

Another big similarity is the Physical Fitness Test (PFT) that we must pass to graduate boot camp. The same three events; running, pull-ups, and crunches (a modified sit-up) are involved in both the VMI and the Marine Corps PFT. Also both VMI and boot camp have a final hurdle before you are officially in the club. Joining the VMI Corps of Cadets involves a ritual called "Break Out." Prior to becoming a Marine we must finish "The Crucible." For VMI's Break Out, the upper classes step-up the harassment for a few days before the march to "break out hill," which is a big dirt slope intentionally turned to mud by fire hoses. The entire freshman class has to work together to make it to the top of the sloppy mess with the upper-classes standing by to keep you from reaching the summit. I don't know much about the Crucible, but I know that you must complete it to graduate. It is the final hurdle on the road to becoming a Marine, the same way that "Break Out" made us full members of the VMI Corps of Cadets.

Another underlying theme here at Parris Island that was a big part of VMI is teamwork. It was said that you couldn't survive the Rat Line without your "Brother Rats." Similarly, the DIs stress teamwork as essential to getting off "the land that God forgot." Before I came, I was wondering what would be harder, the Rat Line or boot camp. I kind of thought VMI would be harder because you had to balance a full load of college courses with all of the military stuff and harassment from upperclassmen. However, after a week of boot camp I would have to say boot camp is much tougher simply because it is non-stop. At VMI you could, to a limited extent, take refuge in the privacy of your room or channel your frustration into your studies. Here, there is no downtime whatsoever and although we have stuff to memorize, there is no real sit-down-and-study time. In addition to no time away from the rule of the DIs, there is no phone usage, whereas at VMI we at least had limited phone access. As far as I can tell, for a recruit to make a phone call would take a miracle or an act of Congress.

One aspect of boot camp that is easier than VMI is the sheer ratio of recruits to Drill Instructors. At VMI the freshman were outnumbered three to one by nosey upperclassmen hell-bent on exposing your tiniest infractions. As a result, there were many more pairs of eyes watching and waiting for you to screw up. At boot camp the recruits outnumber the Drill Instructors more than twenty to one so there are little things like whispering in the chow hall that you can sometimes get away with here that you never could have done at VMI.

***

When I'm feeling really shitty because I'm homesick, lonely, hungry, or tired, I remind myself of just how lucky I am. Most of these guys are eighteen year-old kids who made the decision to enlist as boys and are now locked into this tough lifestyle for the next four years. Many, I'm sure, have doubts about their decision. I made the decision as an adult and I have no doubts. Despite the difficulties and annoyances I have been mentioning, I have no regrets at all about my decision to come to Parris Island and join the Marine Corps. Sometimes I feel like I'm at fantasy camp, doing all of the things I've seen in pictures and movies - the kinds of things I've dreamed about doing since practically the womb. I'm content to be at this famous place that, for some reason, I've always wanted to come to, despite the fact that most of the time it is absolutely miserable. I can actually feel the regret of leaving VMI starting to wither away under the relentless South Carolina summer sun. Of course, I know I must graduate from Recruit Training to finally be relieved of the burden I've been carrying. I guess what I'm saying is that I'm proud of what I'm doing.

CHAPTER 3: Drill

Sunday, July 16, 2000

Yesterday was the worst day yet. There was so much yelling and stress and yelling and frustration. We all learned that rules are rules. There are no exceptions, not even for God. Recruits are only allowed to wear religious medallions or have bibles in our cargo pocket on Sunday. Drill Instructor Sergeant Willis caught a guy wearing a crucifix yesterday (Saturday) and ripped it off his neck, stomped on it then grinded it into pieces with the heel of his boot. Then he found another Recruit with one of those Gideon's bibles that some guy handed out to everybody back at MEPS. Willis, given the nickname *Lucifer* by a previous platoon in his charge, lived up to his title by tearing the pages out of the tiny green-covered bible and scattering the pages of the Good Book to the wind.

Later in the evening some poor guy got a card from his wife to celebrate their one month wedding anniversary. Although the Senior Drill Instructor had distributed the mail, we had not been given permission to open it and were told to store our mail in our footlockers. This guy had his card illegally in his pocket and somehow Drill Instructor Staff Sergeant Erickson found it, opened it and read every sappy word aloud to the entire platoon. I'm not sure why, but it actually made me sick to my stomach to see the poor recruit squirm as the DI mocked him, his wife, and their marriage.

Speaking of sick to my stomach, after a delicious chicken and rice meal with lukewarm, fishy-tasting canteen water, we were pitted. Pit calls always suck but this one was particularly unbearable because I had to piss so badly. Even before we went to the pit, I had to go. Then we worked out in the pit for ten minutes and I thought I might explode. I guess I could have asked to make a head call but whenever a guy asks to make a head call when we are in the pit I always assume he's full of shit and just trying to get out of it. So anyway, after a literally gut-wrenching pit call, I thought I was finally going to get to piss when the bastards marched us out of the pit and back toward the squad bay. But we marched right past our barracks and into a different pit outside a neighboring barracks where we worked out for what had to be another ten minutes. Every time I would dive on the "deck" it felt like my bladder was being raked over a cheese grater. After an eternity, I got my chance to piss and was actually very relieved and a little surprised that there was no blood in my urine.

***

By my calculations, we are about 12% of the way through the boot camp experience. I'm pretty sure that we have seventy-four days until graduation, which is pretty inspiring. When I left home the count was eighty-seven days, so we have cut out a big chunk of time. These are the kinds of things I think about when we are standing around perfectly still doing drill.

So far physically I feel I'm in the top ten percent. Mentally I don't fall for the head games like some of the younger guys because I understand that we are always going to be wrong and the DIs are always going to be right. I realize that no matter how fast we make the racks or run up the "ladder well" it is never going to be good enough because boot camp is designed for the recruit to always be wrong.

Emotionally, however, I'm beaten down. A lot of these kids are probably just happy to be away from home and to have someone besides their parents to boss them around. But I liked my life. I had my own place, and a car, and I did what I wanted, when I wanted. It was pretty cushy. Down here I have to ask to go to the bathroom and have to be told what sock to put on which foot.

***

Between eating only three skimpy diet trays a day, having no booze, drinking only the nasty East River tasting tap water, plus all of the exercise, I have lost twelve pounds already and I bet when it is all over I will have lost thirty or forty pounds.

So far the biggest shock about boot camp is how much time we spend sitting in an actual classroom. Just about every day we go to RTF, which I guess stands for Recruit Training Facility, and have classes on first-aid, Marine Corps history and stuff like that. The classrooms are more modern than my high school or even college. There is a big video screen, stadium seating and air-conditioning. Sometimes I get so involved in the lectures on the Marine Corps' glorious history that I forget the DIs are waiting in the back like caged animals just itching to get at us after the class is over.

At least one DI is with us at all times, including overnight. I see wedding bands on their fingers and wonder how they, and especially their wives, deal with all of the time away from home. My sympathy for the DIs and their wives is short-lived because I remember the hell they are putting all of us through and I'm suddenly glad that they probably have really shitty marriages.

Our first extended period of "relaxation" came today when the Protestant recruits went to church. The Catholic and "no affiliation" recruits got time to shine our boots, organize our footlockers and write letters. When the Protestants got back, we Catholics went to Mass and the Protestants got some free time or what we call "Senior Drill Instructor square away time." In addition to being an opportunity to keep holy the Sabbath, Mass gave us a chance to relax a little, sing hymns, and listen to a homily from a priest wearing a camouflage robe. It was also my first opportunity to see female recruits. For the most part, it was not a pretty sight. I did see a couple of nice looking ones singing in the choir though. Mass was also our first chance to see and talk to other recruits who are at different stages of training. Before mass started, we "First Phase" recruits had a few minutes to quietly pick the brains of the guys who have been on the island a while about what to expect and how to get through it.

At the end of Mass, recruits wearing their dressy uniforms, who I guess are about to graduate, get up and give everybody a pep talk on how to get through boot camp. The guy told us to "live chow-to-chow and Sunday-to-Sunday." That means don't look too far down the road. Look forward to your next meal and to the next Sunday, otherwise you will feel like crap because graduation is so far off. These speeches made me feel better because it reminded me that these guys were in my shoes at one point and now they are about to get the hell off of this island.

The hour or so spent in the chapel was undoubtedly the most relaxing hour I have had since I got here. Although, one thing that surprised me was that the DIs literally scream at you up until the very second you walk through the door of the chapel. When Mass is over, there they are, chomping at the bit outside. Just dying for you to get out there and make you pay the price for your precious hour of stress-free time.

***

The difference between my platoon and the platoons that are more advanced in training is stark. The Second and Third Phase platoons are louder, crisper, in better shape, and a million times better at drill than we are. They also get to do what is called "blousing your boots." This means they take the cuff of their camouflage trousers and tuck it up under what is essentially a green rubber band. It looks sharp and they look like real Marines. My platoon is still in the First Phase, we wear our trousers sloppily rolled up at the bottom like oversized hand-me-downs. I have also seen some more advanced recruits who are allowed to grow standard Marine Corps "high and tights" instead of the bald, down-to-the-scalp look that most recruits sport. My guess is they are close to graduating.

Monday, July 17, 2000

After ten days I'm ready to give an early assessment of the Drill Instructors. Senior Drill Instructor (SDI) Staff Sergeant Jefferson is relatively nice to us. Don't get me wrong when I attribute any benign characteristics to the Senior. Nice is a relative term. The Senior is not actually nice to us, he just doesn't hate us quite as much as the other two DIs. For example, he is the one who gives us our mail each night, although I hate that we are supposed to act like he is giving us a kidney when he sits down after evening chow and tosses out the mail. He is also the one who gives us a "chit" to go to sick call when we are not feeling well and gives the guys any medication that they might be on. I have never been to sick call and don't plan on ever going. Most of the guys that go to sick call are pretty much just pansies either looking to get out of something or they have a pathetically low threshold of pain and discomfort.

In some ways the Senior Drill Instructor reminds me of our "Dyke" at VMI. The term "Dyke" has nothing to do with lesbians, it is a senior buddy that is assigned to each freshman. Just like the Senior Drill Instructor at boot camp, the "Dyke" at VMI was the one who got you your mail and was, although demanding, the only person who seemed to give a crap whether you made it or didn't. Also, you were always supposed to make your Dyke proud, if you didn't, whoever saw you screw up would tell him. It's the same thing here. Other DIs always ask, "Who's your Senior, nasty?" if they catch you talking or looking around the chow hall. Pretty much the worst thing you can do is piss off or disappoint your Senior because you have turned your only ally into an enemy.

Drill Instructor Staff Sergeant Erickson, the pretty-boy, is the weak link of the three because he isn't a terribly bright man. He is the primary one teaching us drill and he is always messing it up. He calls the commands on the wrong foot and gives the order "Right Shoulder Arms!" when the rifle is already on our right shoulder. He makes matters even worse by trying to cover it or make it seem like it was somehow our fault he screwed up.

Drill Instructor Sergeant Willis, as I have previously mentioned, is both mean and downright scary. One day early in training he squished my bananas right in front of me because I took two instead of the allotted one. The reason he frightens me so much is that he seems to bend the rules and, at times, flat-out shatters them. He grabs you, pushes you and slaps you. The other day in the chow hall he smacked a glass right out of a recruit's hand. The glass hit the deck and chards shot everywhere. He is the disciplinarian and seems to relish the role.

***

I have developed a deep, unrelenting hatred for Recruit Advent. Advent is the platoon "Guide." Being the Guide means he has some authority over the other recruits and carries the red and yellow platoon guidon (banner) that bears our platoon number, 1377. When we go to the chow hall, he stands there and lets us know when we can side-step over and get on line to receive our chow. The Guide and the Squad Leaders are responsible for making sure morning clean up gets done correctly and other stuff like that. If we screw up sometimes just the Guide and Squad Leaders get "smoked." Smoked is a term used to describe when the DIs personally and closely oversee the workout of one, some, or all of the recruits because they did something wrong. This term is almost interchangeable with "quaterdecked." The quarterdeck is the area of the squad bay in front of the Drill Instructor's office where recruits get smoked. I'll explain more about this later.

Back to Advent; the first night we slept here Staff Sergeant Oscar told Advent and another guy, Desai, to get the platoon "hygiened" and ready for bed. The way Advent, and to a lesser extent Desai, bossed everybody around I honestly thought they were in some kind of officer training program rather than nasty recruits like the rest of us. A few days later I discovered that Advent and Desai were only put in charge of us because they had been on Parris Island a while. As it turns out, they've been here for a couple weeks because they were in "Pork Chop Platoon." Neither of these guys was fat but you could tell they were weak as hell, even after spending a couple weeks in PCP. Then I saw them at the IST the other day and it was clear these two characters were complete pussies.

To make matters worse, Advent has to be one of the ugliest human beings I have ever encountered. His face is so long that he looks like the guy from that famous painting "The Scream." His eyes are all sunken into his head and he always has the same blank expression on his face; even when he yells or gets pissed off. The reason I loathe him so much is because he treats everybody like he is a DI. He calls guys names and demands that when he tells us to do something we say, "Aye, aye Guide", the way we say "Aye, aye Sir" when we are given an order by the DIs. He also goes and whines to the DIs when we don't do what the pathetic bastard tells us to do.

I am constantly doing everything I can to undermine what little authority he wields. I respond to his orders by saying a "aye, aye PCP" to remind everybody that Advent was so pitifully weak that he couldn't pass the ridiculously easy Initial Strength Test until after he'd been in PCP for a month.

As much as I hate Advent, there are a couple of guys I really like. Recruit Tobego is a good guy. We got to know each other on Sunday because we were cleaning the showers together and got a rare opportunity to shoot the shit. He is funny and although the DIs are for some reason particularly hard on him, he doesn't let it bother him. Tobego is a fellow "fat body" and eats a diet tray like me. Since all of the diet tray recruits go to the front of the chow line we almost always sit next to each other at meals. There isn't any talking at chow but down here pass the salt qualifies as a meaningful conversation.

The other guy I am friendly with is Recruit Stewart. Remember the guy I sat next to on the bus from the airport when we first got here? The guy I said was the dumbest person in the world? I helped him out on the pull up bar the first day of PT and he has kind of clung to me since. He is actually a really nice guy and you can tell he wants so badly to do well. Unfortunately, he is his own worst enemy. He cannot stand still for two seconds without twitching, squirming or scratching and is constantly getting smoked for it. He also forgets where he is and who he is talking to and gets himself in more trouble. For example, a DI will ask him a question and instead of saying "No Sir" he'll say "Na" like he's back on the block.

My rack is next to Stewart's so I do what I can to help him out. We are always ordered to run back and dig some item of gear out of our footlocker or seabag. Stewart can never find anything in time to meet the DI's countdown, so his bunkee (the person with whom you share your bunk bed) and I try and find his stuff for him in an effort to keep Stewart and the platoon out of trouble.

***

Today after breakfast we had PT. They broke the platoon down into three running groups, fast, medium and slow. I am the only fat body in the fast group. That scum bag Advent was kidding himself and joined the fast group but kept dropping back and we would all have to wait for his sorry ass by running in place while he caught up.

In other news, I did seventy-five crunches today which are a lot more than I did on the IST last Saturday.

Today was the first time I was really famished and incredibly tired. It's not even so much that I'm hungry; its more that we eat dinner in the late afternoon and then not another morsel until breakfast the next day. It sucks eating dinner at 4:30 PM and knowing that no matter what, I'm consuming my last bite for at least thirteen hours. I'm not sure why I am so damned tired, it's not like we only get three hours of sleep. We get at least seven hours to sleep each night. Lights out is at 9:00 PM, or as we say 2100. Reveille is at 0500. About every other night each recruit is required to stand one hour of Fire Watch. Fire Watch is awful because it is so boring and because it deprives you of sleep, the only enjoyable thing we get around here.

Basically the Fire Watch paces back and forth in the squad bay or in the head for an hour shift, trying not to fall asleep. If we had PT that day, the Fire Watch washes and dries our PT clothes and delivers them to our footlocker while everyone else sleeps. This is a very efficient way to get the laundry done and redistributed. During your shift, you have to count all of the rifles, seabags and recruits to make sure nothing – and no one - is missing. If a DI comes on deck, you report your post as follows: "Sir, Good Evening Sir. Recruit 'Schmukatelli' reports Post One all secure at this time. There are seventy rifles, seventy seabags, and seventy recruits on safe and secure at this time. The platoon is currently engaged in Taps. Good evening Sir!"

***

In the ten days that we have been here on Parris Island we have gone to the pit four times but I have only moved my bowels three times. I realize this is a gross thing to be keeping track of but I'm trying like hell to lose weight and every time I make what we call a "sit down head call," I feel I'm shedding some more pounds. I think there are a couple of reasons my bowel movements have been so few. First of all, I don't eat a fraction of what I was accustomed to eating in my civilian life. Also I only eat healthy stuff so I guess there is very little waste. Plus the DIs really frown upon "sit down head calls" because unlike a "stand up head call," a dump takes a few minutes and the DIs think you are sitting on your ass relaxing. You pretty much only have time for a sit down head call after Taps (lights out). But when the first Fire Watch shuts off those lights and the DI on duty finishes berating us and gives the order to "Adjust" and we can get under the coarse olive-drab green blanket, the last thing I want to do is put on my shower shoes and trek to the head.

Now is a good opportunity to explain our nightly ritual. The last five minutes before bed usually go as follows: First we pray. When the DI yells "Lay Readers Post" we all bow our heads, crisply thrust both fists in front of us with our arms straight and elbows locked. In unison we chant "GOD, COUNTRY, CORPS." Next we meet with our Lay Readers, recruits who run the nightly prayers for their respective denominations. There is one for the Protestants and one for the Catholics. We are supposed to say a quick prayer but mostly guys bitch about how miserable they are. After we disperse from the prayer meeting, we stand on the side of our racks and the DI commands "Prepare to mount!" We then pound the top rack three times and chant "HONOR, COURAGE, COMMITMENT." Then we get the order "Mount" and we jump into our racks and lay at attention as the DI drones on about how miserable we all are and how none of us will ever become Marines.

At this point each Drill Instructor has a pet lullaby that they have made us memorize so we can sing it when the lights go out. When the Senior Drill Instructor has duty we sing all three verses of the Marine Corps Hymn:

From the halls of Montezuma To the shores of Tripoli,
We fight our country's battles In the air, on land, and sea.
First to fight for right and freedom, And to keep our honor clean,
We are proud to claim the title Of United States Marines.

Our flags unfurl'd to every breeze From dawn to setting sun;
We have fought in every clime and place Where we could take a gun.
In the snow of far-off northern lands And in sunny tropic scenes,
You will find us always on the job - The United States Marines.

Here's health to you and to our Corps Which we are proud to serve;
In many a strife we've fought for life And never lost our nerve.
If the Army and the Navy Ever gaze on Heaven's scenes,
They will find the streets are guarded By United States Marines.

I just love how even in the hymn, the Marine Corps has to stick
it to the Army and Navy.

When Drill Instructor Staff Sergeant Erickson is babysitting us
we recite the Rifleman's Creed:

This is my rifle. There are many like it but this one is mine.
My rifle is my best friend. It is my life. I must master it as
I master my life. My rifle, without me is useless. Without
my rifle, I am useless. I must fire my rifle true. I must shoot
straighter than any enemy who is trying to kill me. I must
shoot him before he shoots me. I will ...

My rifle and myself know that what counts in this war is not
the rounds we fire, the noise of our burst, nor the smoke we
make. We know that it is the hits that count. We will hit ...

My rifle is human, even as I, because it is my life. Thus, I will learn it as a brother. I will learn its weakness, its strength, its parts, its accessories, its sights and its barrel. I will keep my rifle clean and ready, even as I am clean and ready. We will become part of each other. We will …

Before God I swear this creed. My rifle and myself are the defenders of my country. We are the masters of our enemy. We are the saviors of my life. So be it, until victory is America's and there is no enemy, but Peace.

Drill Instructor Sergeant Willis is the most creative and has an original ditty for us to sing:

Yea though I walk through the valley of the Shadow of Death, I shall fear no evil, for I was trained by the meanest, baddest mother fucker on the island.

Our Senior Drill Instructor trained us to be lean mean fighting machines. Shock troop devil dogs, devastating killing machines.

Ready to fight, ready to die but never will.

Finally when choir practice is over the DI on duty says "Adjust" and we can stop laying at attention and we can get under the covers and go to sleep.

***

The quarterdeck is an infamous area in the squad bay because it is the area across from the Drill Instructor's office where recruits often go to get smoked, usually by Willis, but occasionally by Erickson. A recruit can get smoked for any infraction he may or may not have committed. There are always massive puddles of sweat from the unfortunate recruits who have been worked out there. Basically the quarterdeck is a lot like the pit, except that you work out individually or in small groups instead of as a platoon. I have only been on the quarterdeck once and I'm not even sure what I did, but I wasn't going to demand a reason from Drill Instructor Sergeant Lucifer. I don't want to be summoned to the quarterdeck ever again because in some ways the quarterdeck is worse than the pit. At least when you hit the deck in the pit the sand breaks your fall. On the quarterdeck there is nothing but a slab of concrete to cushion your landing. Also, when you are in the pit the whole platoon is in there with you and the DIs have to keep an eye on everybody to make sure they are "putting out" (working hard). On the quarterdeck, the DI stands right over you and at most only has to keep track of a few guys. If you let up even a tiny bit, the DI notices and his wrath is severe.

Tonight was the first night of what is called EEP or the Evening Exercise Program. EEP is basically extra PT for the guys who are fat or who did poorly on the IST. While everyone else is writing letters or polishing boots during square away time, we are doing pull-ups, push-ups and the like on the quarterdeck. Whether it is the pit, the quarterdeck or even EEP, I try to remind myself that it will make me stronger and bring me closer to my goal of a perfect PFT score at the end of boot camp. A perfect score is twenty pull-ups, one hundred crunches in two minutes and a three mile run in eighteen minutes. Right now I'm at five pull-ups, 75 crunches and I ran 1.5 miles in 10:19.

These are very average stats, so obviously I need all of the extra help I can get.

This is the second day in a row we were afforded the opportunity to write letters. It is so funny how you grow to appreciate the simplest pleasures when you are on this island. Tonight I received a piece of mail from my mother which was great. My mom e-mailed my address to my five brothers and sisters so hopefully the mail will start pouring in any day now. Aside from meals and, of course, graduation, Mass and mail are the only things we have to look forward to.

Tuesday, July 18, 2000

You would not believe the tension in the squad bay when the Senior Drill Instructor is passing out the mail. As the Senior reads the names off of the envelope I feel like we are a pack of starving dogs and the Senior is swinging a piece of raw meat in front of our noses. The tension exists because if you have not gotten any mail on a particular day, and the pile of mail begins to dwindle, you become overwhelmed with a profound sense of disappointment. It will be at least another twenty-four hours before you have another shot at contact with your loved ones and, even then, there is no guarantee. Mail is so important because it is an escape. When I get a letter I completely forget where I am. It puts a coat of armor around me that shields me from the DIs and everything else on this island. Unfortunately, the armor withers away by the next day so we are in constant need of letters.

***

Boot camp time isn't like civilian time. The days seem to drag on endlessly but weeks fly by. I can't really explain the paradox, but everyday seems like it is going to go on forever and the next thing you know you've been here for almost two weeks. It's really a crazy phenomenon.

I can already feel my arms starting to get harder from all of the push-ups, pull ups, pit calls and PT sessions. I can even start to feel my ribs and I can't remember the last time I could do that.

***

Today turned out to be a pretty good day because at dinner they were out of diet tray food so I got to eat what everybody else got; a sorry excuse for a BBQ rib. To me the rubbery, bland rib was a feast compared to the dry, tasteless boiled chicken I usually get for dinner.

Wednesday, July 19 2000

Today we did pugil sticks for the first time. My first bout was against a gangly white guy from my platoon named Daily. I thought for sure I would pummel this goofball, but his arms were so damn long I couldn't get close enough to give him too many good shots. The winner is the first one to inflict three "killing blows." A killing blow is a shot across the throat, in the chest or a clean head shot. He beat me three killing blows to two.

The second fight was against a guy from another platoon. I don't know what is name was because we only encountered each other long enough to beat each other over the head. He was a black guy, about twenty-one years old and weighed 245 pounds.

He looked athletic, like he could have played middle linebacker for the New York Giants. The instructor tried to get somebody else to fight him because he had at least twenty-five pounds on me. I said I wanted to fight him anyway and to my surprise and I'm sure everyone else's surprise, I beat him rather handily.

The best part about pugil sticks was watching Advent get pummeled every time he fought. I swear it was like watching an eleven year old girl fight Evander Holyfield the way those guys beat him silly. Advent winced in fear every time his opponent swung at him. After this pathetic display I'm sure his reign as Guide is over.

***

When the platoon went to RTF for a class, I was assigned to stay back and stand Fire Watch. Our rifles, although they are padlocked, can never be left unattended. Therefore when we go to chow, two recruits go to "early chow" before the rest of the platoon. A few minutes later the rest of the platoon leaves for chow with the exception of the two so-called "late chow" recruits who remain behind to stand guard over our rifles until the "early chow" recruits relieve them. We usually bring our rifles to RTF but on this day we didn't so Recruit Desai (Advent's buddy from PCP) and I stood Fire Watch alone in the barracks. It was so nice to have an hour and a half of peace and quiet.

Desai is what is known as the "Platoon Scribe" and I am his "Scribble" or "Assistant Scribe." The Scribes are basically the DIs' bitches. We handle all of the paperwork for the laundry, write sick call chits, and make up the Fire Watch roster. The best part about this job is that I don't have to stand Fire Watch at night. Desai is a control-freak so he handles almost all of the responsibilities and all I do is make up the Fire Watch roster each night.

I learned quickly why Desai gave me the job of making up the Fire Watch roster. It is a hell job. Number one, it has to be done neat, which is not my strong suit. Also, guys are always bitching that they get Fire Watch every night even though I just go around the squad bay in order and pick up where I left off the night before. Sometimes I'll get the whole roster done, complete with the necessary recruit signatures, and somebody will get in trouble and get assigned Fire Watch in the middle of the night. When this happens, I have to do the whole thing over. This requires me to go around in the dark waking guys up to get their signatures on the new time slot. Signatures are required because it is an indication that you knew you had watch and when your shift started. This way if some guy doesn't show up, or abandons his post, there is no way he can play dumb. The whole process makes sense; it's just a pain in the ass.

***

After eating barely edible liver for evening chow, we did what is called footlocker PT. Basically the DI utilizes our old, wooden footlockers to make our lives miserable. One of the exercises that comprise footlocker PT is dips. A dip requires you to put your hands behind your back and on top of the footlocker, with your feet straight out in front of you and your body almost parallel to the ground. Then you lower and raise yourself at the DI's request. The corners of the footlocker are pointy and kill your hands. The DI holds you in the up position for minutes at a time. Lucifer held us up there so long guys were actually crying and begging for mercy. One guy's hand slipped off the footlocker and he went to medical and returned with a cast on. I'm pretty sure he is badly hurt and is going to get discharged soon.

Thursday, July 20, 2000

After PT, we went to RTF and I had a close call with the very notes you are reading. Senior Drill Instructor Staff Sergeant Jefferson saw me writing intently during the lecture and assumed that I was writing a letter home, which of course is not allowed. I wasn't writing a letter but I was documenting the events of the day on a scrap of paper from my notebook to compile this journal, as is my custom. The Senior grabbed the paper out of my hand and began to examine it. I thought this journal, and my life, was over. The Senior looked at the side where I scrawled my notes and I guess because my handwriting was so awful he had no idea what it said. On the flip side were some legibly written notes I had taken on the lecture on Marine Corps history. The Senior was able to decipher:

1st Commandant:	Sam Nichols
USMC Birthday:	10 November 1775
1st Amphibious Assault:	New Providence Bahamas 1775
Grand Old Man of the Marine Corps:	Archibald Henderson
First Sergeant Major of the Marine Corps:	Archibald Somers
1st Marine to win the Medal of Honor:	CPL John Mackie

Upon seeing my copious notes, the Senior actually applauded my efforts. It was a close call, but in a way it was good because I think the Senior was a little embarrassed that he accused me of writing a letter in RTF, when it turned out I was actually, as far as he knew, being a very diligent recruit. In the future, I doubt he will rip any pieces of paper out of my hand expecting something incriminating. I guess you could say I dodged a bullet, or in the words of the super-motivated ooh-rah instructor giving today's lecture, I dodged a "flesh ripper."

***

Today I was put on the quarterdeck for the second time in my recruitship. I lost one of my canteens and, as a result, I was punished. This trip to the quarterdeck was more exhausting and brutal than my first one. I have no energy to explain the details. Just imagine all of the crappy PT stuff I have explained previously and multiply it by ten.

Although it is easier to say than do. I try to stay optimistic and remind myself that all of this exercise is getting me into better and better shape.

***

One of the ways I cope with this place is to count my blessings and realize how good I have it compared to others. Today I found out that there is another twenty-four-year-old recruit. Only this guy, Imish, was a factory worker in Ohio, and is married with kids. He got laid off when the factory he worked for closed down. He is a real nice guy but he has a lot on his mind besides just surviving boot camp.

***

Today a platoon nearing the end of boot camp had what is called "Family Day." Family Day is the day before graduation when your loved ones come and tour the base with you. Although they try to keep nasty recruits like us far away from Family Day, I caught a glimpse of the festivities out the window of the squad bay. I saw those guys walking around holding hands with their girlfriends and showing their parents Parris Island's hot spots. I can actually see pure joy beaming from their faces. I hate those bastards so much. They have one more day on Parris Island and I have more than seventy.

***

The training itself isn't that bad really. In fact it is kind of fun. I especially like hand-to-hand combat and the history lessons. The part that sucks is when we are in the barracks with the DIs fucking with us. They yell and yell and physically torture us by overworking our bodies. I hear that all of that ends by like the fifth week, so that is something to look forward to.

***

I did ninety-five crunches today, a personal best and only five shy of a perfect score. I feel so strong and healthy from all of the exercise and because I eat just three, small meals per day and only drink water. It does get pretty hot down here but most of the outdoor training is done between 0600 and 0900, so it is not all that bad. Today it is so hot that they put up the black flag which means we can't do anything outside because it is over 105 degrees.

Friday, July 21, 2000 (10 Weeks Until Graduation)

We speak our own Marine Corps language down here. If we are given an order to do something we don't say "Yes Sir!" like you would think or like we did at VMI. You respond to an order by saying, "Aye, aye Sir!," which sounds more like "Ice-er" because we say it so fast and we are trying to be as loud as possible.

We don't wear sneakers or write with pens; on our feet are "go-fasters" and our letters are written with "ink sticks." There is also no such thing as a flashlight. On Parris Island, we use "moonbeams" to illuminate the darkness. In the morning, when we march to chow, we bring our moonbeams with us because it is still dark. When the DI says, "MOON BEAMS ON" we respond quickly and loudly, "MOON-BEAMS-ON-AYE-AYE-SIR-CLICK" and then we flip the switch.

We are so worthless that we are forbidden to refer to ourselves in the first person. A normal person would respond to the pretty typical question "Why are you so fucking stupid?" by saying "I don't know, Sir." However, recruits on Parris Island must respond, "This recruit does not know, Sir." It is annoying and awkward and a pain-in-the-ass in general, but what are you gonna do? I messed it up once and uttered the word "I." As a punishment *I* was forced to point to my *eye* and then to my chest while chanting, "This is an eye. This is a recruit. This is an eye. This is a recruit. This is an eye. This is a recruit." It sounds harmless, but it lasted for forty-five minutes. It made my arm ache from the repetitive motion and made me hoarse from the constant talking without water.

My last name is Lalor, pronounced Law-Ler. For obvious reasons, people mess it up and say Lay-Lor. At VMI, there was a senior cadet who, for no particular reason, hated my guts and liked to do what he could to erode my self-esteem. He used to make me sing the words, "Lay-lor, stupid piece of shit, Lay-lor" to the tune of the Eric Clapton song Layla. That bastard didn't even bother to make up any other versus, it was just "Lay-lor, stupid piece of shit, Lay-lor" over and over. The DIs have not reprised that humiliation, but they use the same pronunciation and Drill Instructor Sergeant Willis, who also hates my guts, says "Lay-lor" with a particularly heavy dose of disdain in his voice. It could be worse though, Recruit Palowski is known simple as "Polack" and Recruit Bowles (pronounced "bowls") was known as "bowels" as in, I have to move my bowels.

Another thing that really pisses me off is that the Drill Instructors are such egomaniacs that we are required to open all doors for them. If any DI starts heading for the door, or as we say the "hatch," we have to sprint past them, practically kill ourselves and open the door for them and give them the proper greeting of the day, "Good Afternoon Sir." If nobody notices a DI leaving the squad bay and he has to open the door for himself, he will sarcastically say "No problem, I'll get my own hatch."

***

I made another sit-down head call today. That's four in case you are keeping score at home. 197 pounds here I come. I'm not sure what my current weight is, but I feel my love handles getting a little bit smaller and my pants getting a little bit bigger every day.

***

We made another lovely pit call today. When we are in the pit, I always try to stand in the front row right under the Senior Drill Instructor's nose. I try to do everything as fast as I can, to outdo the others. I am embarrassed to admit but I want to impress the Senior and I'm not sure why. I guess because my brother was the Honor Graduate of his platoon, there is a big part of me that wants to do the same. I remember my brother telling me that the pit was the place where he started to make the DIs take notice of the fact that he was an outstanding recruit.

***

A few days ago one of my fellow recruits, this guy Floyd, asked the Senior if he could bunk with another guy, Kistemaker, whom he discovered was from his hometown in Ohio. I thought this was kind of a faggy thing to do and was shocked when the

Senior allowed them to bunk together. Since we had the squad bay rearranged a few days ago, I was no longer bunking near Stewart and he really needed some help or somebody was going to kill him for constantly getting the platoon in trouble. I asked the Senior if I could bunk with Stewart to help him out and the Senior said yes. I know I'm going to regret this but it's the right thing to do, and I really like the guy. We have been together since the very beginning when we sat together on the bus from the airport. Plus, this kind of gives me a higher cause here at boot camp. It is one thing to just survive boot camp yourself, but to help another guy out in the process makes the experience much more fulfilling.

Saturday, July 22, 2000

Today is Saturday but that doesn't really mean anything to us on Parris Island. Saturday is a training day like any other day. Up at 0500 and on-the-go until 2100, at the earliest.

When we first got here we were issued two pairs of boots and we alternate wearing them. The pair we call "jungle boots" are killing my feet. At the end of the day when I take them off, my feet are throbbing from the beating they have endured. I'm getting worried because at first I thought they just needed to be broken in but it has been two weeks and they kill my feet more than ever lately. I'm afraid that I'm going to suffer some kind of injury, get dropped in training, and be on this shitty island longer than I have to.

In addition to my ailing feet, today was a particularly miserable day for a few reasons. After a pretty rigorous PT session this morning, we had a drill session from hell. We were doing such a crappy job, or so they said, that the DIs marched us right off the sweltering concrete parking lot where we practice drill and into a nearby pit. After the pit call we went back to drilling with sweat-soaked sand covering every inch of our exhausted bodies.

The bright spot in the day came when drill finally ended at around 1300. Drill Instructor Sergeant Willis gave us a class on how to iron our uniforms. It was a very weird to see the source of so much misery standing behind a fold-up ironing board with a can of spray starch in one hand and an iron in the other explaining the nuances of ironing cammie trousers and blouses.

***

To save time, many of us have started to put our combination into the padlocks on our footlockers so that when we need to get something out in a hurry all we have to do is pull down on the padlock and it opens. This became a problem this afternoon and caused all hell to break loose. On the heels of a second substandard drill session, Drill Instructor Staff Sergeant Erickson found an unlocked footlocker and then began checking all of the others. This lead to a dismantling of the squad bay at the hands of Drill Instructor Staff Sergeant Erickson, who went ballistic. He dumped the contents of the "unsecured" footlockers onto the deck and kicked and threw boot polish, hygiene gear, letters and whatever else all over the squad bay. When Erickson's temper tantrum ended, about one third of the footlockers, mine included, were emptied and turned upside down. The squad bay looked as if a tornado had blown through the way everything from toothbrushes to skivvy drawers were strewn up and down the "Drill Instructor Highway," which is the open area in the middle of the squad bay where the DIs roam.

After the dust settled, Drill Instructor Staff Sergeant Erickson generously allotted sixty seconds to return the squad bay back to order. When the platoon failed to meet the impossible deadline, we were told that we were worthless as individuals and that we needed to learn how to work as a team. To teach us team work, Drill Instructor Staff Sergeant Erickson thought it best to flip over as many steel bunk beds as he could. When he was finished the squad bay resembled a shantytown even more than after the previous tirade. Believe it or not this time we were given a reasonable period of time in which to restore order to "the house." Amazingly, in ten minutes the squad bay looked better than it did after "early morning clean up." Drill Instructor Staff Sergeant Erickson came out to inspect. He patrolled up the port side of the squad bay and seemed rather impressed with our work. He then proceeded down the starboard side finding nothing out of place until he reached the second to last rack. The rack belonging to Recruits Alvarez and Chan was "unsat" (unsatisfactory) because one corner of the blanket was not tucked and folded at the requisite 45-degree angle. As a result of this heinous infraction of Marine Corps obsessive compulsion, the squad bay was once against turned to rubble. This game of make-the-rack, tear-the-rack-apart, make-the-rack-again continued for the balance of the afternoon.

I hate to admit it, but, while this tearing apart the squad bay over and over again only hurt the camaraderie of the platoon instead of promoting unit cohesion, which I think was the DIs intent, it did teach me to make my rack quickly and properly. In addition to making my rack, I had to make Stewart's rack on the top bunk because he is helpless and probably hopeless. The poor kid can't seem to get out of his own way. I feel bad about it afterward, but I'm constantly losing my patience with Stewart's incompetence. I want to help the kid, but I don't want to do everything for him. Despite the frustration of dealing with Stewart, I still like him. It's impossible not to like him because he is a good guy and actually trying his best but sadly, probably doesn't have a whole lot to work with.

Before evening chow, I felt the wrath of Drill Instructor Sergeant Willis directed exclusively at me. I brought both canteens to the formation, which is the norm. Unfortunately, on this occasion we were specifically told to only bring one. When Willis saw my mistake he proceeded to dump the entire canteen of water in my face and down my shirt before hurling the drab green container into some nearby bushes. This was the first time I have been singled-out for an infraction and it kind of shook me up. I hate the fact that I have to stand there and be berated and mocked with no recourse whatsoever.

Evening chow wasn't much better than the formation that preceded it. On this night we "ate duck." "Eating duck" has nothing to do with the menu. It means we are only going to be in the chow hall long enough to duck down for a few seconds, gulp a couple bites and then it's back to training. As far as I can tell the DIs are required to bring us to meals three times per day. However, I don't think the length of time we have to eat is regulated. Usually meals provide a relatively relaxing escape from the rigors of training but "eating duck" eliminates any chance of relaxation.

We literally sprint through the chow line. In addition to the DIs, the Guide and Squad Leaders are strategically stationed to expedite the chow hall process. By this point we have eaten enough meals in the chow hall to know how to get the most of every second we have and, although we are in constant motion, we manage to get some produce from the salad bar on our plates. A Squad Leader is posted around the salad bar to be sure that we only get one tong-load of lettuce, one tong-full of tomatoes, one piece of fruit, and one salad dressing packet. Unfortunately the diet trays don't get dressing, nor do we get croutons, or Bacos which, on occasion, are available to non-diet tray recruits, if they are quick.

To get the most food I possibly can, I spread the tongs as wide as I can in an effort to corral as much lettuce as possible. After those of us eating diet meals pass through the chow line, a DI inspects our tray to ensure that we have a diet tray and none of the trimmings. Even cottage cheese is off limits to us "fat bodies" because it is a dairy product. For some reason they always have cake or cookies on the chow line, even though no one in my platoon except for the double rations guy, is allowed to partake. My guess is that platoons further along in training get to eat dessert after meals.

Although I have never been much of a salt eater, the food is so bland and we are encouraged to eat salt to avoid dehydration so I drown my food in salt on the rare chance it is available.

***

After evening chow we drilled yet again and the sand fleas were relentless in the humid South Carolina dusk. A kid named Carlos got caught scratching during drill so we all had to kick the dirt with our feet and chant "Wake up sand fleas, Wake up sand fleas." We did this until every one of us was being eaten alive by the extremely persistent and annoying insects. A few minutes later Carlos got caught "digging" his face again. Drill Instructor Staff Sergeant Erickson tore into him for a good three minute causing Carlos to cry. Afterwards he claimed he only cried because his ears hurt so much from the yelling. Yeah right. He cried because he is an absolute wuss with no pride and no self respect.

As the day came to a close, and Senior Drill Instructor time approached, I knew the only thing that could salvage this brutal day was some mail. I sat impatiently as the Senior, perched on his swivel chair behind a desk of stacked footlockers, called the names off of the letters and threw them in the direction of the addressee. As the pile of mail on the Senior's makeshift desk began to shrink, I began to realize that my chances of getting mail were getting low. When the last envelope came flying out of the Senior's hand and it wasn't for me, I became overwhelmed by a deep sadness and disappointment. There is no mail on Sunday so my next shot at a piece of mail won't come for another forty-eight hours, an eternity on Parris Island.

Sunday, July 23, 2000

69 Days and Counting.

The only day that has a so-called "feel" is Sunday. Sunday, although not a day off like I thought it would be, is nice because we get to sleep in until 0600 and the morning is pretty much all square away time and church. Every Sunday afternoon we "field day," which is not what it sounds like. "Field day" is the term they use for a really thorough cleaning of the squad bay. During field day, all of the racks and footlockers are moved to one side of the squad bay so the floors can be completely "scuzzed" and then transported so that the opposite side can be taken care of. A little vocabulary note: scuzzing the deck basically entails recruits leaning over in a pyramid position and running up and down the squad bay pushing a rag on the deck.

The head, including sinks, shitters and showers are completely cleaned. A tall recruit puts a small recruit on his shoulders and they walk around dusting the light fixtures in the ceiling. Unfortunately there are only a handful of mops, brooms, and other cleaning supplies so a majority of the platoon is left just trying to look busy which is much worse than actually being busy.

After field day is over, Sunday afternoon is every bit a training day. We drill, get pitted, visit the quarterdeck and study knowledge. Even on the Lord's day of rest we are constantly "moving with a sense of urgency." Unfortunately, this half-day of training on Sunday afternoons and evenings doesn't count toward the sixty-four training days required to graduate from boot camp.

I think I mentioned earlier that we never see female recruits except at church. Well, there is a guy in my platoon named Ruiz from the Bronx whose fiancée is a female recruit in Fourth Battalion. Today at Mass I was sitting a few seats down from him and he told us that the female recruit on the alter doing the reading was his fiancée. At first I thought he was joking but then I realized he was serious. After Mass I thought for sure he would go up to her and hug her, or kiss her, or at least say hello. He didn't because, technically, it's against the rules to have any contact with female recruits even at church and, evidently, even if you are going to be lawfully wed.

This girl is going to be Ruiz's wife in a few months and he can't even utter a word to her in church of all places. I can't even fathom what that would be like. I'd like to think if I had a fiancé in boot camp I'd say the hell with the rules and run up and plant one on her. But that is a lot easier to say than to do. Parris Island has a way of making you timid and unsure of your every instinct, so I honestly don't know what I would do in that situation.

I don't even like Ruiz. In fact, I think he is a bit of a jackass who doesn't take anything seriously, but when I saw him sitting there so paralyzed by the fear of the Drill Instructors, I genuinely pitied him.

***

There is no way to know what time it is down here and we are not privy to the training schedule. This makes it difficult to operate because we never know exactly how long it is until our next meal, how long we have to get the squad bay in order, how long we have left to write letters, or how long until we go to RTF. I'm constantly trying to get a glimpse of the DI's watch but it is both difficult and dangerous and, as I mentioned, the watch might not even give the correct time. Just this morning, I had so much free time while the Protestants were at church that I didn't know what to do with myself. Unfortunately, I have no concept of time and couldn't enjoy it, knowing that at any minute a DI could put an end to our square away time.

The only time you have access to a timepiece is on Fire Watch. The Fire Watch is furnished with an old, fake, gold plated wristwatch, likely bought at Wal-Mart around 1972. The Fire Watch needs to know the time so he can wake up the guy who is relieving him. Also the last Fire Watch of the night is responsible for waking up the DI on duty. This job flat out sucks because you are literally waking up the sleeping giant and you just know he is going to be more ornery than usual having spent the night on the office cot.

To wake up the DI you pound on the hatch three times and shout, "Sir, the time on deck is 0430." You feel bad that you're shouting at the top of your lungs while your buddies are enjoying their last half hour of sleep before reveille at 0500, but what are you going to do? If the DI hollers back "Go away" it means he has woken up. If he doesn't say anything you must repeat the process every five minutes until he responds.

Fire Watch can be an eerie job and it's easy to get freaked out. It's the middle of the night, pitch black except for your red lens moonbeam and guys are constantly yelling in their sleep.

Sometimes you just hear groans and moans above the chorus of snores but other times you can clearly hear words. Sleeping recruits can't even escape the omnipotent DIs and the low hum of snores is frequently and suddenly shattered by a sleeping recruit yelling "Aye, aye Sir" or "Yes, Sir … No, Sir."

***

Daydreaming is the only way to pass the long hours of drill and most of the other monotonous and mindless things we do at this place. I am becoming such a world-class daydreamer that, every once in a while, I get so engrossed in my trance I forget where I am for a while. I love to fantasize about Family Day and graduation the next day and my annual trip to a Notre Dame football game, which I'll be taking the week after I get off this island. Like all recruits I am constantly dwelling in detail about how I'm going to gorge myself with pizza, burgers, buffalo wings, ice cream, and my favorite, Mike and Ike candies, when this whole experience ends. From what I've heard, on Family Day you get to spend six hours with your family. I'm not sure if you can leave the island but I kind of doubt you can. Graduation is over by like 1030 and then it's "Free at last, free at last, thank God almighty" I'll be free at last.

***

I weighed in at slender 206 pounds today which means I lost close to twenty-five pounds in three weeks. I also cranked out eight pull-ups today. For the first month or so after I signed the enlistment papers I was practicing pull-ups almost on a daily basis. I was too embarrassed by my weakness in this area to practice them in the gym where I worked out, but I accidentally found a pull-up bar while jogging along a trail at a local park. Some days I would drive straight from the school where I taught and do a couple of sets. There were always mothers with little kids playing on the swings who would give me weird looks. I don't blame them for the puzzled stares. Here was a twenty-four-year-old guy who looks more like thirty, walking into the woods in a shirt and tie with a pair of wing tips on his feet for a few minutes and then walking back to his car.

Back in the spring I was doing twelve pull-ups, although I don't think they were regulation pull-ups so that figure is probably inflated. A regulation pull-up requires that you start at a dead hang, pull your chin completely over the bar and then return to a dead hang before you start your next pull-up. Sometimes when the whole platoon makes a trip to the head at one time to piss or fill canteens we all do a max set of pull-ups on the way out. We only do this once in a while but I really think it should be required every time you exit the head. This would improve everyone's pull-up output and cut down on weasels who go to the head when the shit hits the fan.

Late this afternoon the entire Series, which consists of three platoons, got a demonstration on the Marine Corps Obstacle Course. The Marine "O," as it is called, is basically about a hundred yards long and consists of a lot of walls and bars to climb over. The grand finale is the rope. The rope hangs down from a beam which is approximately thirty-five feet above the ground. To complete the "O" course you must shimmy your way up the rope using your arms and legs, until you climb high enough to slap the beam that holds the rope. I did this obstacle course at VMI and despite being six years younger and twenty-five pounds lighter I was only able to complete it once despite many tries and, even then, I barely finished. I have no problem with any of the obstacles other than that dammed rope. Maybe because I have bad technique, or weak hands, or duck feet, but the rope always kicks my ass. Even the one time I completed the "O" course at VMI, it was by the skin of my teeth. At VMI I only got high enough to nip the bar with my fingertips. I was so exhausted after my hand nicked the beam that I didn't have the strength to slowly make my way down the rope. Instead I slid down the rope, out of control at about five million miles per hour and burned the hell out of my palms and inner thighs. There's an image for ya.

We are doing the "O" course later this week and I'm very pessimistic about my chances of getting to the top of the rope. Even though they probably let you try the rope over and over like they did at VMI, I know that for me it's a one shot deal. If you can't scurry up the rope when your arms are relatively fresh why would you be able to do it after you've tried and failed and your arms are aching? My plan is to concentrate on my technique, using my legs and feet to push me up rather than my arms to pull me up. To be honest though, I'm worried because I'm a proud guy and it ate me alive when I couldn't do it at VMI, and I know for some reason it will be even worse this time.

Monday, July 24, 2000

To quell the constant complaints when compiling the Fire Watch roster, I gave myself Fire Watch. When someone complains that they are getting Fire Watch too often I can respond by saying that I gave myself Fire Watch even though I don't have to, just to shut them up. As it turned out, I had the last shift of the night, or morning depending how you want to look at it. This meant that I had the unenviable task of waking up the drill instructor. Like a lot of things on this island, the anticipation of the event was worse than the event itself. At 0430 I pounded on the DI's hatch just as hard as I could and shouted the obligatory spiel. "Sir, the time on deck is 0430. Good Morning Sir." Luckily I got the response "Go away" right off the bat and didn't have to repeat the process every five minutes, which happens often.

Being the last Fire Watch wasn't all that bad. First of all it's better than Fire Watch in the middle of the night because at least you get about six and a half consecutive hours of sleep. Also, when everyone else was scrambling to get dressed in the morning still half asleep and with the DI screaming his head off, I was already dressed and standing at my post watching the morning routine from a much different perspective than usual.

Every Monday we turn in sheets to be washed, and today, for some reason, I was designated a "laundry recruit." Along with three other recruits, I went around in a bus following a long, flat-bed truck picking up sheets from various barracks on Parris Island and piling them onto the flat bed. Until this tour of Parris Island, I hadn't seen anything but the same one hundred square yards that encompass our barracks, the chow hall, the chapel and RTF. This excursion was a welcomed change of pace from the usual routine.

After all of the sheets were picked up, we went to this building that looked like a factory from the turn of the last century (1900). There were these huge old contraptions everywhere making so much noise. Old civilian men manned the ancient machines and recruits, including me, loaded, unloaded, folded, stacked and carried about ten million sheets this morning. I didn't mind though because it was better than drill, or anything else, the rest of the platoon was doing.

I felt like I was in a prison movie, working on a chain gang. You couldn't talk, or move about freely and this guy who, I guess, is a Drill Instructor, because he wears the campaign cover of a DI, was constantly bitching at us. I forget his name but you could tell he was pissed off at life. The guy probably tells all his friends at home that he is a hot shot DI on Parris Island when all he does is supervise recruits doing laundry. This horrible inferiority complex probably explains why he was such a prick. He is trying to show the world that just because he's a glorified Laundromat clerk, he's still tough.

In between the wash cycle and the drying there was a little down time and we were supposed to be studying knowledge. When Drill Instructor Sergeant Low Self-Esteem wasn't around I got to talking to some recruits who were on "Team Week." Apparently Team Week is a week about two-thirds of the way through training when the Marine Corps takes advantage of its enormous pool of free labor. Platoons are assigned to work in the chow hall, pull weeds, and work in the laundry. There was one guy there who felt so bad that I was in such an early stage of training, and such a long way from graduation, that he gave me a piece of gum to chew after lights out. A month ago a piece of Trident would have meant absolutely nothing to me, but on Parris Island a piece of gum might as well be a $100 bill.

Late this afternoon, Senior Drill Instructor Staff Sergeant Jefferson marched us to the Parris Island Museum. The museum was pretty cool and it had a lot of old uniforms, pictures and weapons. My favorite part was the exhibit on famous Marines. A few of the guys surprised me. Captain Kangaroo, Gene Hackman, Tom Seaver, and John Glenn were all Marines. Also, I had heard him talk about it on his radio show but I forgot that Don Imus of *Imus in the Morning* fame was also a Marine at one point.

The most surprising Marine was pro-wrestler Sergeant Slaughter. Sergeant Slaughter was not only a Marine, but he was actually a Parris Island DI. When they announced him before wrestling matches they would say he hailed from Parris Island. He was my favorite wrestler for years but as I got older and learned that wrestling was fake, I wrongly assumed that because the Iron Sheik wasn't actually a sheik or from Iran, that meant that Sergeant Slaughter wasn't actually a DI or from Parris Island. I guess I was wrong.

When I was in third grade and my brother Pat was a senior in high school, he took me to a pro-wrestling match. The year was 1985 and the Cold War was white-hot in the Mid-Hudson Civic Center in Poughkeepsie, NY. The main event pitted super-patriot Sergeant Slaughter versus Soviet commie Nikolai Volkov. Moved to action by the "Russia Sucks" chant and wearing the DI's campaign cover that I purchased the year before at a military surplus store with my First Holy Communion money, my brother hopped the barricade and jumped up on the ring apron while the match was in progress. Just as "the Sarge" was about to give Pat a high-five in recognition of his, albeit overzealous, support, a swarm of security guards tackled Pat and basically beat the crap out of him. I thought for sure Pat was dead, or going to jail at best. My brother's friends took care of me and we watched Sergeant Slaughter, no doubt moved by Pat's support, go on to defeat the no-good Bolshevik. When it was over we found Pat waiting outside the civic center a little banged up but nothing serious. Four years later Pat enlisted in the Marine Corps.

I mention all this because seeing my favorite wrestler's picture in the Parris Island museum was the latest reminder that I was fulfilling a boyhood dream.

***

After the Senior took us to the museum, he unfurled the guidon. I could care less about whether our platoon number is displayed as we march around this island, or rolled up tightly in rubber bands as it has been since we got here. However, some of the idol worshippers are all excited about it. Similarly, a lot of guys are starting to talk like the DIs. They use lingo like "lock it up" instead of shut up and they say "Good to go!" every other sentence. I can't really explain why it annoys me so much but I hate hearing these guys speak almost exclusively in jarhead jargon. I guess it's because I'm resistant to anything that seems like brainwashing and although I want desperately to claim the title of Marine, I don't want this place to change me from an individual who thinks for himself into a sheep following the herd.

***

I haven't had anything sweet to eat since the airport in D.C. and as I write this, lying in my rack, I'm savoring every last chew of the piece of gum that recruit gave me at the laundry this morning. The way I figure, if you're going to write an illegal journal under your blanket with a flashlight in the middle of the night, you might as well have fresh breath and quietly chomp on some illegal gum.

Thursday, July 25, 2000

We had a couple of classes on Marine Corps history, specifically Vietnam, at RTF today. Everything they told us was so positive and glowing that you would think we won. I'll bet half of the kids in the room don't know that Vietnam was a tragic episode in American and Marine Corps history and that we lost the war (police action). The way he was talking about it, I don't even think the instructor knew that we didn't achieve our objective of stopping communist expansion into Vietnam.

The other twenty-four year old guy, Imish, who has a wife and kids, got caught writing a letter in RTF today. Apparently he mentioned some of the specifics of boot camp that the DIs are so protective of. I guess they're worried that somehow it will get back to their superiors that they bend the rules concerning the treatment of recruits. Don't get me wrong the DIs don't do anything sinister. I think there are some rules that are put in place for public relations reasons. For example, technically they are not supposed to swear at us, but the toilets are called "shitters," so you have an idea of how closely that rule is adhered to. I suppose they are worried that somebody's mom is going to call the General and show them what their son wrote, which would likely be an exaggeration of the truth.

Anyway, all three DIs took turns "smoking" Imish for at least two hours when we got back to the barracks. I think Imish is one of the tougher guys down here and even he was wailing with pain and then sobbing uncontrollably as he flooded the quarterdeck with his sweat and tears. It was the harshest anybody has ever gotten it. They probably wanted to make an example out of him and stop other recruits from telling tall tales about boot camp.

This incident affected me so much for a couple of reasons. Number one, Imish is the only guy I know of my age. Also, I came close to getting caught with my notes for this journal during RTF last week. If not for my awful handwriting, I would have been on the quarterback all afternoon as the merciless DIs worked me out.

Because of Imish getting caught, I'm more nervous than ever about this journal. I can't wait to get this set of notes in the mail and relieve some of the pressure. If they ever found out that I was keeping a daily journal of everything that we do, I don't even want to think about what they would do.

Drill Instructor Staff Sergeant Erickson is always bitching about the "Mothers of America," which I believe is a non-existent organization hell-bent on destroying the Marine Corps. Erickson goes on and on with his "Old Corps" war stories about how we don't have boxing anymore because the Mothers of America lobbied successfully to get rid of it. I agree that the Marine Corps, like everything else, has been weakened by political correctness but I can't stand how he exaggerates about how much tougher boot camp was when he went through. He acts as though he went to boot camp in a completely different era even though he told us he enlisted during the Gulf War, which was less than ten years ago.

Drill Instructor Staff Sergeant Erickson was kind enough to put the platoon through about a half-hour of footlocker PT after evening chow. Then, after evening chow, me and the other EEP Recruits got to do more footlocker PT while the rest of the platoon had square away time, which was really a treat. Usually EEP is a good, hard work-out but not excruciating. With Drill Instructor Staff Sergeant Erickson, EEP is always a pain in the ass because the insecure bastard is desperately trying to prove that he is as tough as Drill Instructor Sergeant Willis.

Just before bed I got into some trouble for laughing. I was standing on one side of the rack and Stewart was directly across from me. I couldn't help but laugh from staring at that goofy bastard's face. Drill Instructor Staff Sergeant Erickson came running over screaming his head off and put me in a headlock. It wasn't a real headlock though. It reminded me of professional wrestling because although his arm was completely wrapped around my noggin, there was no real pressure put on my head. I don't think the other recruits could tell, but I'm pretty sure it was all for effect. That headlock perfectly crystallizes the major difference between Erickson and Willis. Erickson allows himself to be constrained by the regulations and puts recruits in faux headlocks while Willis puts you in a no-shit, this-crazy-bastard-is-going-to-pop-my-head-off, headlock. Willis's extremely blunt motto, "You don't like how I make Marines? I don't give a fuck." says it all.

Wednesday, July 26 2000

We did the "O" course this morning and I'm proud to report that I made it up to the top of the rope. I was honestly surprised that I did it. I concentrated on my technique, using my feet and legs to generate the preponderance of my power and it worked out. I am pretty sure I was the only "diet tray recruit" to complete all of the obstacles.

I have been debating back and forth whether I should go to Officer Candidate School (OCS) and become a commissioned officer. That is the usual way a guy with a college degree goes into the military. I guess there are two reasons why I didn't go to OCS. To be an officer, you must do four years of active duty and that's not really what I was looking for. As a history teacher, I've always had great admiration for the Minutemen of the Revolution and non-professional soldiers throughout our history who put aside their civilian occupations and picked up a rifle during times of trouble. I want to be there for the county if the shit hits the fan but I also want to go to law school next year, not after four years of active duty. VMI viewed as its mission, the training of citizen-soldiers and even had a monument to Cincinnatus the Roman general who epitomized the concept of ordinary men stepping up to defend their country if the times required it. I guess that mentality stuck with me since leaving VMI.

The other thing that led me to a reserve enlistment, rather than an active duty commission, is this god-awful shitty place, Parris Island. A big part of my Marine Corps dream involved going to boot camp on Parris Island, as my father did in 1962 and my brother in did 1989. For me, the road to claiming the title of U.S. Marine had to go through Parris Island.

All that said, if I had to decide right now, riding high from my success on the "O" course, I'd go to OCS and become an officer but who knows how I'll feel a few months from now when I have to make that decision.

Another positive byproduct of the "O" course today was Imish getting a chance to redeem himself. Each of the three platoons in our Series chose their fastest guy to represent them in an "O" course race. The platoon whose guy wins gets to carry the Series guidon. I could give two shits about the stupid flag, but I knew it would make the DIs happy and maybe they would lighten up. Imish got out to an early lead but got beat on, of all things, the rope. I bet if Imish hadn't got the smoking of a lifetime yesterday he would have won. You could see in his eyes that he was disappointed that he couldn't totally redeem himself for yesterday's misstep with the letter, but he did a good job and I think he is back in good standing with the DIs.

The RTF lecture today was on post-Vietnam through the 1980s. Today's lecturer was pretty good. He told a story about a Marine that was severely injured in the Beirut bombing of the Marine barracks. Apparently the Commandant was visiting the guy in the hospital and, although the Marine couldn't speak and could barely move, he managed to scrawl "Semper Fi" on a scrap of paper and pass it to the Commandant. This anecdote made the hairs on the back of my neck stand up and reminded me of why I have always wanted to be part of this proud organization.

***

Drill Instructor Sergeant Willis does all of the teaching and reviewing for the big First Phase test we will take in a couple of days. The test covers everything from first aid, to how many stripes a sergeant wears, to who was the first Commandant of the Marine Corps. I have to say, Willis has some teaching methods that, although they would certainly get him fired from a school, are effective. He tries to simplify everything so everyone can remember and understand the material. He calls this "breaking it down, Barney style," a reference to that big purple children's show character. For example, Willis's way of helping us remember the Battle of Bladesburg during the War of 1812, where Marines protecting Washington D.C. repelled the British three times, was particularly effective. He told us that when we hear Bladensburg just remember "We kicked ass three times." To remember that the extortion of U.S. ships was the reason Marines fought in the Barbary Pirates War, Willis told us to remember "I aint payin' you shit." Like I said before, a school board would have about a million heart attacks if he tried this brand of teaching at a school, but it suits boot camp just fine.

***

This evening, in lieu of square away time, we had a practice test on all that we have been taught in RTF so far. I got a 100% and as a reward I got two hours of Fire Watch to tutor those who are struggling. As much as it stinks having two hours of Fire Watch, which by the way I'll be starting in about fifteen minutes, I did like the recognition and responsibility, two things that are hard to come by for a recruit on Parris Island.

We will take the First Phase test in a couple of days. If you don't pass (80%) I hear that you get dropped back three weeks in training. But honestly, if you can't pass this test you shouldn't be dropped in training, you should be dropped on your head because you are a moron. There are four versions of the test in existence. We don't know which one of the four we are going to get so we have been practicing all four. As with everything in boot camp, if we do something poorly or fail a test, it is a direct reflection on the DIs. Since DIs never want to be embarrassed, especially Willis, they will do everything they can to get you through it, including cutting my sleep by 25%.

***

By the way, we got our fourth haircut today and I finally got a pair of new jungle boots to replace the ones that were killing my feet so much.

Thursday, July 27, 2000

As I predicted, that scumbag Advent was relieved of his duties as the platoon Guide after his pitiful display of pugil sticks. But this morning, desperate to get back in the good graces of the DIs, he took it upon himself to report Tobago for taking a tiny packet of peanut butter from morning chow. Peanut butter is not a banned substance, like cake is, but it is off-limits to diet trays and no one is allowed to pocket a pack and take it back to the barracks. As we were filing into the chow hall, Advent turned in Tobego before he even ate the now-infamous peanut butter, or anything for breakfast. The DIs seized this opportunity to show everyone what happens when you try to eat something you are not authorized to eat. Drill Instructor Sergeant Willis took Tobago back to the squad bay with his scrumptious breakfast of scrambled eggs and rice in a Styrofoam container. When the platoon arrived back at the squad bay, there was poor Tobago on all fours doing mountain climbers, crying and throwing up. Willis was making him eat his chow while getting smoked. Even after he began to puke it up, he was still ordered to continue eating. It was awful to see a guy who you really liked being tortured three feet away from you.

The scuttlebutt was that Advent sold him out and I knew it was true because Advent would sell out his own mother if he thought he would help him. As Tobago puked and moaned on the quarterdeck, I stared daggers across the squad bay at that no good bastard Advent. He tried to pretend like he didn't notice my glare but I know he did. After PT, I got the opportunity to confront Advent in the head. I probably have fifty pounds on the guy and ordinarily wouldn't mess with someone so much smaller than me, but Advent was such a filthy, low-life, dirt bag that I didn't care. I threw him up against the wall and called him every name that came to my mind. I was afraid of the repercussions if I punched him so I refrained. However, I'm sure he got the point.

***

This afternoon we did the confidence course. The confidence course is pretty famous because you see "Private Pyle" struggling with it in *Full Metal Jacket* and almost everything you see about Parris Island includes some clips of the confidence course. It is a lot of climbing, hanging and balancing on obstacles spread out over about a half-mile loop. I have always had success in sports, but largely because I practiced a lot to develop good fundamentals and not because I had much natural athleticism. If I got a chance to practice all of the obstacles on my own for a while I might have fared better. Unfortunately, it is a one-shot deal and I pretty much shot myself in the foot.

I guess I'm pathetically making excuses for myself, so to be perfectly honest, I didn't fare much better than Private Pyle did. We split up into groups of about ten and I failed right from the start. The first obstacle, called the "Dirty Name," kicked my ass. Basically you stand on a log about two feet off the ground and have to pull yourself up and jump over a horizontal log that is approximately ten feet off the ground. It would be kind of like standing on a foot stool and climbing over the crossbar of a football goal post. Everyone else in my group did it, most on the first try. Drill Instructor Staff Sergeant Erickson gave me a bunch of chances and finally he disgustedly said to skip it and "move on to the next failure." For the first time since I've been here, I feel like a below average recruit.

The first obstacle of the confidence course destroyed all of the confidence I had gained earlier this week on the Marine Obstacle Course. After a couple of successes on the easier obstacles, and a few more failures, a thunderstorm swooped in on us so we had to stop for the day. I have to admit I was relieved that we were done with the course because at this point I don't think my self-esteem could plummet any further.

Every so often on Parris Island a voice will come over a loudspeaker and say "Lightning within five miles of Parris Island." When this happens, as it did today while we were on the confidence course, we stop what we are doing and either go back to the squad bay or go to a pavilion known as a "Thunder Dome."

While the rain poured down and the thunder crackled we sat and waited out the storm in the Thunder Dome. Drill Instructor Staff Sergeant Erickson saw this as a good opportunity to show the DIs from the other two platoons in our Series just what a hard-ass he was. He made us put our soaking camouflage blouses in the sawdust, which served as the floor of the wall-less Thunder Dome, and then put the shirts on and run in circles. We were getting screwed with for no reason whatsoever. Most of what we do, although often miserable, serves some purpose, but this activity was pointless. While we were wasting our time during the rain delay, the other platoons used the opportunity to drink water and prepare for the First Phase test. We wore these damp cammies filled with sawdust chaffing our skin for the rest of the day. It absolutely sucked and was all because Erickson knows he is a shitty DI and that the recruits don't respect him as much as we do the other two DIs.

It's safe to say that today pretty much sucked all around. When we finally got back to the squad bay we played a few rounds of tear-apart-the-rack-then-make-it-again, which is absolutely awful. The only thing more frustrating than making and remaking the rack is getting dressed "by the numbers." This is what we do every morning when we get out of the rack. The DI says, "Put my left sock on now. Put my right sock on now." We'll be half dressed and then some idiot can't get his boot tied in time so we have to strip down to our "skivvy drawers" and do the whole thing over. This can go on for as long as forty-five minutes depending on the mood of the DI, how slow we are, and what time we are scheduled to eat morning chow. This kind of stuff makes everyone turn on each other because it exposes the weak links. It's frustrating because it erodes a lot of the camaraderie that has developed during the more important training exercises.

After making the racks over-and-over, we had some footlocker PT, which is becoming routine and a little less excruciating, although I still hate it. The Senior didn't give out the mail, which was a major disappointment.

The one bright spot today was Drill Instructor Sergeant Willis giving us a sexual harassment class. Listening to Willis talk about what you can and cannot say to and about female Marines was hysterical. You could tell he dreaded giving this class and that he was just going through the motions to get it over with. I'm not sure how it was relevant, but he told us about how they gave a guy a bunch of "blanket parties" when he was in boot camp. He said that they used to rough up the platoon screw-up pretty badly but he never told on them. One time it was so bad, the DIs just knew that the guy was getting his ass kicked at night so they transferred him to another platoon. Willis also told us that the term "code red" to describe a blanket party never existed in the Marine Corps until the Tom Cruise move *A Few Good Men* came out.

Before I left, my brother warned me not to have anything to do with blanket parties, even if the DIs encourage it. He said the DIs could be testing you and that punishing a bad recruit is not worth getting in trouble over.

Friday, July 28, 2000 (9 Weeks Until Graduation)

In the middle of the night last night the DIs woke us all up and took a head count. Apparently a recruit from another platoon tried to escape. One of our Fire Watches saw him crouching behind a wall and woke up the DI on duty. The DI called the Military Police and they got the guy. I guess they wanted to make sure none of us snuck out during all of the confusion.

Ruiz, the guy with the finance in 4th Battalion, got a letter from her today. The DIs noticed the return address and the Marine Corps issue envelope and knew the letter was from a female recruit. The DIs thought he met her in church and became pen pals so they smoked him pretty good. They made him hang from the pull-up bar with his chin over the bar for twenty minutes. Even after he would fall off they'd make him jump back up and hang some more.

Apparently two guys wrote letters to their recruiters asking to get them out. Senior Drill Instructor Staff Sergeant Jefferson didn't mention the names of the recruits in question. Instead he took the whole platoon to the pit to punish us all for the two anonymous recruits who, according to the Senior, "betrayed the Drill Instructors and the Corps." Recruiters do a good job of making you feel like they are you're their best friend. They will do anything to get you to sign up and make sure you get to Parris Island, like go to your high school and get an original copy of your diploma or get you out of any pending legal problems that are an impediment to your enlistment. Regardless, you'd have to be a moron to think that your recruiter, a guy whose job is to get guys to boot camp and ultimately to become Marines, would and could somehow miraculously absolve you of your commitment. As Drill Instructor Sergeant Willis always says quite poignantly, "USMC stands for U Signed the Motherfucking Contract."

***

Things down here are up and down. There are times when everything is okay and other times when I'm absolutely depressed and think the day, let alone the next two months is never going to end. I have met some great guys down here and, because we are together all day everyday under such stressful conditions, it feels like we've been friends for years. The weird thing is nobody knows anybody's first name.

For the first time since I've been here, I am physically exhausted. Everything aches, especially my hamstrings and my shins. Rocky Balboa explained to Adrian how he felt after a fight by saying, "I'm nothing but a large wound." That's pretty much where I am at this point.

Saturday, July 29, 2000

25% of the way done.

At VMI we called them "forced marches" and here on Parris Island we call them "humps." Basically we put our packs on our backs and sling our rifles over our shoulders and walk all over Parris Island as fast as we can in two long columns. As with anything else that we do, there is a lot of yelling but most of it is motivational. The worst part about the hump, which was only about three miles with a ten minute break in the middle, was that we are constantly spouting knowledge as we trek along. Shouting takes more out of you than the marching, the heat, or the weight of the pack. It would be so nice to just march and daydream and check out the scenery but that would be too much to ask for. The whole time we are yapping away. The DI asks the question, "E-4 in the Marine Corps?" We respond loudly and proudly, "Sir, E-4 in the Marine Corps is a Corporal, backbone of the Marine Corps. He wears two stripes with cross rifles, Sir." "E-5 in the Marine Corps?" "Sir, E-5 in the Marine Corps is Sergeant, heart of the Marine Corps. He wears three stripes up with cross rifles, Sir." The whole point of this is to prepare us for First Phase of testing which, I think, is in one week.

Before the hump, the shit hit the fan when Advent got caught stealing cookies from the big gear locker. You are probably wondering why there are cookies sitting around a boot camp squad bay? Sometimes we eat packaged lunches with sandwiches, a little bag of chips, and a small pack of Oreos or Chips Ahoy. The DIs confiscated the snacks and stored them in a footlocker for safekeeping. Advent is the "big gear locker recruit," which means he is responsible for keeping the room where we keep stuff like laundry detergent, extra canteens, and miscellaneous uniform items neat. I guess Advent was given the locker combo and decided to stuff his face during Fire Watch.

Since the Tobago peanut butter caper, Advent has pretty much evolved into the platoon anti-Christ because he screwed Tobago, a well-liked recruit. Advent, or as we now call him the "Cookie Monster," is his own worst enemy because he tried to implicate other unnamed recruits, whining "A lot of others have taken cookies too, Sir." Shortly after he tried to drag some others down with him, a bunch of guys roughed him up a little in the head. Although I think he knew Advent acted alone, Drill Instructor Staff Sergeant Erickson decided to punish all of us for the Great Cookie Caper. We must have done five hundred to six hundred straight push-ups. It was pretty brutal although surprisingly, after a few hundred push-ups, my arms went numb and I was as good as new.

***

It is amazing how intolerant this place is. If you cough when the DI is talking or during drill or at formations, it is a Cardinal sin. This intolerance is rubbing off on me. When I'm compiling the Fire Watch list and some guy gives me a hard time, claiming he is getting Fire Watch "every night," I will call him every awful name that comes to my head. One time recently, I tore into some geeky seventeen year old kid for bellyaching about his Fire Watch assignment. I roared, "Shut the fuck up you filthy cock-sucking son-of-a-bitch." Never has such a river of obscenity come flowing out of my mouth as it did onto that poor kid. I could see in his face that he was shaken up. He apologized to me for complaining, but I also apologized to him for being so brusk with him.

I would hate to think this place is affecting me in such a negative way. The sign that arches the road when you first drive onto Parris Island reads "The Change is Forever." When I saw that I vowed that I wouldn't let this place brainwash me or change me in any negative way. I like to think that, at twenty-four, I'm a pretty well-developed person and that I will leave this island at the end of September a skinny, more disciplined, finely-tuned instrument of warfare, but essentially the same man I was when I got here. Is it even possible not to change even while being transformed? I hope that when I get out of here I can still relate to my friends and family the same way I did in the past.

**

My day brightened up considerably when I received a bunch of letters from friends and my sister, Meg. I spent every second of square away time reading my mail. I was so engrossed in my letters that I lost track of time and didn't even shine my boots. I put my dirty, scuffed-up boots on my footlocker and waited for Drill Instructor Sergeant Willis to walk by during his nightly inspection. I figured there was a chance I would get caught but I really didn't care because I had gotten so much wonderful mail.

Sure enough Willis saw that I hadn't touched my boots. He laughed in my face with his trademark sinister chuckle and calmly said, "You must be out your fucking mind boy. Fourth Fire Watch!"- meaning I was assigned to the worst Fire Watch shift because it comes exactly in the middle of the night. By the time you fall into a deep sleep, it's time for your shift. By the time you fall asleep after your shift, it's practically reveille. Saturday night, however, is a relatively good night for Fire Watch because we get nine hours of rack time.

***

Poor Stewart. He has the craziest family life I have ever heard. His dad, a Gulf War vet, is in prison for some kind of sexual assault. His little brother is fourteen and in "Juvy" for stealing a car. His family can't afford a phone or cable TV. He joined the Marine Corps to help support his family. The saddest thing is that he never gets any mail. There is another recruit named Stewart who always gets mail. When the Senior reads "Stewart" off a letter, I see my buddy perk up and then I see his face sink when he realizes it's for the other Stewart. One time he actually got a letter. It was a form letter from his recruiter asking how things were going. He was thrilled. Other than that he has never once gotten any mail.

I wrote some friends to ask them to send him a letter. I feel guilty reading my letters in the evenings when he has nothing so, if he got a couple of token letters, even from a complete stranger, it would mean a lot to him and me. I told my friends to mention how I told them what good buddies we are and how I think he'll be a great Marine one day, to give him confidence and an ego boost.

***

The night went steadily downhill beginning right before lights out at 2100. I had my folder with all of my mail under my pillow poised to read and reread my letters after Taps. Just as the Fire Watch was counting down to shut off the lights. "10, 9, 8, 7, 6…" Willis saw the folder sticking out from under my pillow and took the whole folder. In that folder was every piece of mail that I have received since arriving on the Island some four weeks ago. Willis is a cruel motherfucker too. I didn't know what he was going to do. But having those letters confiscated was like having my gut rung out like a sponge. I am pretty certain I will get them back after some sweat, pain and the obligatory humiliation of having letters from my mother, siblings and friends mocked in front of the entire platoon. I'm not even sure if Willis will bother to read the letters because he is mostly concerned with physical, not emotional, pain.

Also, one thing I have been noticing about Parris Island is that the days are so long here that an event that seems so important in the morning is irrelevant by afternoon chow. Basically I'm going to try not to lose any sleep over this non-incident. Incidentally, I'm glad that I had the foresight to send these journal entries home and not have them lying around my footlocker. If Willis had in his possession my journal I would not be nearly as calm as I am being right now. I'd be shitting a brick.

Sunday, July 30, 2000

I lucked out again. During my Fire Watch last night I got my letters back. I don't know why. Maybe Willis likes me, although I doubt it. Maybe he was in a good mood. I don't know, but I'm so happy he gave them back and without any punishment… yet. He just threw them at me and said, "That's your warning."

I learned a lesson at VMI that most of these other guys don't understand and that is absolutely invaluable here on Parris Island - VMI taught me never to try and explain myself when I am getting yelled at. Even if I know I am right and the DI is wrong I simply respond, "No excuse, Sir." I think that might be why I got the letters back. Guys are always trying to state their case to the DIs when no matter what they say they are going to be in trouble and talking back only fuels the DI's fire. So many times I hear some idiot try and explain why he messed up, not realizing that the yelling and the punishment is all part of the game. When this happens I stand there thinking to myself, "Shut up moron. Don't you realize you are only getting yourself in more trouble?"

Sadly, my buddy Tobago wasn't as lucky as me. He got caught looking at some photos he had been sent while on Fire Watch last night. I guess this was a more egregious infraction than me having my letters in bed, because the Fire Watch is technically supposed to be guarding the platoon from harm. Tobago got his pictures taken away and was given another Fire Watch shift for his crime. On his second Fire Watch shift he was assigned to Post 2 which is the head. Guys are always reading and writing letters in the head late at night because the DIs don't usually check out the head after midnight. However, on this night Drill Instructor Sergeant Willis came barging into the head and Tobago tried to make like Paul Revere and warn the guys who were writing letters that Willis was on his way. Believe it or not, the only guy in there with mail was Advent. Tobago was helping out a guy who, only a few days earlier, sold him out and got him severely smoked. When Willis realized what Tobago was doing he gave him a verbal smoking like you would not believe. He said he was a disgrace to his family, that he was destined to be a failure all of his life, and that he never should have been born. Tobago normally handles this kind of stuff with amazing ease but something Willis said must have gotten to him because he broke down sobbing loud horrible sobs. Willis told him that he had Fire Watch every night for the rest of recruit training and that anytime he reported to a DI he had to say, "Sir, Piece of Shit reporting as ordered, Sir." Tobago was sobbing so hard you didn't know if he was ever going to stop. It was so bad that Willis assigned an extra Fire Watch to keep an eye on him so he didn't kill himself.

***

This morning the other fat bodies and I had our weekly weigh in and I was a svelte 203 pounds, nearly thirty pounds less than when I set foot on Parris Island more than three weeks ago.

I used to think the food, or lack thereof, was the worst part about Parris Island. At VMI you could go through the chow line as many times as you wanted and eat anything you wanted. You could also get cookies and brownies mailed to you and keep them in your room. Here it's slim pickins. As bad as the lack of food is, it is not the worst thing about PI. The worst thing is being on-the-go all day, every day. Every minute of every day is stressful. Some parts are less stressful than others, but even at church you cannot truly relax. In the back of your mind you always know that the DIs are going to be there waiting for you when Mass is over.

There is also no privacy at all. Every place you go is public. There are no doors on the stalls in the head. When we are outdoors drilling or moving from place to place, we have to double and triple up in the port-a-johns. Port-a-johns are notoriously nasty in the civilian world, imagine one on Parris Island where two and three recruits with bad aim are forced to squeeze in.

It amazes me that Parris Island has made me appreciate how good life was at VMI, a place I really didn't like that much. But the reason VMI was so hellish was that I had regrets. I regretted going so far away from home. I regretted not going to a regular college and being able to live it up like my friends were doing. I regretted going to an all-male school and feeling like I was missing out on something. I regretted that my dad got cancer and I was in Virginia and had to go ten links up the chain-of-command to go visit him. Ironically, leaving VMI made me regret abandoning my lifelong dream of becoming a Marine and leaving VMI has a lot to do with why I am here now. I guess what I'm saying is that although boot camp is more difficult than VMI, I'm happier because I have no regrets.

Monday, July 31, 2000

At PT this morning we had an individual-effort run. In civilian terms that means we had a timed race. Usually we run in three groups, slow, medium and fast, but today we ran two miles for a time. My time was a very respectable 13:20. Not quite on pace for an 18:00 minute three mile but enough to put me in the top thirty out of the two hundred or so guys in the Company and a big improvement on the 10:30 mile and a half I ran at the Initial Strength Test.

I believe my speed has improved for a couple of reasons. The obvious one is the weight loss. Losing all of that weight has made me feel so agile and quick. However, I think the biggest contributor to my improved speed is the PT runs with the fast group. Drill Instructor Staff Sergeant Erickson is a fast runner and he really pushes us. He will jog at a normal pace and then take off, practically sprinting, for a quarter mile or so. Sometimes I honestly feel like my heart is pumping so fast that it is going to pop. My chest hurts so much that I always want to drop out but I know I'm too proud to get demoted to the middle running group. That type of training has really built up my wind and stamina. It has also taught me that even though it really hurts when you run as fast as you can for two or more miles, it's not going to kill you and the pain will subside soon after the run is over.

***

As usual, a crappy showing on the drill field led the platoon to the pit not once, but twice. It seems like all we do lately is drill, go to the pit because we suck at drill, drill some more and back to the pit. It's a vicious cycle. I wish I was eloquent enough to articulate how awful drill is and how much I dread it. Just imagine being forced to do something you hate and then getting screamed at and punished because someone else cannot do it well. Then multiply by ten. That is how much I hate drill.

After hours and hours of drill in the morning and early afternoon, we went to Leatherneck Square for some more close-combat training. Learning the proper way to counter an aggressor and properly choke a guy so you can actually kill him was a great opportunity to get out some of the frustrations of recruit life. Then, we went directly from learning how to choke the life out of another human being to a class on Core Values taught by the battalion chaplain. The Core Values of the Marine Corps are Honor, Courage, and Commitment. The chaplain basically told us how these three ideals have been the thread that has tied the Corps and the country together for 225 years. He touched on a lot historical events which was great because I love history and feel like my brain is turning to mush constantly thinking of only my recruit knowledge.

***

Our Platoon has what Drill Instructor Staff Sergeant Erickson terms, a "volume problem." We don't respond to commands loudly enough, so he says. After the chaplain's class we spent at least an hour and a half screaming, "Aye, aye Sir" at the top of our lungs. Erickson was pretending like he couldn't hear us and would respond "Oh hell no. I can't hear you" and we'd yell "Aye, aye Sir" again. This screaming went on so long that half the platoon is now hoarse.

Now you know why I'm worried about my brain becoming a worthless pile of goo.

Tomorrow is the Senior Drill Instructors' inspection. From what I understand, we will be inspected by each of the Senior Drill Instructors from the six platoons that make up Alpha Company. A year at VMI, and three and a half weeks on Parris Island, have taught me that no matter how perfectly our trousers are pressed or how neatly our covers are starched, we are going to catch hell tomorrow from the DIs inspecting us. If you think about it, they have no choice but to ream us tomorrow, if they don't, what is our motivation to improve and do better for future inspections. Also, boot camp is all about recruits failing everything at first and eventually getting it right after a lot of screaming, sweating, and sand.

***

Another recruit got caught taking a peanut butter packet today. Recruit Henri, a four foot ten inch Haitian immigrant, got caught smuggling peanut butter packets out of the chow hall in the battery compartment of his moonbeam. It was pretty ingenious actually and I'm not sure how they caught him, but they did. If he wasn't from another country, I would assume that he picked up the idea from Bobby Brady who pulled a similar stunt with hot dogs on the *Brady Bunch* when the Brady's went to the Grand Canyon. The DIs said that they knew that Henri was not the only peanut butter thief and that others had taken peanut butter, but they had no integrity because they wouldn't come forward. This accusation caused a genuine witch hunt and, in classic boot camp style, recruits started parroting the words of the DIs, accusing their fellow recruits of "integrity violations." It is sort of funny that a little one ounce packet of peanut butter has led to the downfall, at least temporarily, of our platoon on two separate occasions.

Other than what I have mentioned above, today was pretty uneventful. I'm glad I don't have too much to report because I want to go right to sleep because I have Fire Watch at 0100 to tutor. At least I'll be tutoring Tobago, so it won't be that bad. Oh yeah, Tobago is off suicide watch and back to his old self. Somehow he swiped a piece of cake today at dinner and was kind enough to share it with me. I never met anyone with a pair of balls as big as this guy's.

Tuesday, August 1, 2000

We practiced what to say at inspection all morning. When the inspector, a Senior Drill Instructor from another platoon, walks in front of me, I am supposed to shout, "Sir, Good Morning Sir. Recruit Lalor, Wappinger Falls, New York, NY, 0300 - Infantry, good morning, Sir." After that you are supposed to get to what is called "inspection arms." Basically you pick the rifle off the ground, pull the bolt to the rear, checking to make sure there is no round in the chamber before you present the rifle to the inspector. When it became my turn, I choked and froze up like the proverbial deer in the headlights. After saying my name, hometown and military occupational specialty (MOS) I was so happy with myself for not stumbling over my words that I forgot to present the rifle, which is really the whole point of the inspection. I just stood there and then three inspectors jumped all over me calling me a "retard" and a "moron." What killed me was practicing what to do over-and-over in my mind while the guys in front of me were being inspected and then screwing it up.

While they checked my weapon, uniform, boots, and how close I shaved, they quizzed me on knowledge. I got all of the questions right from the first DI inspecting so another guy came over and tried to stump me with a question on something that had not yet been covered. He asked, "What are the three goals of terrorist organizations?" Fortunately, I had gone ahead in the Green Monster and knew the answer. I blurted out, "Sir, the three goals of terrorist organizations are Religious, Political and Ideological, Sir." I know the guy was impressed because he begrudgingly whispered "Outstanding!"

Hearing this exchange, a third inspector approached me and asked me, "What is the cycle of operation of the M-16 A2 service rifle?" I didn't have a clue so I responded in the manner we were told to respond when we didn't know the answer. I said, "This recruit was instructed but does not recall at this time." That was absolute bull because I am certain we have never been instructed on that question, but, like a good recruit, I followed orders.

As if standing for inspection wasn't boring enough, we had a three-hour, indoor drill session this afternoon. I think it was too hot to train outside so we did three hours of non-stop, "right shoulder arms", "port arms", "left shoulder arms", "order arms." I thought outdoor drill, which involves a lot of marching around, was the worst thing in the world - until today. Indoor drill is cruel and unusual punishment. You stand in the same place for so long that, at first, your feet start to tingle. Next they start to get hot until finally, they just ache unbearably. I thought it would never end, but eventually it did, although I'm pretty sure it burned years off my life and cells out of my brain.

After the drill-session-from-hell, a nice looking woman in her late twenties came to give us our travel brief. Actually, I'm not sure if she is attractive or if I haven't seen girls in so long I've lost my frame of reference. Either way, it was very exciting to hear her talk about graduation and how in a few weeks we would be purchasing plane tickets to go home and how soon our families could buy their tickets to graduation. Up until this point, graduation seemed to be light-years away. The Drill Instructors, and everyone else we encountered, acted like we would probably never graduate. They would always say stuff like "If you ever get off this island, which most of you won't, you will be a part of the Fleet Marine Force." Finally someone, albeit a civilian woman, was telling us what we wanted to hear, graduation was finally in the distant future.

This evening was a record setting day as far as mail goes. I got a letter from my Mom, my little sister, my friend Goober, Goober's Mom, and my brother Danny. I have never felt so loved in my whole life. Square away time was not nearly enough time to read all of this mail, so, although it was dangerous, I read my letters in the rack with the flashlight. Tonight was also the first time Willis has been on duty since the night that he briefly commandeered all of my letters. Still it was worth the risk. I didn't have a choice in the matter. I would lose my mind if I had to go all day tomorrow with all of those letters burning a hole in my footlocker. Fortunately, I have developed a pretty good system of keeping my flashlight dim and laying in such a manner that I'm able to read the letters and keep an eye on the door to the DI shack. I use my torso to block the view the DI might have of my flashlight or the letters. This system successfully concealed my activities so well that even Drill Instructor Sergeant Lucifer was oblivious as I read my letters and as I finish today's journal entry.

Wednesday, August 2, 2000

The hours and hours of drilling are starting to get to me. It is not that it's difficult, because it's not. It is just so dammed boring. In another week or so we will go out to the rifle range for two weeks. I'm hoping that we will be so busy learning how to shoot straight we won't have to worry about marching straight. What a welcome change of pace that will be.

***

For the first time since I was a young kid, I pray religiously. Every night I thank the Lord that another day is behind me and ask him to make the time move swiftly. Although it doesn't always seem like it, for the most part that prayer has been answered. In my civilian life, I rarely prayed, but here on Parris Island I look forward to the quiet minutes of prayer before I fall asleep. It is one high points of my day.

It is so ironic that working at a Catholic high school for two years made me cynical and less religious, because although there were many good people there, I came across some appalling hypocrites. Then, I come to Parris Island and have a religious revival. I guess it is as my father always used to say, "There are no atheists in fox holes."

***

I have had Fire Watch almost every night lately to tutor the struggling recruits. Thankfully, this Saturday is what they call First Phase testing, so all of the hours of Fire Watch / tutoring will come to an end soon. Today we set up different stations to work on the prac-ap (practical application) portion of the test. Prac-ap requires recruits to, among other things, tie a tourniquet, dress a sucking chest wound, and demonstrate how to properly board a Navy Ship. When boarding, you salute the American flag and then the captain of the ship. Drill Instructor Sergeant Willis's memory device for this bit of knowledge is, "Salute the flag then the fag." Brilliant!

Along with two other recruits who have a good handle on the knowledge, I was put in charge of running these prac-ap stations. I learned from coaching football, the more game-like you can make practice, the better so I yell at my guys while they were attempting to complete each station because I'm sure that the Marines grading the prac-ap will be rushing us to get all two hundred of us through it in a timely manner. Plus we get yelled at during everything we do so why would the prac-ap portion of First Phase Testing be any different? Drill Instructor Sergeant Willis took notice of my initiative and even gave me a compliment, saying "Good work, shit bag." That is the difference between Willis and Erickson. Willis is confident enough to appreciate when a recruit's idea aids his instruction. Erickson is too insecure to do anything like that. Erickson would have either claimed the idea for himself or dismissed it as a stupid idea just to protect his own ego.

***

Along with a handful of others, I have been designated a burly recruit. This means that I have to shave twice per day. I shave during hygiene time every night, like everyone else, and then again when we brush our teeth in the morning. This is such an inconvenience because although the burly recruits are required to shave in the morning we are not given any extra time. In the same time that everyone else gets to wash their face and brush their teeth, we have to wash, brush and also shave. It is just the latest example of boot camp injustice. It is not my fault I've been shaving every day since the 8th grade and grow a thick crop of red stubbly five o'clock shadow.

I also have a similar problem with sun block. My skin is pretty much as pale as human flesh can be. I burn easily and when I sunburn I peel in layers and layers of nasty, flaky skin. Therefore I go through a lot of sun block. I try to apply every couple of hours, which isn't easy. I keep the bottle of 45 SPF sun block we were issued in a Ziplock bag in my cargo pocket wherever I go. A lot of the other guys noticed that I am always asking permission to apply sun block. Some of the black guys and others not worried about sunburn gave me their issue of sun block. In the first month, I have already finished five or six bottles.

***

Parris Island, and everyone who works here, is obsessed with dehydration or hydration, depending on how you look at it. Marine Officers, Navy medical personnel, DIs, and veteran recruits stress the importance of drinking water. Apparently if you become dehydrated the corpsman has to insert a tube in your rectum called the "silver bullet." This was more than enough to motivate me to drink water even when I wasn't thirsty and even when it made me a little nauseous. In the head on the wall above the urine trough where we crowd together to relieve ourselves is a urine chart. The chart has several different shades of yellow. We are supposed to match the color of our urine with one of the colors on the chart. Once you have matched the colors, the chart tells you how many canteens of water you need to drink in the next few hours to avoid dehydration. The darker shade of yellow the more water you need. For example, if you're pissing apple juice, you better pound some canteens ASAP. If your piss looks like white wine, you're good to go.

The DIs love making us pound canteens the way a frat boy pounds a beer. Some guys puke from too much water but my Rugby days taught me the finer points of slamming a beer and I used the same principles to down canteen water. By simply opening wide the back of your throat and throwing the beverage directly into the throat bypassing the lips and tongue, one can consume an amazing amount of liquid in a short period. The DIs walk around and make sure our canteens are empty, so some guys beg me to swap canteens and drink the water they can't finish to keep them out of trouble. I do it to help out the guys I like and also to fill up my stomach to combat ever-present hunger pangs.

Thursday, August 3, 2000

We have been so busy around here lately that I have not had much time to write letters and have had to do almost my entire note-taking for this journal at RTF, late at night in the head, or in my rack. Normally I get a decent amount of note-taking done during square away time. I'm sure everyone thinks that I'm just writing letters although lately some of my buddies, especially Ryan, a sharp seventeen year old kid from Connecticut, have been inquiring about what I am always writing. Because we are a similar height, Ryan and I stand next to each other in formation.

As a result, he and I sit next to each other nearly every time we go to RTF. I always catch him looking over my shoulder and trying to see what I'm intently scribbling.

Don't get me wrong, I like Recruit Ryan a lot, he is one of my best friends down here, but I don't want to risk getting caught or jeopardize the journal in anyway. I just tell him, in a joking way, to mind his own business. I guess I'm afraid he'll mention that I'm keeping a journal to one guy, and that one guy will tell another recruit, and before I know it everyone will know and it will all blow up in my face.

***

Today we got fitted for our dress uniforms. We spent a lot of the day in a big supply warehouse walking around in T-shirts, tighty-whities, black socks and shiny black dress shoes trying on trousers and the gabardine service uniform. It was real treat to look in the mirror and see myself trying on the uniform I have wanted to wear my whole life. We didn't try on the famous dress blues, but we did get measured for the green Service Alphas like Ollie North wore while testifying at the Iran/Contra hearings and like Jack Nicholson wore on the stand in *A Few Good Men*, when he uttered the famous line "You can't handle the truth."

***

Two days from today we have what is called Series Drill. This is where we compete with the other two platoons in our Series in a drill competition. I usually don't care too much about a lot of the manufactured boot camp motivation stuff, but I am taking this seriously because if we win the DIs, especially the Senior, will be extremely happy with us and our quality of life is likely to improve. Shockingly we actually had a good drill session today. Maybe we are peaking at the right time. The DIs were so happy with our performance on the drill field that they let us have juice and chocolate milk with lunch today. I think the juice here is too sweet and syrupy but I drank it anyhow because we don't get very many privileges so I have to take advantage of any treat we get. I would rather the chocolate milk than juice but fat bodies are barred from drinking "brown cow."

***

Starting tonight I'm going to do some pull-ups on my own after lights outs. I like to think I have a pretty strong upper body but I have always been pretty weak at pull-ups. The fact that I have thick thighs and a really big ass doesn't help. Pull-ups are all upper-body strength and a lot of my weight is concentrated in my lower body, which in terms of pull-ups, is all dead weight.

***

I almost forgot the real highlight of the day. I called Drill Sergeant Willis's bluff on knowledge today. While reviewing for First Phase testing, Willis told the Platoon that the U.S. had never lost a war. I guess the confident Social Studies teacher in me overcame the submissive recruit in me because I called him on it. I asked, respectfully and using the best military lingo as I could muster, "Sir. Didn't we fail to achieve our objectives in Vietnam?" Willis said, "What do you mean?" I responded, "Sir, we fought in Vietnam to stop the spread of communism and Vietnam is a communist country today, Sir." Willis said that Vietnam was not a communist country because we trade with them. I informed him that we trade with almost every communist country except Cuba. Finally Willis backed off his early statements and said, "I'll look into it."

I'm sure everything Willis knows about Vietnam, and history in general, he learned here at Recruit Training and, as I mentioned earlier, those lectures have a lot of holes in them. I guess I took a big risk disagreeing with the DI, especially Willis. I didn't make a conscious decision to contradict him, it just sort of popped out. Fortunately, I think Willis realizes that all of the tutoring I've been doing is going to make him look like the greatest instructor in the world when we take the First Phase test, one week from tomorrow. If I was not the platoon tutor, I don't think he would have been so understanding of a recruit disagreeing with him in front of the entire platoon.

***

Amazingly it is approximately 2130 and I have yet to do one push-up all day, and it is highly unlikely that I'll have to do one until tomorrow. Come to think of it, we didn't really do anything physical today. First juice then no push-ups? This has to be the best day I have spent on Parris Island.

Friday, August 4, 2000 (8 Weeks Until Graduation)

Today started out as a relatively easy day mainly because I got to go to the dentist. In my civilian life, I loathe the dentist. I guess I have weak teeth because I have had a ton of dental work done in my life. In the civilian world the dentist sucks because you go sit in the waiting room forever, finally the dentist does what he has to do, makes your teeth feel worse than when you got there and you leave with a mouth full of gauze. However, Parris Island is such a screwed up place that going to the dentist and getting a filling is actually a treat.

You are not allowed to talk or sleep in the waiting room at dental, but there are TV's in the waiting room and, although technically I don't think you are allowed to watch them, it is almost impossible not to. The TV was permanently on ESPN 2 and some awful car racing show but I guess that's to be expected in South Carolina. The good thing was that the previous nights scores are constantly being scrolled across the bottom of the screen. I don't have a clue what place the Yankees are in or how they have been doing over the past month, but I know they beat Oakland 3-2 last night.

While I was at dental with a few other guys in my platoon I missed a long and, I'm quite certain, an excruciatingly boring, drill session, which was absolutely fabulous. From what the other recruits have told me, I also missed a pit call, which kind of disappointed me. I'm not saying I like pit calls. Anyone who claims they like to go to the pit is a liar and an asshole. However, missing a trip to the pit made me feel like a weasel, like those guys who go to sick call in the morning. But it's not like I asked to go to dental or could have declined the opportunity. Besides a bunch of other guys from my platoon went to dental with me so I probably won't lose any sleep over it.

***

Since the last time I mentioned the platoon Guide there have been a bunch of changes. After Advent was relieved of his command, there were a couple of guys who held the position for less than a day. Imish even got a shot at being Guide before being removed after only a few hours. The Guide basically has to have a big mouth, not mind bossing people around, and be willing to do the DI's bidding.

After a couple of Guides with tenures lasting only a few hours, Recruit Kistemaker got the nod. Kistemaker is no ordinary recruit. He is what is known as a prior service recruit. This means that he was a member of another military branch before joining the Marines. As it turns out, Kistemaker who is also twenty-four, was a Sergeant in the Army. That means he was the same rank as Willis and just one rank below Erickson and the Senior. Why he would give up being a Sergeant in the Army with men under him to become a Marine Recruit, who has to ask permission to piss, is a mystery to me.

Kistemaker was a good Guide because he had instant credibility because of his Army background. You could tell just by the way he conducted himself and by his maturity that he had been in the service before. For some reason he got fired, probably because the DIs thought having an ex-soldier as Guide was sort of a compliment to the nasty Army. Anyway, after Kistemaker got canned the DIs installed this guy Hans. Hans used to be my bunkee before I started bunking with Stewart. The best way to describe him is to call him a bitch. He is always whining and feeling sorry for himself. I'm sure he, like the rest of the platoon, was shocked when he got the job.

***

One of my favorite ways to pass the time down here is to make calendars and count the days until graduation. I keep track of how many calendar days stand between graduation and me, as well as how many training days I have left. I keep track of how many weeks remain and what percentage of boot camp is behind me and how much lies ahead. At present I have fifty-six days left and I have completed exactly four weeks or 25% of boot camp.

One of the few bright spots in my day is when I get to cross off the previous date in my countdown. I enjoy drawing an "X" through the most recent day completed so much that I keep a bunch of different calendars just so I can duplicate several times that tiny sliver of euphoria that goes with knowing I have one less day on Parris Island.

***

You wouldn't believe how many recruits are engaged to be married. The DIs once told us that the average age of our platoon is nineteen and I know at least ten guys who are engaged. Some guys use the term engagement loosely and haven't even given the girl a ring yet. Others have rings, a date picked out and, at least one, has a banquet hall rented. Why do these guys want to get married so young? Don't they realize that most of them are going to be traveling around the world for the next four years and meeting all sorts of girls? Why would they want to be tied down to someone they are barely going to see for the next couple years? This marriage thing must be contagious because yesterday an eighteen-year-old recruit named Dexter told me he planned to propose to his girl on the parade deck at graduation.

Other than girlfriends, fiancée's and, in a few cases, wives, the other big subject recruits discuss on the rare occasion when we get to chitchat, is food. I know guys who know exactly what food they want to eat first when we get off this island. Some guys have even sent letters home requesting a long list of goodies that their mother or girlfriends should bring to Family Day. I guess when you go a month without any home cooking or even any snacks other that a piece of fruit, young men become almost obsessed with food.

***

For some reason, I have an easy time remembering dates. It was fifteen years ago today that my brother Danny and my sister Christine took me to my first Major League Baseball game. It was Yankees versus White Sox. Before the game they retired Phil Rizzuto's number "10" as part of Phil Rizzuto Day. Ironically, the White Sox pitcher that day was former Marine Corps Reservist Tom Seaver, who, that day, became one of only a handful of pitchers in history to get a 300th career win.

Saturday, August 5, 2000

This morning we had that drill competition. After morning chow we donned our neatly pressed "inspection cammies" and boarded a bus to take us the short drive to a gymnasium on the other side of the island where Series Drill was being held due to rain. The fact that it was a relatively cool and foggy Saturday morning, and because we were on a bus silently getting psyched up to compete, reminded me so much of high school football. Despite my hatred of drill, I wanted so badly to win this competition because I'm a very competitive person by nature. Also, I was pretty sure if we won the DIs would cut us a little slack for at least a short while.

When we entered the gym another platoon was drilling and it was unbelievable how absolutely silent it was. It made me nervous to see how close the big-wig judges were to the platoon. The worst thing you can do in a drill competition is to have an "unnecessary movement." That means that even if you put the rifle on the right shoulder when given the order "left shoulder arms" you don't correct it until the DI commands, "Recruit Schmukatelli, correct yourself." The platoon before us had some real obvious unnecessary movement and we all cringed in silence and realized we could definitely beat this platoon.

After watching and waiting in utter silence for a few minutes, it was our turn to drill. It seemed like our platoon did well, better than the platoon that went before us, because we had no unnecessary movements. But like a lot of things around here, Series Drill was anticlimactic. I thought that we would know where we placed immediately after all the platoons had finished. But it wasn't until late in the afternoon that we learned that we had come in third place out of six. They called it Series Drill which had led me to believe that we were only competing against the other two platoons in the Series. For some unknown reason, the competition pitted the platoons from both Series' in the company against each other. Third place out of six. Right in the middle. Not great but not bad either. Our platoon didn't get cake at evening chow, as the winning platoon did, but we also didn't spend an hour in the pit as the 6th place platoon did. Life didn't improve for us because of Series Drill, but it also didn't get worse. I guess our performance at Series Drill is most accurately described as a push.

***

I got a letter from my friend Goober's mother today. She gave me an update on the presidential election. Apparently George Bush chose former Defense Secretary Dick Cheney as his running mate. Nothing against Cheney, but this news made me so homesick. I follow politics closer than I do sports and I have been following this election for over a year as a good citizen and as a social studies teacher. Now that things are starting to heat up, I'm upset that I'm missing out on history. After all, presidential elections only come around every four years and this will be only the second presidential election that I can vote in. I guess there are greater tragedies in the world and missing one campaign isn't a huge sacrifice, but the current events update was just another reminder of how far I am from the world I lived in before I came down here.

Damn! I just realized that I'm going to miss the Olympics in addition to the baseball pennant race too. Oh well, I'll get over it.

***

This afternoon I got the biggest scare I have gotten in the twenty-eight days I have spent on this island. We were doing drill in the squad bay and the Series Gunnery Sergeant came and got me. The "Series Guns" as we call him is above our DIs. He runs the PT sessions in the morning and remarkably, he is way more intimidating than even Drill Instructor Sergeant Willis. Words just explode out of this guy's mouth when he says something. When he gets pissed off it is as though his eyeballs are going to come shooting out at you.

He is a white guy, in phenomenal shape, and looks like the prototypical Marine Corps Drill Instructor with his lean build and square jaw. When he called my name, my heart stopped for a good three seconds. "What did this nut want from me?" I asked myself as a million things ran through my head. I wondered if I was in trouble because I didn't tell my recruiter about the traffic ticket I had pending or maybe something awful had happened back home. I even considered the possibility that this guy, who looked about my brother's age, served with my brother and recognized my name.

When we got outside, I was relieved to find out that the Series Commander, 1st Lt. O'Neill, wanted to speak to me about going to OCS (Officers Candidates School). 1st Lt. O'Neill noticed in my paperwork that I had a college degree and wanted to recruit me to go to OCS. The Lieutenant and I discussed my plans to go to law school and the opportunities available to me for tuition assistance if accepted a commission as an officer. It was weird talking to this guy who was about my age, maybe younger. Had I stayed at VMI I would be at least a 1st Lieutenant by now, or maybe a captain. When I got dismissed I rejoined the Platoon in the squad bay and everyone was looking at me wondering why the psycho Series Gunnery Sergeant took me away.

***

It's funny how the term college is used down here. If a recruit "has college" it could mean a whole range of things. It could mean he took a couple of junior college courses, or it could mean that he has a PhD in astrophysics. Down here a guy with eight college credits and a guy with a master degree both "have college" and both get the same automatic promotion from Private to Private First Class.

***

It's been a wild and crazy Saturday night here on PI: footlocker PT, boot polishing and brash shinning. I'm so tired I can't wait for lights out and I'm just praying I don't somehow end up on

Fire Watch. Nine hours of pure unadulterated sleep would be the greatest thing in the world right now.

Sunday, August 6, 2000

I am pleased to report that for the first time in what seems like forever I didn't have Fire Watch. I slept from almost the moment my head hit the pillow until the lights came on this morning without any interruption. Sleeping straight through the night is almost unheard of because of Fire Watch and because we drink so much water it is common to get up three or four times to piss during the course of a night. Then this morning, we had a good two or three hours of square away time before Mass and I was able to catch up on my letter writing. I wrote back to everyone that has written me since I have been here. I vowed to reply to all the letters by Sunday. I tell myself that I'm doing this because it's polite, but deep down I know I'm just doing it so everyone will continue to write to me.

This was a banner day because we were actually allowed to march to church without any DIs overseeing us. I guess it's a sign of the times but we were split up into groups of ten with one recruit in each detail calling the cadence. I think this type of autonomy is going to be the norm for getting to church from now on. Words cannot describe what a welcome change it is.

A lot of the recruits in the platoon are getting a little full of themselves lately. I guess because we are almost finished First Phase and we are starting to see recruits who just arrived on the island in the past few days, we think we are big shit. As a result of our cockiness the DIs are starting to tighten the screws. This morning Drill Instructor Sergeant Lucifer gave me a "Blood Choke" for improperly requesting a head call. We were on our way out to formation before morning chow and I didn't have a drop of water in either of my canteens. I was in a hurry so I just said, "This recruit requests permission to make a head call." This drove Lucifer mad because I didn't ask for the requisite permission to speak. He put me in a textbook "blood choke", a move we had just learned a few days ago out at Leatherneck Square. The second I made the flub he came sprinting over to me wrapped his meaty paws around my neck, and applied pressure to the jugular area just like they taught us to do. The other day Drill Instructor Staff Sergeant Erickson put me in a token headlock, but this was not for show, it was a legitimate chokehold. For a split second I honestly thought this crazy bastard was trying to kill me. Then, just as I started to gasp for air Willis released his death grip and shoved me in the direction of the head.

I couldn't believe that Willis would do something like that. Even in the movie *Full Metal Jacket* the DI doesn't use his own strength to choke a recruit. He forces the recruit to use his hand to choke himself, I guess to cover his ass. Willis didn't seem to care about covering himself; he only cared that I be severely punished for the heinous crime of not asking permission to speak to the almighty Drill Instructor Sergeant Lucifer.

***

At church today I talked to a couple of guys who are going on the Crucible this week and graduating next week. The Crucible is the final test before you become a Marine. I'm not sure what it entails but I'm sure it is tough. The guys I spoke with told me that so far the hardest part of training is A-line. A-line comes after the rifle range. According to these guys it sucks because you basically crawl through mud, under barbed wire and through puddles all day. They also said that, although it sucks, the time flies by.

***

I got a letter from my little sister Meghan today. She gave me a Yankee update and I found out that they are still in first place. It seems like a million years since I left home and I can't even remember what place they were in when I left.

***

I have developed the worst farmers tan in history. My forearms, biceps and even my hands are a golden brown while the upper portion of my arm remains roughly the same color as copy paper.

***

While the Platoon was doing field day, I was selected to go on a working party. Along with ten or twelve other recruits from all six platoons in the Company, I got to do a little landscaping outside the barracks. I was hoping to use the lawn mower because I have always loved mowing lawns, but instead I got stuck pulling weeds from the cracks in the sidewalk. I can't complain though, being outside working on my own was much better than being inside field-daying the barracks with the rest of the platoon.

***

I'm disappointed that not only didn't I lose any weight in the past week but that I actually gained two pounds. This morning the Senior weighed me in at 205 pounds. I pray to God that I haven't hit a plateau and reached my lowest possible weight. I am starting to worry that I might never reach the 197 pound mark, the maximum I can weigh for my height. If I don't get down to 197 pounds I will never get off of this island.

I'm not trying to make excuses or come across as a hard ass, but I feel like we don't do enough long distance running and that is why I'm not losing the weight I need to. At most, we formally run three times per week, usually Monday, Wednesday, and Friday. If we ran everyday, which I am convinced we should, I would probably be under 197 pounds by now. I can do pull ups and crunches on my own after lights out but I can't run, the best fat burner of them all, except when we do it as a platoon.

I'm pissed off that I didn't lose any weight at all this week and that I'm still a diet tray because I'm seven or eight pounds above my max weight. Last night the platoon got cake with dinner and this morning they all got Boston cream donuts. It killed me to sit there and watch the other recruits in the platoon enjoy those desserts, while the other diet trays and I ate our usual scrambled eggs and gooey rice that remains in the shape of the scoop, even after you digest it.

I have a plan though to lose more weight. In the past I have been taking an extra piece of bread at every meal by squishing all three pieces together so it looks like only two pieces. I also snag a packet of salad dressing from time to time if I'm reasonably certain that I can get away with it. No more though, I'm off bread and completely. If I can avoid all of those carbohydrates, how can I not lose weight? I'm also going to strictly adhere to the diet tray rules, not so much because I don't want to get caught, but because I desperately want to get off diet tray and avoid the stigma that goes with it. Diet trays have two big, white stripes spray painted on either side of all of their T-shirts. At PT, in the squad bay, or whenever we are not wearing our camouflage blouses, the white stripes are a constant reminder to me and anyone who sees them that I'm a fat body. At PT, other DIs, recruits from other platoons, and onlookers in general have no idea that I'm one of the better runners in the platoon. All they see is that I am branded with the stripes of the fat body.

Aside from not being allowed salad dressing, peanut butter and, recently, dessert, diet tray is really not all that healthy. Breakfast often includes three strips of bacon or eggs in one form or another. How can they expect us to keep losing weight if we eat a dozen eggs per week and a half pound of bacon every day?

I got a letter from my brother Pat last night but just got a chance to read it today. His letters are designed to torture me. He likes to recap his day by telling me how he went swimming, shot hoops, went to McDonalds, took a nap, and watched TV. My favorite part was when he explained how he was going to go for a run but it was too hot and he was kind of tired so he went to Friendly's and got a sundae instead. Actually those letters don't really torture me, they crack me up. What aren't so funny are the threats my brother made before I left about sending nasty food to me while I'm down here. If you get a package with food in it you have to eat everything in one mouthful so that you can't enjoy it. My brother told me he was going to send Vienna Sausages, pickled eggs, and sardines so I would have to down all that nastiness in one gulp. I was never sure if he was kidding or not, but every time I see the Senior with packages I get a little sick to my stomach. So far so good though.

The only thing we are allowed to get sent is "letter writing gear", hygiene items and medial items like cough drops. If you get a package or even an envelope that looks a little bulky the Senior makes you open it in front of him and inspects the contents. We are allowed to get powdered Gatorade sent because sometimes when the Senior is on duty, he has the Fire Watch fill up a big jug and make the weakest Gatorade you ever tasted. It has just slightly more flavor than water but, unlike the warm, fishy tap water we are used to, the Gatorade is at least cold because the Senior scores some ice for us.

I had concocted a scheme to smuggle in a Snickers bar. I was going to have one of my buddies put a candy bar in a toothpaste box and glue the box back shut. I figure a Snickers is roughly the same weight as a tube of Crest and I could probably get away with it. Ultimately though, I decided against it because the risk wasn't worth the reward. All of the worrying and stress about getting caught would sap any of the enjoyment out of it. Besides, I am in relatively good standing with the DIs, don't have it as hard as a lot of the others, and a candy bar isn't worth jeopardizing that.

***

It is so weird how sometimes it feels like the end of boot camp is right around the corner and then other times I get so depressed because there is still so much time left. I try to tell myself that, although the DIs have control of everything else here, they can't control time. No matter what those bastards do, the clock is always ticking. Every second, minute, hour and day that elapses brings me closer to civilization. This thinking sometimes helps a little but I feel like I have been here forever and I'm only one-third of the way done. Sometimes I try to play games with myself and I vow not to think about what time it is or what day it is. But I break the vow almost immediately every time because I can't resist.

I remember when my brother was in boot camp. For me, a thirteen year-old kid, the three months seemed to zip by. Pat left for boot camp and before I knew it he was graduating. But I was on the outside, at home, enjoying all the late 1980s had to offer a rambunctious seventh grade boy. My brother however, was here, mired in this Hell and I'm sure as miserable as I am.

***

Tomorrow is swim qualification. A lot of guys are worried because they aren't good swimmers. Some of the other recruits in my platoon have never swum in their lives. I'm not worried because I grew up with a pool in my backyard, was on a swim team in elementary school and, believe it or not, I have a half credit of survival swimming from VMI.

From what I hear, some guys qualify on the first day and other guys may take all week. Someone at church told me that, after you qualify, all you do is go back to the squad bay and study knowledge for the rest of the day, because First Phase testing is less than a week away.

Monday, August 7, 2000

After morning chow we had PT. I did 114 crunches, which is fourteen more than I need for a perfect score. I'm so happy because now I really only need to work on pull-ups and the run. What sucks is that I can't practice running on my own like I can crunches and pull-ups. Given that reality, I have decided to just about kill myself during the runs at PT to get the most out of it. For the past few nights, I have been doing pull-ups after lights-out. It takes a lot of discipline to put on my shower shoes, get out of bed, and do pull ups at the end of a grueling day, but for the past few evenings I have managed to do it. I'm getting demoralized though because I am still in the single digits in pull-ups after a month here. I think losing thirty pounds so quickly took a toll on my upper body strength and therefore my pull-ups.

***

A lot of guys went to sick call today which pissed off the Senior. I don't blame him; this is Marine Corps Boot Camp, if you have a cold or a fever - suck it up. Although he didn't go to sick call, Stewart has a horrible cough. He is always hacking away, usually at the most inopportune times. The Senior will be giving out mail or giving his end of the night diatribe and Stewart will be coughing his head off. The other recruits are always angry with Stewart because his coughing, twitching, and general incompetence is constantly getting us all in trouble. Today, at PT, Stewart stepped in a hole and twisted his ankle. The Senior thinks he is malingering but I'm sure he is genuinely injured. The Senior even told me that he is going to begin smoking me, instead of Stewart, when Stewart screws up. This latest attempt by the Senior to straighten Stewart out has made me even more intolerant than before. I am constantly yelling at him when he screws up and impatient when he futzes around making the rack in the morning. Even when he doesn't get caught for moving in ranks, I voice my displeasure and sometimes I give him a quick punch in the shoulder. I feel bad about always bitching at my friend, but he has to improve.

The other thing that pisses me off about Stewart is that I don't think he appreciates what I do for him. I guess he just assumes that I like making his rack every morning or showing him the proper way to set up his shoe display. But sometimes I'm tired or have my own stuff to do. I still take care of Stewart's stuff before my own because I know the DIs, especially Willis, would scrutinize Stewart's stuff much harder than my own gear. I still like the guy, but he is really grating on my nerves lately. The bright side is that babysitting Stewart gives me something to do and think about other than the Marine Corps minutiae that dominate almost every minute of every day.

***

Swim qualification was a nice change of pace. Don't get me wrong, it was still a lot of the usual hurry up and wait, but at least we were hurrying and waiting to do something besides drill. To qualify we had to swim twenty-five meters without touching the bottom of the pool. Then we had to jump off of a ten foot diving board. Then a two minute dead man's float followed by treading water for another two minutes. Finally, we had to inflate our cammies and float on with them for another two minute period.

I was shocked by how many guys flunked the twenty-five meter swim. I guess if you have never swum before it is hard to learn on Parris Island when you have been stripped of all of your confidence and don't trust anyone. One guy in the platoon, Nathan, who was one of the guys I thought was a pussy when I met him on the flight down from Albany, started crying during the two minute water tread. This guy has got to be the biggest pussy I have ever met. During a lecture at RTF a few weeks ago, Nathan stood up in front of three platoons and asked the Marine giving the lecture what he had to do to get sent home. Of course the lecturer referred him to our DIs and the entire platoon got smoked for it. This guy cries on a daily basis. Willis, who hates all recruits, has particularly strong disdain for Nathan and does everything in his power to make his life hell. When Nathan has a hissy fit, Willis mocks him by making a loud crying baby sound, like "WAAAAH!" Whenever we are doing drill, Willis always pulls Nathan aside and smokes him. He even made him stay in the squad bay during chow to eat a hot tray because Willis was ashamed that he was in our platoon and didn't want to be seen with him.

There is actually a small part of me that feels sorry for Nathan. He came down here on the buddy program with his best friend from high school. The night we got here the friend got in trouble for a fraudulent enlistment, he withheld information about his medical history. Everything got worked out, but it took a couple of days, so Nathan's buddy didn't start training with us and got put in a different platoon. Plus, I don't think Nathan, like a lot a guys, had any idea what he was getting himself into. What makes Nathan's situation so bad is that he thought he would have his friend here with him at least. Instead, he is all alone and is among the most hated guys in the platoon because of all the times he gets the platoon into trouble. Plus he is a pretty effeminate guy, which makes him an immediate target for all DIs.

Back to swim qualification. I was amazed with how nice, and how modern, the pool was. It seemed to be a state-of-the-art, Olympic-size pool. This shocked me so much because everything else down here is old and pretty shitty. We do pull-ups on rickety old bars and sometimes we lift weights, which are nothing more than coffee cans filled with cement attached to a steel bar. This beautiful, heated indoor pool, that looked like it was built last week, seemed out of place on this stinky little island.

All reservists and guys who have an MOS (Military Occupational Specialty) other than infantry are done with swimming if they passed today. The guys who failed keep going all week until they pass. If, at week's end, they still go "UNK," or unqualified, they get dropped back a week in training. The active-duty infantry guys have to qualify on more difficult things. I think they have to swim with a full pack and rifle on them and other stuff like that. Because I am a reservist and because I passed all of the tests today, swim qual is over for me.

For the rest of the week half the platoon is either at the pool if they are still doing swim qual or in the squad bay with Willis studying knowledge. We have gone over the same questions over and over and still guys are getting them wrong. Most guys when Willis asks how many they got wrong say one or two to avoid his rage. Some guys are honest and end up getting screwed for being honest. Stewart for example, gets more than half wrong on every test and always tells Drill Instructor Sergeant Willis exactly how many he got wrong, even though Willis goes bananas on him every time. Although, I began tutoring Stewart after lights-out a few nights ago and he has shown some improvement.

The way we do practice tests is so painfully boring and inefficient. The questions are on an overhead projector. Only six or seven questions fit on each slide so we have to wait forever while all of the slow guys answer all of the questions on each page before we can move on to the next slide. Also, you can't skip a question and go on to the next page because how are you going to go back and answer the ones you skipped when they are on the overhead projector?

***

I successfully abstained from bread all day and plan to do that until I reach my magic number of 197 pounds. It's probably all in my head but I feel skinnier than I did just yesterday. I can't wait until weigh-in on Sunday.

Tuesday, August 8, 2000

We woke up this morning to Drill Instructor Sergeant Willis mopping the floor with Recruit Lane's face. Lane, a lanky bastard, at least 6 foot 6, who is all knees and elbows and rail skinny, didn't know how to properly report his post and Willis made him pay for it. When we woke up, Willis was pushing and pulling at his clothes and dragging Lane up and down the squad bay. Lane tried and tried to come up with the correct words to report his post.

Each time he failed, Willis got madder and madder. A couple of times Lane stumbled and fell but Willis kept on dragging him along until he got back to his feet. It was like watching an episode of Cops. Finally, Lane got it right and, in his squeaky high-pitched voice said, "Sir, Recruit Lane reports Post 1 all safe and secure at this time. There are sixty-eight recruits, sixty-eight rifles and sixty-eight seabags on safe and secure at this time. The platoon is currently engaged in Taps. Good morning, Sir."

I got in trouble this morning too for having an improper shave. I'm a hairy guy and sometimes my chest hair pokes its way up above the rim of my skivvy shirt. Senior Drill Instructor Staff Sergeant Jefferson made me shave all the way down below my collarbone. This sucks because it takes longer to shave and it has caused a nasty rash. I think it is all bullshit because I see DIs all the time with some chest hairs peeking out to the light of day. Anyway, it's not that big of a deal. I guess if having to shave a few overzealous chest hairs is the biggest problem I have today, that is a good thing.

All reservists and active duty guys with MOS's other than infantry who passed yesterday are finished with swim qual, so I completed the entire swim tests required of me but got roped into being the doorman at the pool. Basically it was my job to keep track of all of the recruits in my platoon as they came and left the pool. When a guy who went "UNK" yesterday finally passed, he could go back to the squad bay and study knowledge with Lucifer. When the infantry guys finished they were sent back also. I had to wait until there were ten recruits ready to go back and then I would choose a responsible recruit to march the platoon to the squad bay.

That is a new thing, marching without a DI. As of this past weekend, unless we are going as a platoon, we can march to and from where we have to go without a DI. On Sunday we marched in details of ten to church, which was a welcome change, although certainly not a free-for-all. We march in two columns of five with a Squad Leader, the Guide, or somebody halfway competent calling the cadence. I have called the cadence a few times and it is a lot harder than it might seem. I am not at all musical and have no rhythm to boot, so my cadence is kind of herky-jerky. Real fast, then real slow. I won't volunteer to march a detail anymore because I am embarrassed at how bad I am at it.

I sat outside the pool all morning in the heat and humidity and must have gone through a half bottle of my trusty sun block. I was allowed to sit down and study knowledge when there was nothing for me to do. This was a pain though, because every three seconds a Marine would go in or out and I'd have to get up and open the door, shouting the greeting of the day, "Good Morning, Sir!" Getting up and down got to be such a nuisance I decided to stay standing and study my knowledge. Predictably, the Senior banned this little convenience because apparently standing in the sun too long would make me pass out. As if getting up and down to open the door five hundred times an hour wouldn't take its toll.

After swimming, we had a few endless hours of drill which, as it always seems to, lead us straight to the pit. This was no ordinary pit call; this was far more brutal than normal. I'll bet we spent a good forty minutes flopping around in the sand as the sun beat down on us. The Senior went out of his way to make this not only the longest pit call but the sandiest. When we did jumping jacks, or side-straddle-hops as we say down here, we were required to hold a fist full of sand in each hand. It is impossible to keep all of the sand in your hands when you are flailing away like a mad man, so sand was going everywhere. I got sand in my eyes, deep into my ears, and even in what little hair I have.

We also were practically break-dancing in the pit. The Senior would make us roll around from left to right and from our chests on to our backs, again and again. When we were done you couldn't even tell we were wearing camouflage pants because there was so much sand soaked into the sweat-drenched material. The pants looked like they were covered in oatmeal the way the clumps of sweaty, mushy sand covered every inch of the cammie trousers.

For some reason, whenever we go to the pit we take off our blouse and are left with just a green skivvy shirt on. When the pit call is over we put the blouse back on which is just gross. Underneath the relatively clean cammie blouse were gobs of sweaty mud soaking through the skivvy shirt and chaffing so bad I have a rash on my shoulders and back.

When we got back to the squad bay we were standing at attention "on-line" in front of our footlockers when one guy, who I couldn't see because he was so far down the line on my right, started to hyperventilate. Then, in a chain reaction another guy passed out and finally a third joined in by passing out briefly and then hyperventilating.

The third guy was the new platoon Guide Hilbert. The first two guys regained their composure rather quickly, but Hilbert, who has to be the most shameless suck-up I have ever met, had to be taken into the showers by the Senior to get cooled off. When the Senior returned he was praising Hilbert as a great example of a motivated recruit. This logic was ridiculous. Every one of us was in that pit doing all of the same stuff. Hilbert couldn't handle it and starts to freak out afterwards and somehow he is this shining example of the super-recruit.

I never liked Hilbert to begin with. I used to call him "wannabe" Guide before he became Guide because he was always bossing everybody around in his whinny pathetic voice. Hilbert is one of those guys who stands up when we are being chastised for being ungrateful during Senior Drill Instructor square away time and says stuff like, "Sir, this recruit believes that Senior Drill Instructor Staff Sergeant Jefferson is a great Senior Drill Instructor and the platoon should do more to make him proud." If you would have told me before I got here that this kind of brown-nosing went on at boot camp, and that it actually worked to some degree, I would have said you were nuts.

Since we've been here we have heard people say that the pit works on a schedule, meaning that no matter what we do we are going to go to the pit a certain number of times and on designated days. I have always tended to believe this and today reinforced it. We were doing quite well at drill today and then some guy makes a tiny mistake, the kind of mistake that usually barely gets noticed, and the next thing you know we are in the pit for close to an hour and guys are passing out. I think it is safe to say that this pit call, and probably all of the other ones, was pre-meditated.

Wednesday, August 9, 2000

Today was a typical day on the island. Up early, Tobago swiped some extra chow and Advent pissed everybody off. I am getting used to the routine around here which is good. At VMI I don't think I ever really got into the routine in the whole year I was there. Speaking of VMI, there are so many parallels between boot camp and that experience. The most obvious one is the shaved head. Another one is the pit. Here the pit is the dreaded place where intense exercise leads to intense pain. The pit's VMI counterpart is the sweat party. A sweat party was when the upper classes would wake us up at some ungodly hour and either bring us out in the courtyard and make us do the things we do in the pit; up-downs, mountain climbers, side-straddle-hops, run in place and, of course, push-ups. I learned at VMI that the anticipation of the sweat party is in fact worse than the sweat party itself. When a rumor would float around the VMI barracks that a sweat party was going to take place, we would all lie in our racks unable to sleep and every creek of the old barracks would startle us. It's the same thing here really. We dread the pit so much and waste time trying not to go there, but trips to the pit are inevitable so why resist?

One difference between Parris Island and VMI is how we eat. At VMI we had to eat by the square, meaning we would scoop food off our plate with a fork, bring the fork straight up above the plate until it reached the level of our mouth and then bring the fork into the mouth on a straight horizontal line. Then we repeated the process in reverse to get another mouth full. At VMI we also sat on the front two inches of our chairs. Here we shovel the food into our mouths and no one is looking at how much of our asses are actually on the chair.

***

The new Guide, Hilbert, is starting to drive me crazy because he is such a whiner. Today, he failed to get us ready in a timely manner for chow as the DIs ordered him to. Instead of taking it like a man he cried, "Sir. Some of these recruits are just lazy and don't care." We all got smoked pretty good for that lame excuse.

***

I guess it's inevitable when you put seventy guys in a room for three months, but there is some nasty stuff here on Parris Island. I think I already mentioned how we have one big urine trough we gather around to piss in instead of using normal individual urinals. And I'm sure I mentioned how the "shitters" have no doors on them. Other nasty byproducts of all of us being cooped up in here are the development of some hacking coughs, nasty rashes, and a couple of cases of ringworm. If we didn't obsessively clean the squad bay and have mandatory "hygiene" time in the morning and at night, we would have revived the bubonic plague.

Thursday, August 10, 2000

I went to dental again this morning, which was actually a pretty good experience. Even though letter writing is forbidden at dental, it's not really enforced, so I had a lot of time to write letters while I sat with the thirty or so other recruits who were also waiting to see a dentist. Despite this quasi-ban on letter writing at dental, I penned a lengthy letter to my buddy Goober seeking answers to all of my questions on the state of the New York Yankees and the presidential election. At one point while I was writing and a DI barged into the waiting area screaming and yelling his head off at the recruits who had dozed off or who were watching TV. These bastards stick you in a waiting room for a matter of hours, sit a TV right in front of you, turn it on and then bitch at you when you watch it.

The TV in the waiting room is both a blessing and a curse. The blessing is that the TV is tuned to CNN Headline News, so I can catch up on current events and the baseball season. For example, I just found out that Gore picked Connecticut Senator Joe Lieberman as his running mate. The impact of this decision gives my brain a little something to chew on while I'm trying to forget how miserable drill is. I also caught some Yankee highlights and my eyes actually welled with tears because it depressed me so much. Seeing the Yanks and the rest of the news was a vivid reminder that as I waste away down here the world is passing me by and I'm missing out on two things I love; presidential politics and pennant race baseball. That's just one of the curse parts of watching the news at dental. The other thing that stinks about the TV in the waiting room is that they preview upcoming shows, movies, and the Summer Olympics. For a second I get excited and think "that show looks good" and then I quickly realize "shit," there is no way I'll be able to watch it.

***

Seven weeks from today is Family Day, which is the day before graduation. Then I have a total of ten days off before I have to report to Infantry School on October 10th. I should have a decent amount of money when I get off of this island to pay for my flight home and my trip to Notre Dame. This will be our 3rd annual trip out to South Bend, Indiana to see the Fighting Irish on the gridiron. Rumor has it that eight of my buddies from home are going to chip in and rent a Winnebago. I'm a little worried that my weight loss and the fact that I will not have had even a whiff of alcohol in three months will make my tolerance pathetically low. I'm sure I'll get by. That trip out to see ND is another one of the things I daydream about when I'm really bored or really miserable.

***

I just found out that we are going to actually live at the rifle range for the next two weeks. From what the guys at church tell me, time really starts to fly once you start the range. God I hope they are right.

***

For the first time in probably three years I am below the two hundred pound mark. Not by much however. I weighed in today at a trim 199 pounds. That means I have lost thirty-three pounds in a little over one month and I only have to lose two more pounds and I'll be off of diet tray.

When I first got here I couldn't even wrap the government-issued towel around my waist because either the towel was too small or my waist was too big. I have gotten so skinny that I don't even have to unbutton my pants to take them off. I feel stronger and quicker than I have ever felt before, even when I was in high school and in great shape. I don't think my arms have ever been this big and this defined. Imagine if we waited in line less and did more running, I'd probably be less than 185 pounds by now.

***

We got our pictures taken yesterday. The boot camp portrait is so important to me and I'm not sure why. I guess because I'll be looking at it for the next fifty years. Also, because as a little kid I used to look at my dad's boot camp mug shot and I knew that someday I'd wear that same uniform. I guess the photo is sort of tangible proof that I am getting closer to putting my face on the Marine Corps family coat of arms.

The way they take the pictures is a little crazy because they make you put on a modified dress blues that only covers your neck and the top of your shoulders- the parts that are in the picture. On our heads we wore a white garrison cover that, for some reason, has no top. Wearing camouflage pants, a sweaty green skivvy t-shirt with the dress blues dickey over it and that topless hat made everyone look ridiculous, but I'm confident that these guys know what they are doing and I'm sure the pictures will make it look like we are in a perfect uniform.

The photographer had us tilt our head just right and then he snapped the picture. The picture itself took less than thirty seconds but amazingly it took over four hours to get the whole platoon through. This kind of boredom and standing in line is murder on a fidgety, impatient guy like me.

After the pictures we ordered those boot camp books, like the one of my father's that I used to look through regularly as a kid. The books have everybody's portrait in it and some action shots of us training. The photographer told us that the average recruit appears in ten action pictures. I'm kind of surprised that they are doing all of this so early because there are some guys who are still so out of shape or so undisciplined. I can't imagine they are going to get through the rest of training.

***

I'd say about 85% of the guys in my platoon are going to be active duty when we get out of boot camp. The rest are like me, reservists. Basically reservists graduate boot camp, go to our MOS (Military Occupational Specialty) School and, when that is over, we have to train one weekend per month and two weeks each summer for six years.

***

Tomorrow we have the First Phase test. If you get a 100% on both the written and the prac-ap Drill Instructor Sergeant Willis will give you a *Whopper* with cheese. Aside from a day off or a trip home, I can't think of any better motivator than a hot, juicy

Whopper. I also can't wait until this test is over so I don't have to stand Fire Watch at night tutoring the "Rock Recruits."

To motivate the platoon for the big test, the Senior Drill Instructor decreed that we could begin to blouse our boots. We now look like real Marines with neat trouser cuffs bloused around our shiny black boots instead of, as Drill Instructor Sergeant Willis colorfully puts it, looking like a "bag of ass."

Friday, August 11, 2000 (7 Weeks Until Graduation)

Two kids, who just two months ago were my students, were supposed to arrive on the island for Recruit Training last week, but I have not seen them. There are more people here than I imagined. I guess it was pretty stupid of me, but, before I came here, I thought that there was just one platoon here at a time. It turns out, from the best that I can tell, that a new Company, which is made up of six platoons, arrives here each week. The new Company replaces the company that graduated the previous Friday. If there are, on average, seventy recruits per platoon and six platoons per Company and four companies per Battalion and three battalions of male recruits - I estimate that there are more than 5,000 male recruits on Parris Island at the present time. Fourth Battalion – the female battalion – is a total mystery to me so I won't even guess how many are in it, but I will say there seems to be less female recruits per platoon, so 4th Battalion is probably smaller than the other battalions.

***

Last night I had Fire Watch to help this kid Guerra study for the First Phase test which we had today. This morning I volunteered to eat a hot tray back in the squad bay with Guerra so we could study for today's big test. Guerra is a Dominican from the Bronx and a fairly old guy by boot camp standards, around twenty one or twenty two years old. He's also in great physical shape. Despite the outward appearance that he may be a tough guy, he is the meekest, most timid guy in the platoon. He is constantly getting in trouble for not sounding off. Drill Instructor Sergeant Willis hates him more than he hates the rest of us, probably because Willis considers Guerra weak and a disgrace to his hometown of New York City. This timidness and the fact that Willis has a particularly vehement disdain for him are the reasons for Guerra's problems with remembering the knowledge. He is as smart as the next guy, but he gets so flustered and intimidated that his mind goes blank. Evidently, the DIs don't know that when under pressure Guerra's brain ceases to function. They were peppering him with questions all morning and I watched this pre-test interrogation knowing that they were destroying what little confidence he had in himself. Telling someone like Guerra to "learn or else" is probably the most counter-productive thing they could do, but this is boot camp, not kindergarten, and ultimately Guerra will have to shit or get off the pot.

I found the test this morning to be pretty easy. The written part was the standard stuff: Marine Corps Birthday (10 November 1775), Grand Old Man of the Marine Corps (General Archibald Henderson), First woman Marine (Opha Mae Johnson) and so on. For the prac-ap portion we had to make a tourniquet, a splint, and pretend to dress a sucking chest wound and a few other applications which we were well prepared for. The First Phase Test is the first of the graduation requirements. There are others, like rifle qualification and final PFT and probably still others but I just don't know what they are.

Like a lot of things here, it was much ado about nothing and our whole platoon, including Guerra passed. Eighty percent is considered passing, so for all seventy of us to pass is a pretty good accomplishment. We found out that everyone passed immediately after the test but had to wait until tonight to find out what our individual scores were. I got a 100% on both parts, which entitles me to a *Whopper* with cheese from Willis and the Senior promised a phone call home to those of us who got double 100's. We didn't get the burger or the call yet but I'm sure they will be coming pretty soon and I can already taste that juicy burger and feel the wonderful grease dripping down my chin.

The average score in the platoon is important because our DIs, especially Willis, are in competition with the other DIs. Because this test has been Willis's primary responsibility all along, our performance is a very direct reflection on his abilities as an instructor. Rumor has it we came in second or third out of the six platoons in the company but we have not gotten any definitive word yet.

How well we do in these platoon competitions also determines what job our platoon gets for Team Week. The better the platoon does in drill, First Phase testing and a couple other events, the better job we get. That guy who gave me gum at the laundry a few weeks back must have been in a platoon full of "shit birds" because working in the laundry like inmates has to be the worst assignment of them all.

I am a little ticked off at guys like Stewart and Guerra, as well as the others who I worked with during my free time and on Fire Watch to prep for the test, because they have not even acknowledged that I helped them pass. I guess they don't know any better, but it still irritates me. Also, the DIs were so shocked that Guerra passed, they gave him shrimp from the Drill

Instructor's chow line at dinner. This made me mad because they are rewarding this kid because he did well today but they have ignored those of us who have been on top of the knowledge from the beginning and tutored Guerra. What about us? We didn't get squat for our efforts. Oh well. What are you going to do? The only one who thanked me was Tobego, which didn't surprise me because he is a rock-solid guy and mature beyond his years.

I actually got a little recognition from Drill Instructor Staff Sergeant Erickson today, although not for tutoring. He commended me for my ability to sound off loudly. He made me sound off a bunch of time for the platoon so he could show them how loud they should be. It sounds stupid to be proud of having a loud voice and the ability to shout loudly, and before I came here I wouldn't have thought anything of it, but down here any positive feedback you get helps motivate you.

Tomorrow we go on a five-mile hump out to the rifle range. I'm concerned about the range because I know myself well and I am aware that I am a late bloomer when it comes to a lot of things. I have had success in sports only by practicing on my own after the team practice finished. If I could go on my own and figure out a strategy for myself, I think I'd be fine on the range. Unfortunately, I know damned well that there is no way they are going to let me fire a rifle on my own. The reason I'm so worried is because passing the rifle range is a graduation requirement. If you don't pass the range they drop you back two weeks to try it over again. Two weeks on Parris Island is like two years in the real world, not to mention how embarrassing it would be to have to write my parents tell them that I failed the rifle range and didn't know when I would be coming home. Also, failure means my trip out to Notre Dame is gone. We're not even at the range yet and already I'm feeling the pressure.

Friday evening parade at the Virginia Military Institute when I was a cadet in 1994. I'm the third man from the front.

Mr. Kieran Lalor
Social Studies

From the yearbook at Our Lady of Lourdes High School where I taught for two years before enlisting.

My official boot camp photo.

My Dad, Dan Lalor in his boot camp picture from 1962.

My older brother Patrick Lalor was the platoon
Honor Graduate when he was a "Boot" in 1989.

The late, great Mike Glover's boot camp photo from 2004.
He was killed in action by a sniper while on patrol outside
of Fallujah, Iraq two years after this photo was taken.

Dave Mahoney, one of my oldest and best friends.
He enlisted in 2006 at the ripe old age of 32
and served in Iraq in 2008 and 2009.

Taking aim at Saddam Hussein during the early
days of Operation Iraqi Freedom in 2003.

Making a new friend in Nasiriya, Iraq
on Easter Sunday 2003.

With the love of my life Mary Jo at the 2004 Marine Corps Birthday Ball. We were engaged at the time and got married the next summer.

On the campaign trail in 2008.

Aboard the USS Intrepid at the inaugural Iraq Veterans for Congress Victory Dinner in 2010.

CHAPTER 4: The Range

Saturday, August 12, 2000

Today sucked. I lost my cover before the hump out to the rifle range and had to suffer the humiliation of being excluded from the platoon tug-of-war team. When finally we got to the rifle range barracks Drill Instructor Sergeant Willis amputated my boot and nearly my foot. Now that night has fallen on another Parris Island day, I am starting to realize just how shitty this new squad bay is. Don't get me wrong, the old squad bay sucked, but at least we had all gotten acclimated to it and felt it was our own crappy squad bay. This foreign squad bay out here at the range is smaller and dingier. In this shit box, when the DI walks down the DI highway (the path in the middle of the squad bay formed by the gauntlet of recruits standing online) he is that much closer and capable of seeing more discrepancies. The DI can also intentionally bump into a recruit and then pretend the recruit tried to assault him providing an excuse to put us on our faces or in the pit. Also, we were, literally and figuratively, stepping on each other's toes in the old squad bay and that has only worsened here. On top of all that, a lot of things don't work, like three of the twelve showerheads. This hell hole is so old and shitty it will be impossible to sanitize it enough to meet the DI's standards.

In Hamlet during the famous "to be or not to be" speech, Hamlet says that it is better to "bear the ills we have then to fly to those we know not of." To use a modern cliché: "Better the devil you know than the devil you don't know." Bottom line: Our old barracks was shitty but this one is shitty *and* foreign to us, so it sucks more.

Sunday, August 13, 2000

I was reprimanded last night for talking at dinner, and today I got punished with a little quarterdeck time with Lucifer. But I have to say, I really don't mind that stuff anymore. It just rolls off my back.

Today was a pretty light day, even for a Sunday. We just cleaned the new squad bay, did a little drill, a little PT, and had a class on shooting to prepare us for the rifle range. I'm really getting worried about my inability to sit Indian style for a long period. By the way, we don't use the term "Indian style." We use a politically correct term, "cross legged." Anyway, I can't bring my legs in as far as I am supposed to, but hopefully I'll become more flexible over the next week as we practice the shooting positions more.

It seems like every Sunday I get organized while the Protestants are at church and we Catholics get Senior Drill Instructor square away time. I arrange my footlocker with my uniforms perfectly folded, my boot polish and "dobber" placed just right and my letter writing gear stacked neatly. I try to get a jump on the upcoming week but the problem is this organization only lasts until about 0800 on Monday because we are always frantically diving into our footlockers and grabbing whatever item the DI gives us two seconds to find and my neat footlocker gets torn to hell.

Another thing that annoys me about this place is how the DIs make everything theirs. That is, when they tell us to get something, they'll command us to, "Get *my* canteens now." Often they'll take possession of the whole island or the entire Marine Corps by saying stuff like, "If you get off *my* island." If they don't like somebody they'll say, "Why did you join *my* beloved Marine Corps, shit bag?" This quirky possessiveness by the DIs is nothing life or death but one of the many things that frustrates me about this God forsaken place.

On a positive note, I am so pumped about my dramatic weight loss and my prospects for further weight reduction. I noticed that the chow hall out here at Weapons Battalion serves smaller portions than our real chow hall, so I will likely lose weight even faster while we are out here for the next two weeks. My preoccupation with weight loss is ironic since all we seem to talk about around here on the rare chance we get a minute to shoot the shit is how many donuts, cookies, and Big Macs we are going to eat when we leave Parris Island.

***

My new rack is next to the DI's hut so the first rack they see every time they leave that place is mine. This sucks, because my stuff has to be perfect at all times. Also, I'm the first recruit they see, so I get sent to other decks (floors) to get stuff from other platoons. When I go to another platoon's squad bay for a mop or something, I get smoked for five or ten minutes by the other platoon's DIs. I think DIs get tired of smoking their own recruits and like to smoke someone new. Variety is the spice of life, I guess. The bright side is this will make me stronger.

Monday, August 14, 2000

Today was the first day of Grass Week, which is a week of formal rifle range instruction and conforming of our bodies into the shooting positions. It was a long, hard, boring day. We rotated from classroom instruction held in an open-air building, similar to a dugout at a baseball field, to what is called "snapping in." Basically, snapping in is taking a shooting position with the rifle jammed in your shoulder and the sling wrapped tightly around your arm for long periods of time. Snapping in is horrible; just horrible. My arms and legs are so contorted in those shooting positions they hurt like hell. Eventually they go numb, but it takes like an hour of snapping in before that happens and even then they don't go completely numb. As snapping in drags on, my limbs just transition from experiencing a spike-like pain that makes you want to scream to a dull pain that makes you want to cry.

Shooting a rifle is more complicated than I ever imagined. All of the knobs, sites, wind calls and shot groups are a total mystery to me. One click the wrong way will put you off the target. In some ways it reminds me of golf. I am a pretty terrible golfer but I have played a few times and understand the basics. In golf, you change clubs depending on the conditions and distance to the green. Adjusting your sites is the rifle equivalent of changing clubs. If you use your 500-yard settings on the 200-yard-line you are going to miss the target completely even if you execute everything perfectly, just as if you used 3-iron for a chip shot.

Throughout boot camp, I have daydreamed during classes figuring I'll pick up what I need to know along the way. However,

I am so petrified of UNKing the range, I hang on every word the PMI (Primary Marksmanship Instructor) says. I take better notes than I ever took in college and I am really trying to understand the entire process.

I got a letter from my mother the other day and I think she may have unintentionally jinxed me. She mentioned how my dad's buddy, who went to boot camp with him, failed the rifle range and got dropped back in training. That hit home. I guess forty years after the fact that guy probably has a sense of humor about his extra two weeks in this hell, but if I flunk the range and get dropped I will be absolutely destroyed.

**

One thing that amazes me is how the DIs can take seemingly innocuous things and make them torturous. For example, a canteen with water weighs a couple pounds, if that. Hold that canteen out in front of you at eye level with your arms perfectly straight for five or ten minutes and you will feel sharper pain than you have ever imagined. For no particular reason, Drill Instructor Sergeant Willis had us do a little of that before lights-out. I hate that son of a bitch.

Tuesday, August 15, 2000

I'm still getting used to things out at the range. We only eat at the chow hall for morning chow and evening chow. Out on the range, we get a bag lunch consisting of one bologna and cheese sandwich, one orange, a package of four Oreos, lunch size Doritos and one mustard packet. It sounds better than it is. These lunches are known unaffectionately as "bag nasties." Granted, it is nice to have the junk food, but the portions are small and I still have to fill up on canteen water. Luckily, I taught myself to like bologna when I was in college as a cost cutting measure.

I heard a rumor that we are going to be staying in these barracks for two more weeks after the range. One week for Team Week to work in the Weapons Battalion Chow Hall and then a second week for what is called A-Line, which I know very little about except that it is a good milestone to reach. I forgot about this until now, but I awhile back I ran into a kid in the chow hall who was my student last year. I think I was in the second week of training and he was about to start A-Line and to me it was like he was the luckiest guy in the world to be that far ahead in training. I've been looking forward to A-Line ever since. The kid's name was Mike Anderson and he called me Mr. Lalor because, in a previous life, he was the student and I was the teacher. But when our paths crossed on Parris Island, I was a First Phase Recruit and he was only a couple of weeks from becoming a Marine. I was like the nerdy college freshman with a beanie on my head and he was a dashing PhD candidate with a hot blond on his arm.

***

A young Marine Lance Corporal paid a visit to the squad bay today. Apparently Drill Instructor Sergeant Willis was his DI last year and Willis was hard on him. At first, the guy hated Willis but grew to appreciate his tough approach to training recruits. I think the Lance Corporal and Willis were from the same neighborhood, or at least both from Brooklyn. After the guy sang the praises of Willis in a little pep talk, Willis let his guard down a bit for the rest of the night and was, at least for Willis, pretty mellow.

Except for what I mentioned above, today was nothing but classes and excruciating snapping in from reveille to Taps.

Wednesday, August 16, 2000

We snapped in all day in the sitting position, which is another way of saying the cross legged position. Now that I have had three days of it, I'm ready to provide a more detailed explanation of snapping in and why it sucks. Basically, snapping in requires you to get in the tight shooting positions, wrap the sling around your arm and aim at a tiny black target painted on an old white oil drum. It is the vice-like tightness of our "loop sling" around our biceps that makes our arms go numb. My legs also go numb, particularly in the sitting and kneeling position, because most of my weight is crushing down on my knees and ankles. The goal of snapping is to teach your body "muscle memory" so that when you go to fire your weapon, your body will instinctively know where all its parts should be and you can properly apply the fundamentals of marksmanship. The fundamentals of marksmanship allow you to get proper "site picture and sight alignment" or, what up until a few days ago, I would have simply called aiming. Snapping in also involves loading an empty magazine into our M-16s, racking the charging handle, sighting in and pulling the trigger, which causes the bolt to slide home. It's called dry fire and it gets old quick.

In between long snapping in sessions, we get class from the PMI. Our PMI is Sergeant Romano from Long Island, New York. He seems like a decent guy. He is probably in his late twenties and has been in the infantry for his whole ten years and looks, to my untrained eye, to be a Marine Corps lifer. He, like all PMIs, wears a DI's campaign cover but he is not a DI and does not have the mean streak needed to be a DI. He knows boot camp sucks and he tries to keep us updated on sports scores, new movies and on what is happening in the real world.

The sitting position has been killing me, and I'm starting to get worried because I can't stay in it very long and moving around makes your shooting less accurate. The kneeling is the most painful of all positions; we start concentrating on it tomorrow. One more thing to look forward to.

I'm so worried about whether or not I will qualify with the rifle that I have ceased counting down days. If you UNK the range you get dropped back two weeks in training. Getting dropped is sometimes referred to as "the time machine," because you think you are forty days from leaving this God awful place and all of sudden that number jumps back to fifty-four days. In the event that I go UNK I want to mitigate the mental heartbreak so, for now, I stopped counting the days, just in case.

***

Eating less bread as a means of losing weight has been working for me so far. I can feel my ribs very easily and now have hip bones sticking out for the first time since high school. There is no scale out here at the rifle range barracks, so I have no idea how much I weigh, but I know I'm skinnier than we left "main side."

***

Periodically throughout the day today, small groups of recruits went and shot at the ISMT (Indoor Simulated Marksmanship Trainer). To my knowledge, the ISMT along with the state-of-the-art pool are the only modern conveniences on Parris Island. The ISMT is basically a video game, which almost perfectly simulates shooting an M-16. I think the thought-process of the Marine Corps is to save money on ammunition by having the first few hundred rounds fired by a recruit on the ISMT. Plus, the ISMT provides a safety benefit because if a recruit has a negligent discharge in the ISMT, the DIs can get all over him and teach him a lesson without anyone actually being imperiled. If that same nervous recruit, holding a rifle for the first time, inadvertently fires a round with an actual M-16, obviously, the consequences could be deadly. For me, the ISMT served as a confidence boost because, although I don't know my score, I feel like I shot pretty well.

***

My platoon just picked up recruits named Bishop and Franks who got dropped for UNKing the range. They are both black guys from Alabama and I think they came in together on the buddy program. Franks seems like a decent guy, sort of quiet. Bishop is a loud-mouth jackass. He reminds me of Advent when we started boot camp, before Advent was humiliated into humility. Bishop is a big know-it-all because he has "been through it before." Like Advent back in early days, he doesn't seem to realize that although he has more experience on Parris Island than the rest of us, this is only because he is a failure and got dropped. He is constantly arguing with the original members of the platoon saying he knows best because he's done it before. Seeing these "drops," as they are called, is a cold reminder that rifle range drops are real and not an empty threat. I'm starting to get nervous…really nervous.

***

Drill Instructor Sergeant Willis went crazy this evening and I'm not even sure why. He was grabbing guys' mail and throwing it around. Then he smashed a bunch of Gatorade canisters on the floor sending the powder mix all over the place. So much for the kinder gentler Willis we saw yesterday when his protégé stopped by. Maybe he knows we saw his softer side and wanted to reestablish is position as an intimidating bastard.

Thursday, August 17, 2000

It's all starting to come together. All of this discipline stuff, the cross-legged sitting for classes, the constant harping upon attention to detail and the demand that we stand perfectly still in formation and when drilling. I now believe all of boot camp up until this point has been designed to help you become a proficient rifleman.

It has also become clear that Bishop, the new guy we got the other day because he went UNK on the range, is the worst thing that ever happened to our platoon. Our PMI is the nicest guy in the world. He never yells or gets mad, but Bishop managed to piss him off by constantly contradicting him during the classes. Imagine a guy who just failed to qualify with the rifle contradicting a person whose occupation it is to teach marksmanship. There is now no doubt that Bishop is a complete lunatic.

I had been under the impression that there were no pit calls out at the range because the DIs don't want to stress you out when you need to qualify, and while you are armed and have access to live rounds. Well, that is not the case. There is a pit right on the range and thanks to Bishop angering our easygoing PMI, we paid a visit this afternoon.

***

Tempers are starting to flare out here at the range. There have been a couple of fist fights in the squad bay between recruits. I almost got in a scuffle with some asshole who was kind of picking on Stewart. I think maybe everybody is starting to get raw after more than a month on this island and with the weight of having to qualify on our minds. Add in a jackass like Bishop, who got into a scrap with the Guide today, and this whole place is about to boil over.

***

After we snap in all day and have classes with the PMI, Drill Instructor Sergeant Willis gives us further marksmanship instruction in the evening. Tonight he made an interesting point about guys being on the firing line praying to hit the target. In Lucifer's theology, "God has more important things to do than worry about whether or not you shoot straight."

He's got a point.

***

These are long, hard days out here at range. Being in the South Carolina sun in August from the minute the sun rises until it sets sucks the life out of you. The way I feel at the end of the day is by far the most run down I have ever felt in my life. On top of that, I have been counting down the days until I am halfway through boot camp and now that it's almost here and I'm like, "Oh shit I still I have another six weeks on this shitty island."

Friday, August 18, 2000 (6 Weeks Until Graduation)

Bishop struck again. Apparently while on Fire Watch he has been sneaking from the squad bay, entering the chow hall, and helping himself. We went through another witch hunt today to determine if he had any accomplices. Bishop has not volunteered any other names of his fellow late night diners. This could mean one of two things: either he acted alone because he didn't want to share the bounty with anyone else or he is not as big a piece of shit as Advent, who would rat out his own mother if he thought it would get him out of trouble.

***

We fired our rifles for the first time today to BZO (Battle Site Zero) them. Basically, a rifle has to be fitted to each person because the lengths of your arms, where you put your cheek on the stock, and a lot of other things unique to the individual affect where the round goes. To BZO the weapon, also known as "doping" the weapon, you shoot three sets of three shots. If you are applying the fundamentals of marksmanship correctly, all three shots from the first set should be in a tight group even if they are not on the target. Once you have a tight shot group you adjust the sights of your rifle and fire another three shots in hopes of moving the shot group onto the target. Then you do the same thing a third time, for good measure.

If you are not properly applying the fundamentals of marksmanship, you don't get a shot group at all and your three shots are scattered. I fell in to the rounds scattered category with all three of my shot groups, so they took my weapon and had a DI fire it to see if the rifle was broken. As it turns out, the rifle was fine and it was me that was broken. Failing this first minor test of marksmanship, with qualification week starting Monday has made me more nervous than ever about going UNK.

***

In other news, it has been about a week and still no *Whopper with cheese*. I hope that was not an empty promise, but it well may have been; after all, this is boot camp.

***

In the squad bay we have what is known as the "mote table" (short for motivation table). The Senior Drill Instructor puts some of his medals, awards and pictures there to motivate us to keep working hard. Recruits are invited to have pictures of their girlfriends sent for the platoon's viewing. A lot of guys have had pictures of their girls sent - some of the guys have some gorgeous girlfriends, but sad to say, some of my other fellow recruits are dating real ugos and, evidently, don't realize it because they put their photos on display.

The mote table reminds me of a little incident that occurred when I was at VMI. We had a company motivation board and all of the Rats (Freshmen) were ordered to put something on the table that motivated them. The upper classmen were thinking along the lines of calendar girls and pin-ups and pictures of tanks and planes and other military stuff. I happened to have a picture of the King of Rock and Roll, Elvis Presley, and like an idiot I posted it on the motivation board. When we got to the chow hall later that day, one of the upper classmen asked us in a painfully slow Virginian drawl, "Who in the hell put a picture of Goddamned Elvis Presley on the motivation board?" There was no sense in trying to hide it, so as soon as he finished the question, I sprung to my feet and exclaimed, "Sir, I did Sir!"

The upperclassman, a Corporal in the Corps of Cadets whose name I have long forgotten, then asked, "God Damn, *Lay-lor*, what is your favorite Elvis song?" I responded "Sir, Hound Dog, Sir." With this, he ordered me to stand on my chair, with the entire Corps of Cadets eating dinner, and sing "Hound Dog." At first I was a little bashful and just went through the motions, softly singing while I stood there rigidly praying the ordeal would end. Then the upperclassman said, "Aw, hell no *Lay-lor*. Sing it with some feelin'." So I started swaying and singing doing my best Elvis impersonation and completed the whole song as all 1,500 or so Cadets watched, mouths agape. This was about two months into the first semester, and up until this point, I had remained pretty anonymous. Thanks to Elvis, my anonymity ended that evening in the chow hall.

Experience is the best teacher so just to be safe I will not be putting anything on the mote table.

Saturday, August 19, 2000

This morning we took the mock PFT. Basically, this means we did the full three mile run, a max set of crunches in two minutes and a max set of pull ups. This is a dress rehearsal for the final PFT, which we will do in September. I cranked out eight pull-ups, one hundred crunches and did the run in a fairly speedy 20:21. As far as scoring for a PFT, you get five points for a pull-up, with a maximum of one hundred points. Each crunch is worth one point and the most you can get is one hundred. The run is complicated, because it sort of works backward. Basically, you start with one hundred points, and for every ten seconds over eighteen minutes (a perfect score) you lose a point. So my score was 226 out of 300, which is respectable.

You have to get a minimum of three pull ups, fifty crunches and complete the run in less than twenty-eight minutes to pass. A guy in our platoon named Kaye did so badly on the mock PFT that he is being dropped. I'm not sure what his numbers were, but they must be pretty low, because getting dropped basically means they don't think they can get you to pass the real PFT, even with four more weeks of training. I'm not sure if he'll be dropped back one or two weeks, or indefinitely, until he gets his PFT score up. I feel badly for the guy. He had to call his parents today and tell them he is not graduating when they thought he was. You can tell he is completely humiliated and looks as if he might cry.

***

It's hard to believe late August is already here. In two weeks my little sister Meg will be a senior in college. That is unbelievable to me. She is twenty years old, but being the youngest of the six, I think of her as a young kid. Actually in a couple of weeks (September 11), she'll turn twenty-one, which is also crazy. Another red letter day on the Lalor calendar is September fourth, my parent's 35th wedding anniversary. My whole family will be together celebrating the occasion, except me. Damn, that made me sad. That Sunday will suck. Come to think of it, by the time I get home, Meg will be up at school in Albany, Christine will be in Boston, Sue and Danny will be in Brooklyn and Pat in Danbury. It's going to be tough getting everybody together.

***

I have started to lose my farmer's tan, because on the rifle range we wear our sleeves down and not rolled up like we do "in the rear." This week it was one hundred degrees each day and there we were in boots, long pants, and long sleeves. I think I have set a record for most gallons of sweat produced by a single human being. The black flag went up around 1000 this morning and didn't come down until sunset. The only problem is that Black Flag doesn't apply out at the range and we shoot no matter how high the temperature gets.

***

It's been a while now and still no *Whopper with cheese*. Drill Instructor Sergeant Willis said the other day that we'd get it before graduation, so I'm pissed off about that. If we don't get it until the last week of boot camp, after we have completed the Crucible, what is the point?

From what I hear, the Crucible consists of fifty miles of humps over three days in the field with minimal food and sleep and a bunch of obstacles we have to overcome. The last day of the Crucible we march back to the parade deck for a ceremony and we officially become Marines. The following week is called transition week and we basically pay bills, turn in our rifles, etcetera. So for training purposes, we are done one month from yesterday. But I am getting way ahead of myself, because I still have the range in front of me.

Other than what I have just mentioned, the rest of the day was pretty much drill, drill, drill, drill. I did get some interesting mail from my brother Patrick though. He sent me a neatly folded McDonald's hamburger wrapper. That bastard knows just how to torment me.

As I sit in this crappy barracks on a Saturday night in the summer I can't help but think about what my friends are doing. Ah shit. That was a dumb thing to think about because it made an otherwise tolerable day end on a downer.

Sunday, August 20, 2000

We went to Mass at the Weapons Battalion chapel this morning and had a different chaplain, who unknowingly gave me a little confidence boost . The priest who says Mass out here used to be a Marine. He is in the Navy now because the Marine Corps doesn't have its own chaplain corps. Anyway, he told a story about how he was a boot on Parris Island and got to the 500-yard-line and needed to shoot each of his last ten shots into the bull's eye to qual. He said he prayed and prayed as he shot, and miraculously did it, earning an improbable fifty out of fifty points in his last ten shots. Not surprisingly, the priest's story directly contradicts what Drill Instructor Sergeant Lucifer said about God not caring how you do on the range.

***

Yesterday, I got a letter from my sister Meg. She is a solid Yankees fan and updated me on all of the new players that have joined the team since I left; Dwight Gooden and Luis Sojo are back, and for some reason, the Yankees acquired Jose Canseco.

***

I wish someone would send me an update on politics. I have not heard one word about the Hillary Clinton / Rick Lazio Senate race since I got here. I know about Governor Bush of Texas being nominated by the Republicans and choosing former Secretary of Defense Dick Cheney as his running-mate. I want to read up on this Bush guy, because I'm not sure how I feel about him. He seems a little wishy-washy to me. My impression is he is a lot like his father and Bob Dole, who both got their asses beat. I'm also not crazy about electing the son of a former President. I'm Irish and inherently skeptical of anything that reeks of England or monarchy. That reminds me - my dad is going to arrange for an absentee ballot so that I can vote in November's election from the School of Infantry (SOI).

If I had to vote today, I'd certainly choose Lazio, because Hillary Clinton and her draft-dodging husband are big government/small military liberals and stand against everything I believe. As far as Bush versus Gore, I will likely cast a protest vote for Allen Keyes or Pat Buchanan or maybe Ross Perot for old times' sake. I am decidedly unimpressed by Bush and Al Gore is only a few degrees better than the Clintons. So what is a conscientious conservative to do?

***

More was revealed today about the stolen chow episode. It turns out that Bishop was not sneaking into the chow hall, after all. He was going into the dumpster behind the chow hall and eating expired bag nasties that were thrown out. When this came out, Drill Instructor Sergeant Willis went crazy on all of us in classical Lucifer style.

***

Surprisingly, we didn't snap in all weekend. We did go to the range and basically replicated the whole qualification course as a dry fire. The course of fire entails five stages. The first stage is from the 200-yard-line. You have twenty minutes to shoot five shots from the sitting, five from the kneeling and five from the standing. For some reason the standing is also called the "off-hand." It is at this stage (the slow fire) where the wind calculations enter in.

Then we go from the standing to the kneeling position and shoot ten rounds total, but you have to split the rounds between two magazines and do a magazine change, which is also known as a "tactical re-load." Changing magazines in the middle is tough, because you only have seventy seconds to shoot ten well aimed shots. This is known as rapid fire. Unlike the slow fire, you basically only aim your first shot per magazine and the rest of the shots somehow are supposed to be on target if you are properly applying the fundamentals of marksmanship. We'll see about that.

For stages three and four, we move to the 300-yard-line for five rounds of slow fire from the kneeling position. Then a ten-round, rapid fire, where we start in the standing position but drop and fire from the kneeling. Finally, stage five, we go back to the 500-yard-line and have ten minutes to shoot ten shots from the prone position, which basically requires us to shoot while lying on our chests. The closer to the ground you are the more stable and therefore more accurate. Thus, the standing is the hardest and the prone is the easiest. However, the Marine Corps being the Marine Corps, the relatively easy prone is made exponentially harder because you are 500 yards away.

The scoring is pretty simple. The dead center bull's eye is worth five points then there are rings worth 4, 3, 2, and 1. 220-250 is an Expert. 210-219 is a Sharpshooter. 190-209 is a Marksman.

Anything below a 190 is UNK and you get dropped. Oh God! I don't even like to think about it.

Monday, August 21, 2000

Today was the first day of qual week. We fired the whole course of fire that I explained yesterday, which I forgot to mention is officially referred to as the "known distance" or "K D course." Known distance means you know how far you are from the target at all times. I guess there are other courses where you have to estimate how far from the target you are. That might be part of A-Line week, but who knows?

I felt like I was doing pretty well on the first stage of fire which is five shots sitting, five shots kneeling, and five shots standing from the 200-yard-line in twenty minutes. Then Drill Instructor Sergeant Willis came up to me and said "Get your head out of your ass." I'm not sure what he was talking about, because I thought I was doing okay, but he knows better than me. The DIs don't let you keep score during the practice runs because they don't want you to be thinking about your score and forgetting the fundamentals of marksmanship. This makes sense. While playing baseball I have always found that not tracking my batting average is the best thing you can do for it. If you go into a game thinking, "If I can go 3-for-5 today, I'll be batting .325", you are going to press at the plate. If you go 0-for-2 in your first couple of at bats and need to go 3-for-3 in your last three, you are going to put too much pressure on yourself. I believe it's the same concept on the range. If you are firing thinking "I need a five" it is going to distract you and have a negative effect on your score. My plan is to apply the fundamentals, and after my last shot goes down range, pray to God that my score is high enough to qual.

On Stage 2, the 200-yard-line rapid fire, I did okay; I got a couple fives, fours and threes. Some guys got what is called a "possible," which means you get fives on all ten rapidly fired shots. I am confident there is no chance I will do that. Stage three and four, I slipped a little. I got mostly twos and threes. I remember doing well when I concentrated on the "front sight tip" as I was instructed to do. I'll have to remember that.

From the 500, I was inconsistent. I got a five and then I got a bunch of complete misses. It is embarrassing. If, after you shoot, the target doesn't drop, the range coach calls to the pits and yells for them to pay attention, pull the target and spot the hole. They pull the target down, search for the hole and then call back "no impact, no idea," meaning I suck and didn't hit the target at all.

***

That guy Kaye, who UNK'd the mock PFT and got dropped, is still with the platoon. But because he is getting dropped he didn't shoot with us today, but he came to the range and did the bitch work for the DIs and PMIs. The poor guy is in limbo and needs to PT so he can eventually get off the island. Instead he is stuck getting water for these guys.

***

Normally, we don't see 4th Battalion (female recruits) up close because they eat and live in their own battalion area. Even at church, when we do catch a glimpse of female recruits, we never see the female DIs. But here at Weapons Battalion, there is only one chow hall and today we were heading to evening chow just as a platoon of female recruits was leaving. Believe it or not, the female Drill

Instructors are, for the most part, good looking. That was the high point of my day; gawking at some female Drill Instructors.

Drill Instructor Sergeant Willis was staying in the squad bay on duty tonight and I thought that there was a pretty good chance this could be the night for the *Whopper with cheese.* Sure enough, during square away time he called all of the guys who got double 100s on the First Phase test up to the quarterdeck and lined us up. Then he told us that it was "Whopper Time". We were all ecstatic and practically drooling thinking about flamed broiled bounty we were about to receive. Willis went back into the DI's hut and when he returned he was holding a box of Whopper *candies* and a can of Cheez Wiz.

He handed each of us a Whopper candy and squeezed a little Cheez Wiz on it and made us stand there, while all the dummies that didn't get double 100s laughed and watched as we were forced to eat that unholy combination of chocolate malt ball and processed cheese. This pissed me off a lot because I lost too much sleep tutoring guys to make Willis look like a fucking superstar Drill Instructor. Not getting the promised reward would be bad enough but getting a non-reward and being mocked for doing well on the test made my blood boil.

Tuesday, August 22, 2000

We were up at 0400, went to chow, and then we were out at the range while it was still pitch black. Then we shot all morning. I felt pretty comfortable with the sitting, but my shooting from the kneeling position needs work. My rifle range coach thinks that it's a waste of time for us to practice from the standing position because, apparently, that is something you can either do, or you can't, and practice isn't going to make a difference. The range coach says almost every guy from the standing position is merely "spraying and praying," meaning they shoot in the general direction of the target and hope for the best. He thinks the extra five shots are better spent working on the sitting or kneeling. By the way, the range coach is a Marine Lance Corporal or Corporal, who works with two recruits per relay. He distributes the rounds and gives us pointers on how to shoot and make the proper wind calls. If he is in a good mood he gives pointers on how to endure boot camp.

When we finished shooting, we ate our bag nasty by the numbers because Drill Instructor Staff Sergeant Erickson was flexing his DI muscles. When I say we ate "by the numbers," I mean we were instructed when and how to eat every item in the bag. First, we were told to "eat my ketchup packet now." Then we ate the orange peel, followed by the orange. Next, we were ordered to crush the bag of Oreos and bag of Cheetos and basically drink the crumbs. Finally, we ate the bread, salt packet, bologna, cheese and pepper packet, individually, in that order. I think this was Erickson's way of punishing us for getting all the junk food that comes in a bag nasty.

After lunch we went to the "butts" to pull targets. The butts are the area down range behind a big mound of Earth called a berm, where the targets are. This area is alternatively referred to as the pits. Basically you stand below a target that is being fired on. It is safe because the berm is thick and because there is concrete reinforcing the earthen berm. Plus, the bottom of the target is about three feet above our heads. Still it is a crazy feeling though, because rounds are quite literally whizzing over your head all day long. You can hear the snap of the round breaking the sound barrier as it streaks over your head. There is a red line on the concrete about 7 ½ feet high which you are not allowed to put your hand above because it could get hit by a low round.

One guy in my platoon, Lane, the guy who got roughed up by Willis because he couldn't report his post a few weeks back, is too tall and might get hit by a round so he is not allowed in the pits. After Lane is done shooting, when the rest of us head down to the butts, he just sits on the firing line and watches, baking in the South Carolina sun.

The way it works is we pull targets in the afternoon for the guys who pulled targets for us in the morning. It is a pretty primitive system. Two guys are on a target standing there looking up and listening to see if round goes through their target. When a round hits your target, which sits in a rusty carriage moved by a pulley system, you pull it down. You find the shot hole and stick an orange disk on the hole and raise the target. The shooter can see the disk on the target and tell where he shot. If the orange disk is, for example, way to the left of the target during the slow fire, the shooter knows to adjust his sites to move the strike of the round toward the right to get it into the black.

Providing "slow butt service" can have a bad effect on the shooter's score and on his ability to qual. For example, if the pair of recruits working a target takes a long time marking your shot, it can eat away at the shooter's time in a slow fire. Also, when the guys pulling the targets are paying attention, within a second of you pulling the trigger, they will pull the target down, mark the shot and send the target back up. When the target drops immediately after you shoot it usually means you got a four or a five because the guys in the pits are looking primarily at the center of the target. If you can get in the rhythm of *target up … site alignment … site picture … trigger pull … target down … target up,* you are going to get a high score. If the guys down there are not paying attention and you shoot, but the target doesn't go down, the range coach has to tell the safety tower to call down to the butts and "mark target 19." This takes time and gets you out of your groove. When you have slow butt service you begin thinking to yourself, "Oh shit, did it completely miss the target, and that is why they didn't pull my target down?"

There is a Marine whose job it is to work at the range in the butts who communicates with the safety tower on the firing line. He has a microphone and if you are providing crappy butt service, he lets you know. Also, there is a DI back there at all times keeping everybody on their toes. When the shooters are moving from say the 300-yard-line to the 500-yard-line, it takes a few minutes, so the DI in the pits will smoke us a little just so we don't forget about where we are.

After the range, we went on a two-mile "mote" (motivational) run. Along the way we stopped to do push-ups or pull ups. I yanked out ten picture perfect pull ups – a personal best - which was motivational indeed.

Speaking of PT, that guy Kaye who failed the mock PFT finally got switched from five days of Limbo and into another platoon today.

***

I'm worried that next week might be a tough one to keep this journal because we will be working at the chow hall nineteen hours a day. I guess working in the chow hall won't lead to too much interesting stuff worth including in this journal anyway, so that problem may solve itself. Come to think of it, I have not been too good at guessing what things are going to be like, so who knows? I may be getting my wisdom teeth pulled next week so I'll try hard to recall the events of the week and jot them down when I'm over at dental.

Wednesday, August 23, 2000

I found out today that I won't have to work in the chow hall next week during Team Week. I'll be doing office work for the DIs all week, which is fine with me except that I don't want to have an easy time when all of the other guys are hating life, working nineteen hours a day in the chow hall. The DIs know I went to college so they think my bachelor's degree qualifies me to sort and file papers. I feel like the guy in the *Shawshank Redemption*; he was a banker, so he got to handle the warden's money laundering operation while the rest of the guy's made license plates.

Everyone says the time starts to fly after the rifle range. We'll find out soon enough, assuming I qual, which at this point I'd put at a fifty-fifty proposition.

Like everything else down here, our success or failure on the range is a reflection on the DIs. If we can keep the UNK's relatively low, compared to the other platoons, I think that Team Week will be relatively easy. If we have a lot of UNKs, all hell will break loose because Drill Instructor Sergeant Lucifer is the DI most responsible for training us to shoot. If we embarrass him, I have no doubt he will go above and beyond to make us miserable.

***

While waiting for my relay's turn to shoot, I was sitting next to a guy in my platoon named Thornton who is from Hazard County, Kentucky where the fictional *Dukes of Hazard* come from. All the men in his family have worked in the coal mines for years and are now stricken with black lung. He joined the Corps to escape the mines and a similar fate. He said the actress who played Daisy Duke comes back to Hazard County for the annual Dukes of Hazard festival but the years had been unkind to her.

Back in the mid-80s, when my brother was jumping into wrestling rings to help out Marine wrestlers, there was an up-and-comer named Hillbilly Jim who was planted in the crowd to harass the wrestlers. He, at least according to the World Wrestling Federation, hailed from Mud Lick, Kentucky, which until today I sort of assumed was fictional. I jokingly asked Thornton if he knew where Mud Lick, Kentucky was. To my surprise he knew because it was the town next to his.

***

Because the range starts so early, we go to bed at 2000 to wake up at 0400. Keeping these hours makes me feel like I am four years old. We go to morning chow and then to the range in the pitch black. We sit there from like 0500 to 0700 until the sun rises. As soon as it is bright enough to shoot, we begin. Shooting takes about three hours and then we work the targets for the other relays for another three hours. I'm doing alright with the shooting and feel I am improving gradually with each day. I'm somewhat optimistic about qual day on Friday. Today I felt a little better in the rapid fires, but I kind of lost it at the 500-yard-line.

Since we got out to the range, I have been very paranoid about being a safety violator. I am always aware of where the muzzle of my weapon is and I am never the first one to fire when the tower gives the order. Just in case I misunderstood, I don't want to have a negligent discharge. A recruit from my platoon named Slavin had a negligent discharge today. He fired his weapon after the tower said "cease fire" because he wanted to get his tenth rapid fire shot off. The DIs, PMIs, and everyone else went ape shit on this guy, and I hear he is being dropped. Slavin is a smug, arrogant guy and not terribly bright. I am not surprised he had a negligent discharge and I'm not at all concerned if he is getting dropped back in training.

***

My "bunkie' right now is Desai. He is the Scribe and was, along with Advent, one of the PCP recruits put in charge of us way back during Forming Week. He got here June 1, but because he was in such poor physical condition he spent a month getting in shape just to pass the IST. He told me that his original platoon graduates this Friday. That sucks! Had he been able to do three lousy pull-ups, he'd be getting off the island the day after tomorrow. It's his own fault, though, because he came down here unable to do one single pull up.

***

Senior Drill Instructor Staff Sergeant Jefferson told me today that I will be getting off diet tray this weekend. It is nice that it is now official, even though for the last week since I got down to 190 pounds, I have been sneaking non-diet tray chow.

***

I have always known I had a top notch mother, but being on Parris Island really makes me appreciate it. She is my most loyal letter writer and keeps me updated on the presidential election and sports. Her dedication reminds me of all the stuff she used to do for me when I was a kid, like drive me on my paper route if the weather was nasty and take me to Burger King for breakfast after I had to serve an early Mass when I was an altar boy.

Thursday, August 24, 2000

Today was "pre-qual," which is basically the last practice run before Qual Day. You do everything as if it was qualification day, but your score doesn't count. You can shoot expert or you can UNK, but it doesn't matter either way. Pre-qual is, however, a good barometer of how you'll do on Qual Day. This is the first time a score was kept for us. On the previous three days, I had an idea of how I was doing, but not a concrete number. Still, we were not told what our score was, although the DIs knew. A lot of guys were getting bitched at for UNKing pre-qual, but I was not among them, so I figure I shot at least the 190 I needed to qual.

For the past couple of weeks, I've had nightmares every night about qualifying, or more accurately, about not qualifying. As Qual Day approaches, the pressure has increased. Relaxation is an extremely rare commodity on this island but there are a few opportunities when a recruit can sort of decompress, like right when the lights go out at the end of a hard day. Early in training I felt a soothing calmness when the lights shut off because it signified another day was over and I was a day closer to getting off the island. Recently, the quiet of the night has left me in a constant state of dread over the whether I will qualify.

After you graduate from boot camp you get ten days of leave and then you have to report in to a school to learn your MOS. Since I am going to be a grunt, it means I'll go to the School of Infantry or SOI. I'm not exactly sure how long SOI is. I heard it's about two months. Anyway, if I get dropped two weeks, I won't start that until late October, which means I won't be done until late December so getting dropped not only means spending more time on this island, but it also means I'll miss my annual Notre Dame football road trip, and probably Thanksgiving, and possibly Christmas with my family.

To make matters worse, I received a letter from my parents last night. I always thought they might come to graduation, but it's a long trip and I'm not a kid, so I was never sure. I remember my dad saying before I left that they wouldn't be able to make it. I didn't really care then because I thought I was too old to have my parents come. Well, according to the letter from my mother today, they are coming. They booked a flight, rented a car, and are all set to come for Family Day and graduation, September 28th and 29th. I can't even fathom the humiliation if I had to call and tell them to cancel their plans because I can't shoot straight.

If I don't qualify, I'll get dropped, which would keep me on the island for two weeks longer, which would be unbearable. If I failed once, the pressure to qualify would multiply. With each failure, the pressure would crush me a little more. I heard they will drop you twice for a total of four extra weeks and if you still can't qual then they give you an "other than honorable" discharge and send you home. Imagine if I had to go home and face my family and friends saying I couldn't shoot a damned rifle well enough, so they kicked me out. I would be too embarrassed to go home.

Tomorrow is for all of the marbles. Tomorrow will make or break me.

Friday, August 25, 2000 -Rifle Qualification Day– (5 Weeks Until Graduation Unless I UNK)

Early this morning we began shooting in hopes of qualifying. About halfway through there was lightening, so we had to stop for two hours, which was pretty much hell. My last two shots before the lightening were fives, the most you can get. I was starting to feel pretty confident and think I was getting into a groove. Then the heavens conspired against me. When I'm shooting, there is less time to think about how much is hanging in the balance. Having to sit there, watching the rain fall, gave me time to think and made the pressure unbearable.

I was not keeping score in my head, because that only messes with you mentally. Plus, we were told not to, so why risk getting in trouble to do something that I know is counter-productive? Another recruit sits on a box behind you and keeps the score on a clipboard. We were not supposed to discuss how well or poorly we were doing, so I'm not sure what my score was when we got interrupted. The guys in the butts keep the official score. If there is a discrepancy, you defer to the score in the butts.

After the lightening stopped, we resumed shooting. I felt like I was shooting as well as I could. Although I didn't know my exact score, I felt like overall I was doing better than in pre-qual which I think I passed based on the fact that nobody bitched at me.

When we got to the 500-yard-line, my rifle coach, who is forbidden to advise or instruct on Qual Day, said, "I hope you're good from the prone." I didn't know what this meant but I assumed it meant, I was mathematically still capable of qualifying but had to get fives on a majority of my last ten shots from the prone. In the previous four days, I usually got about half the possible points from the 500-yard-line. Today, my first five shots from the 500-yard prone were 2, 2, 4, 4, and 3. My last five shots however were 5, 5, 5, 5, and 5. If I had shot like that the whole time, I'd be in the running for high Expert instead of fighting for my life to be a Marksman.

When my last shot was fired I felt good, but I knew it could go either way. The recruit keeping the score was my buddy Ryan. I asked how I did and he said, "Too close to call without adding it up." I knew Ryan pretty well and had a handle on his mannerisms. I noticed he seemed to have answered the question a little strangely. Then my range coach arrived and in a very pissed off manner asked, "Well, don't you want to know what you got?" He had added up the score on the card Ryan had been keeping on the firing line. Oh God, I thought. Ryan is acting weird. The coach is all pissed off. This is not good. Then the coach told me my score. 188. Two points shy of qualification. I UNK'd.

I was crushed, distraught, heartbroken, and embarrassed all at once. The DIs were bitching at me saying I "choked." About 20% of the recruits go UNK, but most of them fail on pre-qual day, so they were not expected to qual. Since evidently I had qual'd yesterday, the DIs assumed I would qual today. When I didn't, they were shocked and more angry with me than the other UNKs. According to Drill Instructor Sergeant Willis I dropped ten points from a 198 in pre-qual to a 188 when it counted.

There was another recruit who dropped twenty-five points between pre-qual and qual. He was sitting on the firing line sobbing.

A million things went through my mind, as I knew I would have to suffer through another undetermined number of days of nightmares, worrying about qualifying.

I mentioned that a while back I was designated the platoon A-Scribe. This basically means I do some administrative paperwork for the DIs when the regular Scribe is not around or is too busy. Instead of going to pull targets during the afternoon relay I was sent to calculate the individual scores, the platoon average score and to find out if there were any discrepancies between the score cards on the firing line and the official score in the pits. Avoiding the afternoon in the pits would have been a great treat had I passed, but because I failed I felt like shit and couldn't appreciate how wonderful it was to sit in an air conditioned office with a calculator. After UNKing, I was not anxious to see everyone else's score and see first-hand so definitively what a shit bag I was.

As I went through the two sets of score cards, I came across mine. The one from the firing line reflected an UNK score of 188, but the official card from the pits said 190. Holy Shit I thought. This is too good to be true. I didn't know what to do because the odds that this could happen were astronomically long. For one thing, it was the only discrepancy in the whole pile and it was in my favor. On the other hand, the Marine in charge doesn't know my name because we don't have our names on our uniforms yet, so he might not even realize that my score card is the one with an error in my favor. Still I was hesitant to show the Marine in charge of confirming the scores, but I had to. What was I going to do? Throw away this miracle for fear I would not be believed? There are no big cross outs on the scorecard or anything so it doesn't appear that I am cheating.

A little nervous, I pointed out the discrepancy to the Marine Sergeant in charge. He didn't bat an eyelash and moved my scorecard from the UNK pile to the qualified pile.

What a relief I didn't UNK after all. What a great feeling. The only worry now is, how long it will take for the message that I actually passed to get back to the Drill Instructor's to clear my good name?

I didn't have a chance to think about it much at the time, because I was so concerned about qualifying, but recall that my last five shots from the 500-yard-line were fives. I didn't realize the significance at the time, because I didn't know my score. Had any of those last shots been anything less than five I actually would have UNK'd. What foreshadowing that priest's story was. He made ten out of ten 5s from the 500-yard-line knowing he had to. I got 5's on each of my last five shots without knowing the significance because I was determined not to keep score in my head. We both qual'd , but by the slimmest of margins.

I honestly think what I experienced today was an honest to God miracle. Within an hour, today went from being the worst day I've had on Parris Island, and one of the worst of my twenty-four years on Earth, to the best day since I have been here. Talk about a rollercoaster.

***

With the range over, I can relax as much as a recruit can on Parris Island. I can also resume my favorite past time of counting down the days.

CHAPTER 5: Team Week

Saturday, August 26, 2000

The Senior came in late last night and was bitching at us for not doing well as a platoon on the range. He said we "gave it away," whatever that means. I guess he thought we would have done better. I am so relieved that I didn't UNK that the Senior being mad doesn't bother me at all. He is definitely aware of how close I came to UNKing because he came up to me and mocked me for only qualing "by the skin of my teeth."

There is a recruit in another platoon in our Series that used to be a Sergeant with the Army Rangers. He UNK'd the range. I'd like to say that Army dogs can't shoot but my platoon's prior service Army guy, Kistemaker, got one of the highest scores ever on the range, so go figure.

Desai, the main Scribe, went UNK so he will have to re-qual next week. I was under the impression that as soon as you UNK you get dropped but as it turns out you get another chance to qual during Team Week. If you still can't muster a 190 by the end of Team Week then you get dropped. As a result of Desai going UNK, I was promoted to full Scribe today, which is not good because being the Scribe is a thankless job. Unlike being the platoon Guide or a Squad Leader, you cannot get a meritorious promotion upon graduating for being Scribe. What you get is a lot of nitty-gritty work and demanding, unappreciative DIs bossing you around more than normal.

Franks, who was one of the two Alabamans who got dropped to our platoon for UNKing the range with his original platoon, qual'd yesterday. I'm happy for him and can only imagine how happy he must be to be relieved of all that pressure. Franks' counterpart Bishop, the cancer on the platoon who rummages through the chow hall trash on Fire Watch, went UNK yet again. He gets a chance to shoot again next week. All the guys who UNK get to shoot next week while the rest of the platoon is working in the chow hall. From what I hear, if Bishop doesn't qual next week he gets booted out of the Marine Corps.

Now that the range is complete we will start doing more combat-oriented training like rappelling, shooting at night, shooting moving targets, and crawling under barbed wire. In the next couple of weeks we will even be going to the gas chamber. I am dreading that because my brother Pat said that was the worst part of boot camp and he is of the rare bread that actually liked boot camp. If Pat is saying that the gas chamber was hell, it must really suck. Since I have been here I have heard that a lot of guys puke and just lose it in the gas chamber and try to pry the door open. That should be interesting.

We did the confidence course again today and it actually worked. Unlike the last time, where it crushed my self-confidence, this time I completed all of the obstacles with relative ease. It's funny because the "dirty name" obstacle, which kicked my ass last time, was a breeze and I can't figure out what was so hard about it. I have probably lost twenty pounds since then so I'm sure that helped. There were some new obstacles we conquered like crawling across a rope which was about fifty feet above water. A few guys fell in the water but I'm proud to report that I made it across.

First the range, and now I redeemed myself on the confidence course; things are going well. However, I see guys make the mistake of getting too high or too low emotionally and I'm not going to do that. Even keel is the best way to get through this or most anything.

***

Team Week started at 1500 today. Most of the platoon is at the chow hall learning what they have to do all week. Me and two others are staying back in the barracks for most of the week. I am assigned to my Scribe duties and one of the guys, MacAndrew, is the platoon artist. He was given paint to do some motivating art work on a cover block for the DIs. A cover block is a wooden frame that DIs use to keep the brim of their campaign covers stiff and straight. They want MacAndrew to paint all sorts of Marine Corps stuff on it.

Since the DIs were not around when most of the platoon was getting their instructions at the chow hall, I quickly completed my Scribe work and began writing letters like crazy. I've written so many letters today that I'm worried I am going to run out of people to write to. One of my many responsibilities this week will be to answer the phone in the DI hut. Obviously, I am not allowed to make any personal phone calls, just to the Military Police if there is a problem. Also, because of the "promotion" from A-Scribe to Scribe, from now on I will be the one who collects everyone's outgoing mail at night and puts it in the mailbox on the way to the chow hall in the morning.

***

It is funny, the first week I was here I met a guy at church who was at the exact point in training where I am now and I thought, "Wow, this guy is the luckiest guy in the world, only one month to go". The guy was nice and gave the advice "live chow to chow and Sunday to Sunday." The guy was younger than me, probably eighteen or nineteen but, in boot camp years, he was like ten years older than me. At the time I thought it was brilliantly insightful for this guy to come up with that "chow to chow" bit. I subsequently realized that, although it is good advice, it is a common expression and not the brainchild of that particular recruit. Even though that guy seemed like a nice guy, he was so much closer to getting off this island than me so I couldn't help but hate his guts.

Sunday, August 27, 2000

We still go to bed at 2100 but now we are up at 0230 to go to work in the chow hall. Good thing for me I don't require that much beauty sleep. I worked over at the chow hall for a while today before I got called back to the squad bay to do Scribe work. I had breakfast while we were working in the chow hall with no DIs. It was amazing. I must have drank a gallon of milk. Plus I had Fruit Loops, Apple Jacks, Mini Wheats, sausages, eggs, coffee cake, two pears, and potatoes. I hope it is like this all week although I am worried I'll put on weight. From what I hear, they PT us every night during Team Week because they know we are pigging out all day. Now that I think of it, last night they tortured us for no particular reason for a good forty-five minutes before hygiene time.

The great meal notwithstanding, the platoon has been so busy with the range and now working in the chow hall they have not given out mail since Thursday. The good part is that even though tonight is Sunday there is a possibility that we'll get caught up on mail tonight. It's hard to believe it's almost September. I was just thinking that this will be the first September in nineteen years that I'm not going to be going back to school. I went Kindergarten through 12th grade, then four years of college, and the last two Septembers I went back to school as a teacher.

Even though it's getting way ahead of myself, I'm starting to think about what I will do in December when SOI ends and I become a Reservist. My first order of business will be to get my law school applications in. Then I'll I have to find work from January to September and, assuming one of the schools lets me in, I'll start up law school in September 2001.

Little by little I'm starting to notice that the tear-us-down phase of this trial-by-fire is beginning to give way to the build-us-back-up-into-Marines portion of boot camp. For example, they used to say, "If you get off my island…" Now they say, "When you graduate…" It is a subtle but meaningful distinction. That being said, we are still not even considered Marines. Only after you complete the Crucible and the Senior Drill Instructors gives you your EGA (Eagle Globe and Anchor, the familiar Marine Corps emblem) are you considered a Marine. That happens about a week before graduation.

***

Now that I am so svelte and in such good cardiovascular shape I am thinking of running in a marathon when I get done boot camp and SOI. Maybe I'll do the Boston Marathon in April. Running a marathon is a goal I have always had, mainly for the feather in my cap. Now seems like the time to do it because I'll never be in this good of shape again.

***

Boot camp has inspired me to do a lot of things when I get the chance. I already mentioned running a marathon, maybe take up martial arts, and maybe get into shooting. The marathon is still at the very top of my list, although we learned some martial arts stuff yesterday that I really enjoyed. The problem with boot camp martial arts training is that you learn a bunch of moves one day and then don't work on them again for a while and I tend to forget what I learned. I'm hesitant to take a Karate class in the civilian world because I don't want to take a class with a bunch of twelve-year-old boys, like that episode of *Seinfeld* where Kramer was "dominating" a do jo full of tweens.

Now that I'm in the best shape of my life I am also thinking about boxing. I really believe if I boxed I could be a good boxer. After all, I have 0.5 college credits in boxing from VMI, which is a pretty unusual thing to have on a college transcript. Plus when my brother was a senior in high school and I was in 3rd grade, I got boxing gloves for Christmas. Pat's buddies would come over to spar with me. I duke'd it out with half of the class of 1985 and although they boxed on their knees to make up for the inevitable height difference, no punches were pulled.

The bottom line is that for some reason boot camp has made me want to try everything out and be a modern day renaissance man.

Monday, August 28, 2000

Today has been a pretty cake day. I stuffed my face at breakfast and then got two lunches. One lunch was good old fashion "pub grub" from the DI's chow line. There were Buffalo wings, French fries, and a mini-pizza. Heaven on Earth. The only thing that ruined the pub atmosphere was drinking canteen water instead of beer.

Most of the day in the squad bay it's just me and two other recruits. The Guide and I are doing the paperwork for the DIs and MacAndrews, the artist, is doing his thing for the DIs. Drill Instructor Sergeant Willis gave MacAndrews a *Maxim* magazine to get ideas for the artwork he was commissioned to do. This gave me a chance to read a few pages, on the sly of course.

One of my duties was to sort the incoming mail, which arrives at the barracks in a big sack for all six platoons in the company. While we broke the mail down by platoon I saw that I had letters from my sister Meg and my buddy Goober. I was tempted to snag my mail but I decided against it because chances are we'll get that mail tonight, so why take the risk?

We are all starting to look like worn out tennis balls because it's been a while since our last haircut. We used to get our heads shaved once per week but since we have been out at the range we are out of our routine and have not gotten haircuts in almost two weeks. At some point, we will be allowed to grow our hair from the current cue ball to a standard Marine Corps high and tight. Maybe high and tight time is near and that is why we have not gotten haircuts lately. I'm going bald anyway so it's not a big deal to me although I would like to have a little something on top when I walk of this island in about a month.

I saw a guy in the chow hall today who rode up with me to Albany with the recruiter on July Fourth. He was the one who had his piss test lost in the lab in Albany so he shipped out a week after me. I don't even remember the guy's name but it was nice to see a familiar face from before boot camp. I'm actually surprised that the kid recognized me because I am forty pounds lighter than when I met him. That's good because I was worried my parents wouldn't recognize me at graduation.

Out here at Weapons Battalion we run into female recruits from time to time. It's weird seeing them doing the same things we do and yelling, "Yes Ma'am!", "No Ma'am!" when talking to their DIs. I still can't get over the women DIs. To see a twenty-something year old woman screaming mercilessly at an eighteen-year-old girl is, to me, a little disturbing. It is still highly illegal to look at, or talk to, woman recruits. Yesterday, a guy in my platoon ran into a girl in church that he knew from home and gave her a hug at the end of Mass. Somehow the DIs found out about it and he got smoked real bad when he got back to the squad bay.

We have some weights in the squad bay so MacAndrews and I have been doing some lifting on our own to try to counteract the dramatic increase in food intake. The DIs don't seem to have a problem with us pumping iron so long as we get their work done and don't appear to be enjoying the limited slice of autonomy too much. The magic number for me is to be below 197 pounds when I have my final weigh in. If I am 198 pounds I'll get dropped but there is no way I am going to let that happen.

I got to take a ride to the tailor shop today with Drill Instructor Staff Sergeant Erickson to pick up the platoon's Service Alpha uniforms which have been tailored. This made the day go quickly because anything out of the routine tends to speed the time along. Drill Instructor Staff Sergeant Erickson took me to our regular squad bay back in the rear and smoked me pretty good. I did all of the usual stuff, push-ups, mountain climbers, up-downs, side-straddle-hops plus, since the squad bay was empty I ran suicides. Suicides are what basketball players do. Sprint to the foul line then jog back to the baseline. Then Sprint to half court and jog back and so on. This was a real ass-kicker but I have been stuffing my face all week so it is probably for the best. In fact, I got weighed in today after lunch and I was 195 pounds. So I have gained a couple pounds this week but nothing to be alarmed about.

This relatively laid back week has given me time to think about my long term plans. There is a lot I love about the Marine Corps and I am considering possibly becoming a Marine J.A.G. (Judge Advocate General) lawyer when I finish law school. I have heard about programs where the Marine Corps pays for law school and, in exchange, you serve in the Marine Corps as a lawyer for four of five years after graduation. It is something I am considering but for right now my plan is to finish boot camp, complete SOI, and get into law school. The other stuff is long term and will work itself out.

The bad news is tomorrow I get my wisdom teeth pulled. The good news is I'll get to catch up on some news because they have CNN Headline News in the waiting room.

Tuesday, August 29, 2000
Exactly 1 Month Until Graduation!

I was already doing paperwork at 0400 this morning. I thought I was getting a break not having to work in the chow hall but my job is much tougher than I anticipated. I have to keep track of the comings and goings of all sixty-eight recruits in the platoon. They schedule all medical and dental appointments for Team Week because there is not much training. My job is to let everyone know where to be and when and to know where everyone is so that the DIs have "accountability," which basically means knowing for certain where everyone is and being able to confirm that everyone is where they are supposed to be and that no one is UA (unauthorized absence).

When Drill Instructor Sergeant Willis told me this was going to be part of my job for the week he warned, "You fuck this up. I kill you." Thanks for the confidence boost, Sir.

Originally, I had an appointment to get all four of my wisdom teeth pulled on Thursday but, for some reason, it got pushed up until today at 0630. When you go to dental you are not supposed to talk to other recruits, which is par for the course. What surprised me is that you are not even supposed to talk to the Navy personnel checking out your mouth. If the dentist or some dental assistant tries to chat you up you are supposed to say, "This recruit was instructed not to engage in casual conversation." I'm a pretty social guy, so I usually disobey this rule because I don't think it will ever make it back to my Drill Instructors that I spoke with a dental assistant about the weather.

The wisdom teeth removal was miserable. They gave me the gas which made me a little nutty. Then they covered my face because there is a lot of water and stuff spraying all over the place. I never even saw the dentist but I heard him. They stick a big piece of rubber in your mouth for you to bite down on and then crank away on your wisdom teeth. Then there is a horrible cracking sound. Then you are done. Afterwards my mouth was bleeding like crazy only I didn't know it because it was numb. I went to the place where they fill prescriptions to get some pain killers unaware that there was blood dripping down the corners of my mouth onto the sides of my chin. After an hour of wondering why all of the Navy medical personnel and civilians I encountered were looking at me with horrified expressions on their faces, I caught my reflection in a shiny silver fire extinguisher. The blood was dripping out of the corners of my mouth like a bad Halloween costume.

When I got back to the squad bay I was still bleeding so much that I ran out of the gauze that the dentist office gave me and had to use moist toilet paper. I guess I could have asked the DIs for more gauze but I am not about to become high maintenance. I was given bed rest for the remainder of the day and I have light duty for tomorrow which, for some reason, I feel guilty about even though I shouldn't. I just don't like the thought of my buddies working all day in the chow hall and me lying in my rack.

I got my lunch delivered to my rack by MacAndrews. My tongue was still numb from the Novocain and my mouth was still stuffed with the improvised toilet paper gauze so I didn't eat and gave away my cookies to MacAndrews and the Guide. I am not that hungry because I ate enough breakfast chow to hold me over in preparation for the removal of my wisdom teeth.

***

In the nearly two months that I have been here I have learned a lot about leadership. For one, you need credibility and respect to get things done and to get people to listen to you. You cannot just order people around and expect them to follow just because you are the Guide or a Squad Leader. The guys here are, for the most part, proud and stubborn and even if they have to listen because you have a billet (position of authority), they can follow your orders in an ineffective way just to spite you. In some respects, the messenger and the manner in which the message is delivered is as important as the message itself. When Advent was the Guide he would say in effect, "Clean the barracks because I said so and I am the Guide and you must listen to me." Everything got done because it had to but when orders are given in a disrespectful manner guys do exactly what they have to do and no more.

Speaking of Advent, I'm not sure why but he had a complete hissy fit in the chow hall today. He threw his cup and then cried.

He was such a prick to everyone in the beginning. Recall when he was Guide and ratted out Tobego for taking peanut butter from the chow hall and when Advent took cookies from the Big Gear Locker, he tried to bring others down with him? Now he is 100% isolated from everyone else in the platoon. He made his bed and now he doesn't want to lie in it. Boot camp is hard enough; to have to go through it surrounded by people who hate you and without a single friend must be difficult. I think the isolation is starting to eat away at him and prompted the odd, even by boot camp standards, outburst today.

I have zero sympathy for the guy because he is a complete phony. He is constantly talking about how he has a top security clearance because his MOS is going to be intelligence. I don't know if that is true and I don't really care. He is a horrible Marine and a complete coward. He was some kind of general or something in the Junior ROTC program in high school. I know this because he has told us all a million times, as if anyone cares. Then he actually put a picture of him in his faux Dress Blues uniform from Junior ROTC up on the "Mote Table." The guy is constantly bragging about this JROTC bullshit yet he came to boot camp unable to do a single pull-up: that should tell you everything you need to know about this phony bastard.

***

Today we found out that the Guide, Hilbert is going to be our platoon honor man. Coming down here one of my goals was to be the Honor Graduate of boot camp because my brother was. I am a little disappointed but I have given 100% to boot camp and I'm proud of my efforts here and that I am well-respected among the other recruits and I think even respected by the DIs. I am a little surprised that they determined the Honor Man so early. What if he gets hurt or can't finish the Crucible?

If I had to pick the Honor Man, I would pick Kistemaker because he has excelled at every aspect of boot camp and never had any problems with discipline. My guess is that there is some anti-Army bias at work here. The DIs don't want to give an ex-soldier an award because it is like saying we could not transform our raw recruits into better warriors than an Army Sergeant who has four years of Army training plus Marine Corps boot camp.

***

I felt bad that I was in my bed half asleep and a little woozy from the drugs when this evening the rest of the platoon was doing rifle PT (calisthenics using the M-16) in the squad bay followed by a round of tear-the-rack-apart, make-the-rack, tear-it-apart-and-make-it-again. I also missed PT today, which I am not happy about because the final PFT is only fifteen days away.

Wednesday, August 30, 2000

I'm always looking to do things more efficiently and the Marine Corps has taught me several good techniques. For example, we tied a pen to our rifle range data books so that there was no way you would be without a pen when you needed to plot your shots or write down a site setting. When I was teaching, it used to drive me crazy when a kid would come to class without a pen. This is a simple but brilliant solution to that problem.

I have worked for hard bosses in the past. My dad, a former-Marine, was a very hard boss with high standards who would stand and watch me as I planted stuff in the yard, or painted one of the bedrooms in our house, or shoveled the snow. My first job, other than a paper route, was when I was twelve years old and I worked with my little league buddy for his father's landscaping business. The father, also a former-Marine, was a tough boss and had high expectations. He was a good guy but we worked hard that summer. I remember the first day of work I was so tired I fell asleep in the truck going from one job to another. Well, neither the landscaper nor my dad can compare to the kind of taskmasters the DIs are. They give you work with impossible deadlines and the expectation that it be absolutely perfect. This has made me much more meticulous, a trait I have always lacked.

One thing I have been working on for the DIs is an updating of what looks like some kind of report card for each Recruit. Most of them have pretty generic entries like "Said Named Recruit is an average recruit." Some guys, like Bishop for example, have entries which indicate that he is a "below average recruit." There were was one superlative about Bilderband's ability to PT. There was also a mention of Kistemaker's prior Army service and a mention that his physical fitness is below average and that he is on diet tray. Marines will take any and every opportunity to stick it to the Army. My own entry mentioned that I was on diet tray but that I was "making strong progress." I was happy with that.

Another thing I came across today while tending to my Scribe duties is a schedule for graduation practice which starts today for the Honor Graduates. That is the main reason why the Guide is not working the chow hall. He and the other five honor men from the company's six platoons have some pretty involved marching to do at graduation and this is a good week for them to practice so they don't mess things up. To me, the existence of a graduation schedule is another milestone indicating that there is a light at the end of the tunnel.

Since it is only me, MacAndrews and the Guide back in the squad bay, Willis doesn't have to supervise us too much and I think this is sort of light week for the DIs compared to the crazy hours they normally work. Willis brought a small TV and VCR into the DI Hut and, although he keeps the door shut, I can hear the TV and him laughing. He was watching *Wayne's World* before and laughing hysterically in his big, loud, scary voice. He was also watching *All in the Family* and cracking up. It was funny to hear him laugh because I honestly thought he was incapable of any kind of benevolent human emotion.

You can tell the difference between the Senior and Willis just by what they asked MacAndrew to draw for them on their cover blocks. Willis wants naked women and the Senior wants only Marine Corps stuff like tanks and helicopters. Both the Senior and Willis are good Marines, but the Senior is very much a boy scout-type Marine while Willis is a maverick and more representative of the gritty side of the Corps.

Overall, things went well today. The DIs were impressed with my resilience after oral surgery. Drill Instructor Staff Sergeant Erickson said that I must be "drugged up or something" because I have so much energy. In the real world such a comment is not considered complimentary. But on Parris Island, coming from a DI, I think it is high praise. I also think I impressed the Senior today. He asked me who was in my immediate chain of command. I knew the answers because that is a pretty easy question. Then he tried to stump and asked who the Secretary of Defense and the Secretary of State was. I follow politics so, of course, I knew that the honorable Richard Cohen and the honorable Madeline Albright were the two secretaries. Then the Senior asked if I wanted to be a politician, and I said "Maybe Sir." This was the first time the Senior ever really showed any interest in me. I'm hoping this means I might even get a Squad Leader billet which would be a real feather in my cap because Squad Leader is the billet held by the best recruits. Scribe is not only a thankless job. it is also a job usually reserved for nerdy bookish types. In fact the other five scribes in the Series look like chess club or A.V. squad alums. I was considering flat out asking the Senior about getting a shot as one of the Squad Leaders but I'm not sure how that would go over so I'll keep plugging along and hope for the best.

Three of the eight UNKs from our platoon finally qualified yesterday and another four qual'd today. Only Desai, my old bunkee and the former-Scribe remained unqualified when the UNKs got back from the range late this afternoon. Desai has already spent more than a month of extra time on the island and if he doesn't qual he is going to spend at least another two weeks in boot. He must have been shitting a brick until it was discovered that he actually qualified in the pits although not on the unofficial firing line score card.

Somehow even Bishop managed to qualify after I don't remember how many attempts and the platoon is now 100% qualified with the M16 A-2 Service Rifle.

Thursday, August 31, 2000

I remember at VMI the upperclassmen talked ad nauseum about how much harder it was when they were in their Rat year and how easy we have it. It's the same thing here. You would not believe the outrageous "Old Corps" stories the DIs tell. Drill Instructor Staff Sergeant Erickson is by far the worst offender. He told us the other day that when he came through Parris Island they had boxing four times per week and that if you didn't break your opponent's nose or give him a concussion you got smoked. I think some of the younger guys might believe that but I don't buy it. Even the rifle range coaches from last week, who were boots just a year or two ago, tell us how much harder they had it when they came through.

My view is that boot camp changes slightly overtime but that ninety-five percent of it remains the same. I base this on my own experiences, coupled with conversations with my dad who came through here in 1962, and my brother who came through in 1989. The three of us basically cover three distinct eras and my experiences have been very similar to what I've heard from my dad and brother.

The Senior was with us tonight and apparently in a good mood so we watched a movie; *Full Metal Jacket,* of course. In case you don't know, *Full Metal Jacket* is the Stanley Kubrick movie about a platoon of recruits aboard Parris Island who go to Vietnam. It was sort of surreal watching a fictional depiction of what we are going through for real. I'm surprised the DIs like this movie. After all, the underachieving recruit ends up shooting and killing the Senior Drill Instructor. I don't think we will do any more live shooting for the rest of boot camp so I guess they are confident that even if there is a loose cannon, disgruntled recruit, he doesn't have any rounds to do anything like that.

Besides, at the rifle range, they conducted an extremely thorough search at the end of every day to make sure we had no rounds. Obviously, they visually and physically ensure that the rifles do not have rounds. They also pat us down, check our pockets, magazines and magazine pouches, and wand us with some sort of metal detector. We also make this verbal declaration, "Sir. This recruit has no brass, trash or saved rounds to report at this time. Sir." Brass refers to the brass shell casing that discharges when you fire the weapon. Trash is any other kind of rifle range stuff like the stripper clips that hold ten rounds nice and neat for easy distribution. It is a good policy to say no ammunition and no ammunition paraphernalia (also known as trash) can come off the range because it is sort of a zero tolerance - plus policy.

If somehow you took a round and it got through or you accidentally had a round that got stuck in the corner of your pocket, they have what are called amnesty boxes all over the place. Basically, an amnesty box is a locked container with a hole where you can deposit a round that you took off the range. So, if by mistake, one got left in your pocket and got by the check, or you had some nefarious intent but came to your senses, there is a way to properly get rid of the round, no questions asked. Hence the term amnesty. The Marine Corps knows that most recruits are not going to want to tell a DI that for whatever reason they have a saved round so the amnesty box is an effective, and brilliantly simple, solution.

When I was on bed rest yesterday I was extremely bored but I had two books to read. I perused *The Guidebook for Marines,* which is basically a manual that covers all of the basics a Marine needs to know. There are chapters on first aid, Maine Corps history, customs and courtesies, how to be an effective leader, how to wear the uniform, and so on. There is a lot of good stuff particularly the history stuff and information on the Universal Code of Military Justice. The other book is a novel called *Rifleman Dodd* that is unbearably boring and mind numbing. The plot involves a rifleman fighting in the Peninsular War of the early 19th Century. Nothing really happens, but the protagonist demonstrates the traits of a good rifleman by always keeping his rifle clean and putting the accomplishment of his mission above all else. I understand why the Commandant of the Marine Corps has ordered that every recruit be issued this book; the moral of the story is a good one. The manner in which the story is told however, is stupefyingly dull.

***

I slept like a baby last night because I took three of the Tylenols I got from dental the other day and it knocked me right out. Steady sleep was great because I have been having trouble sleeping lately. I had to go back to dental again today. CNN Headline News was on and I think I heard them say that President Clinton was disbarred by the State of Arkansas. Good, I'm glad that draft-dodging perjurer can't practice law. When you think of all of the corrupt and shady characters practicing law and then realize the President of the United States is not even allowed to be among their ranks, it becomes clear what a dirt bag he is. I think even Nixon held on to his law license after he resigned the presidency.

***

I have not had a haircut in fifteen days and my hair is long. Other recruits at dental notice this sort of thing and know I must be far along in training and they are asking me all of the questions I was asking a month or two ago. They ask how the range was and if anybody in the platoon UNK'd. They want to know if the DIs ease up during Grass Week or Qual Week. They are disappointed to learn that they don't ease off the accelerator.

It's one of the really odd things about this place; in a matter of weeks you can go from a clueless First Phase recruit, unsure of everything, to Yoda the Jedi Grand Master.

***

I'm not sure what the dentist had to do but I was unable to get numb so they could not do anything. The dentist kept sticking me with a needle deep in the back of my gums and then poking around in my mouth. When I told him I could feel him in there he was incredulous. He said of all the Novocain he had already injected in to me, "We are getting into small farm animal territory here." The Navy dentist sent me back to barracks and said I would have to come back tomorrow and we would try again.

A bus picked me up outside of dental and drove me back out to the Weapons Battalion area. I was the only one on the bus so the civilian bus driver chatted me up a little. He was probably in his early fifties and was a Vietnam Vet. He told me how he was on Parris Island in the late sixties as a recruit and how he hated his Senior Drill Instructor so much that he vowed he would kill him if he ever saw him in 'Nam.

I guess this guy was a burly recruit and, early on in boot camp, he had a bad shave and his Senior got on him about it. For the rest of boot camp, some two and a half months, the Senior dry shaved this guy every morning in front of the whole platoon. He said his face got so raw from the dry shaving it was excruciating just to touch it. Plus, it was a daily humiliation to have the Senior Drill Instructor shaving your face in front of all the other recruits.

Anyway, I guess back during the Vietnam-era when a platoon graduated their DIs sort of graduated with them and in this case went to Vietnam with their platoon of recruits-turned-Marines. As it turns out, the Senior Drill Instructor ended up saving the bus driver's life over in Vietnam and giving his own life in the process. The Driver said, "I cried like a baby over a man who six months earlier I swore to God I wanted to kill."

The driver said this made him realize that the DIs were only hard on the recruits because they knew they were going to be shipping off to Vietnam and wanted to make them physically and mentally tough. He said it also taught him never to hate anyone because everyone has a purpose for what they are doing.

The bus driver, whose name I don't even know, said that he rarely tells this story and I'm not sure why he told it to me, but I'm glad he did. By the time the story was over the driver's eyes had welled-up with tears and so had mine. Running into this man and hearing his story made me realize the old Friedrich Nietzsche quote "that which does not kill us makes us stronger" and sort of put all of the mind games and physical pain of boot camp into perspective and made it all more tolerable.

To lighten the mood the driver next asked if I followed college football, which was about to start on Saturday. It's hard to believe football is starting up already. When I left civilization it was not even the baseball All-Star break, yet now it's almost fall. The driver and I talked a little football and then we were back at the barracks.

***

As I write this, half my face is still numb and my eye is twitching a little bit. I think the dentist may have given me too much Novocain or put it in the wrong place.

Friday, September 1, 2000 (4 Weeks Until Graduation)

58 Down 28 To Go!

I went to dental early this morning and sat around for a couple of hours waiting. Then they said I didn't have an appointment, so I went out and waited for the bus for longer than Forrest Gump. I was hoping for the Vietnam Vet driver from yesterday but it was not him. I think I am getting sick. I have aches and pains and a scratchy sore throat, headache, and a fever.

Our days of being long-haired hippies are over. We were taken to the Weapons Battalion barber today for a round of cue ball cuts. A lot of us were expecting high and tights but not yet. I also got weighed in today and I was 205 pounds. That means I have put on ten pounds since Monday and fifteen pounds since last Sunday. Between the extra chow early in the week and the inability to PT because of dental during the past week, I have a lot of weight to lose before final PFT, which is in about a week and a half.

***

Remember Imish? The older guy from Ohio? I think he is getting discharged because his mother-in-law called her Congressman who called the base General. The mother-in-law claimed that he abandoned his family. The DIs went nuts on him. When I came home from dental all his gear was packed and ready to go. He is in the chow hall with the rest of the platoon working but I'm pretty sure he'll be gone soon.

***

After evening chow we got an outstanding pep talk from a recently retired Sergeant Major. Sergeant Major is the highest enlisted rank and it takes almost thirty years to achieve that rank. But this rank is in no way guaranteed just by staying in for three decades. From what I can tell, a Sergeant Major is pretty much the right-hand man of a General or a Colonel and he is supposed to represent all of the enlisted men in a unit to the top brass.

He gave our group of young, eager Marines, about to hit the Fleet and see the world, some very sound and pragmatic advice based on three decades of experience. When I heard he was going to give us some advice I thought it was going to be along the lines of shoot straight and keep your head down, or obey orders and use your chain of command. I find it interesting that his advice to newly-minted Marines involved women and money. It makes sense. I guess this guy in his thirty years in the Corps saw enough guys mess up their careers and lives over women and money that he made them the touchstones of his advice.

He summed his advice up into three maxims:

1. *"Foreign money is real."* I think what he was trying to say was when you go overseas keep track of the exchange rate and continue to live within your means and don't go broke on liberty and default on your car payments and other financial commitments.

2. *"Bar girls are smarter than you."* Here he was warning that girls hanging out in bars frequented by Marines know what they are doing and they are likely going to either flat out rob you, trap you with a pregnancy, or slowly bleed you dry financially by buying stuff in your name.

3. *"True love does not exist in an overseas bar."* He related stories of guys on liberty not getting back to the ship on time or never coming back to the ship because they met a girl whom they thought was *"the one."*

He also reiterated that although some Military Occupational Specialties (MOS') are more glamorous than others, every MOS is important to the success and readiness of the Marine Corps. We have several guys in our platoon who are going to be in the Marine

Corps band and the Sergeant Major made a point of highlighting how important the band is to recruiting and getting Congress to appropriate funds to Marine Corps projects. I agree that every MOS is important but I have to say that I have noticed recruiters, civilians, and even DIs and other Marine Corps personnel, have a positive reaction when you say that your MOS is infantry which is my MOS. It makes sense. As Drill Instructor Sergeant Willis, himself a supply and logistics guy, once said, "Infantry is where the metal hits the meat."

The retired Sergeant Major also told us, essentially a bunch of federal employees on government time, something that would give the ACLU fits. He said, "If you are religious, stay religious. If you are not religious, get religious." Then he used a venerable saying my father used to say, "There are no atheists in fox holes."

Saturday, September 2, 2000

The whole platoon is moving to a new barracks this afternoon when the new Team Week platoon relieves us in the chow hall. MacAndrew, the artist, and I spent all morning moving the DIs' stuff to the new squad bay. While Drill Instructor Sergeant Lucifer was in the new barracks setting up his stuff, MacAndrew and I were in and out of the old squad bay transporting the DI's gear. I knew the DI's office had a working phone because during the previous week, one of my jobs was to answer the phone, though it rarely rang. MacAndrew and I, at grave personal risk, played look out for each other while we each made phone calls. I was not able to get through to anybody, but MacAndrew spoke to his mother briefly. He said his mom was so happy to hear from him that she was balling and he couldn't even understand what she was saying. As he was talking to his mother, I heard Drill Instructor

Sergeant Lucifer enter the barracks and gave MacAndrew the cease fire hand and arm signal which is simply waving your right hand in front of your face, palm out. MacAndrew understood the signal and abruptly hung up. For a second I thought we were dead men. Had Lucifer been a little quieter he would have walked right in on us. I was watching the back hatch because the DIs almost always come through the back hatch, but on this occasion he came through the front way. I don't even want to think about what would happen if we got caught. MacAndrews called collect but I just called and had anyone answered I would have billed it to the Marine Corps. My reasoning was that on the off-chance that the Marine Corps combs its phone bill for unauthorized calls, I would be off Parris Island by the time they figured it all out, besides going through collect call process wasted time and increased the odds of getting caught.

Even though no one answered when I called home, that MacAndrew managed to get through was a satisfying victory for me. After being in this highly controlled and oppressive environment for two months, it feels great to just beat the system a little and get away with it.

This little bit of excitement made me forget my vicious head cold for a while, but now that the euphoria of having struck a blow for liberty has subsided, my cold is kicking in again with a vengeance. Fortunately, another of my Scribe duties is to distribute cough drops at night to the guys who have colds. Since I have an unlimited supply, and they help a little, I have about fifty per day. I hope by Monday I am better because from what I am told the upcoming week is among the most grueling of boot camp.

By the end of the day we were all settled in our third barracks of boot camp and we have one more relatively easy day before A-Line commences.

CHAPTER 6: A-Line

Sunday, September 3, 2000

I was feeling kind of crappy today because tomorrow is my parents' 35th wedding anniversary and I'm sure my whole family is getting together to celebrate. I hate missing out on stuff like that. I went to Mass this morning and they sang my mother's favorite church song that goes "Let there be peace on Earth and let it begin with me." On the surface, there is some irony about a couple hundred guys training to become Marines singing about peace beginning with them. Then again, the presence of a strong military acts as a deterrent and is a much greater force for peace then any pacifist hoping for the best. My eleventh grade history teacher, Mr. Murphy, used to give us extra-credit for memorizing quotes from historical figures. Since then I have gotten in the habit of committing to memory quotes I like. It was George Washington who said, "To be prepared for war is one of the most effective means of preserving peace."

Of course your internationalist-peacenik-can't-we-all-get-along-hippy crowd will say international cooperation is the way to peace. But as I see it, old General Washington did more for the peace and prosperity of the world than the UN ever will.

***

In many ways, boot camp is a constant personification of the expression "feast or famine." We either don't have enough time to get things done or we have too much time and are bored stiff standing in formation waiting. We are either dying of thirst or we are pounding canteen-after-canteen of water to hydrate. Last week we were, quite literally, engaged in a non-stop feast with our platoon working the chow hall. It was crazy how spoiled we got last week. For the first seven weeks we would fork a guy in the face for an extra lima bean, but last week we were throwing out chicken with half the meat still on the bone and dumping out glasses of milk. Beginning today, it's back to the famine of diet tray and drinking nasty canteen water instead of juice and "white cow" and "brow cow" (milk and chocolate milk, respectively). I'm not sure if I'm on diet tray anymore but until that final weigh-in I am going to stay on it voluntarily.

Today, at the Protestant services, a recruit from one of the platoons on the range tried to hang himself in the head with his belt. A guy from our platoon walked in on him before he got too far. I heard about this early in the day but sort of dismissed it as a rumor. Then, this afternoon, an MP came and took a statement from the recruit who witnessed the potential suicide. My guess is the guy was trying to get out of the Marine Corps by appearing suicidal. We are out on the rifle range. Even the dumbest recruit could figure out a better way to off himself than tying his belt to a pipe, so I think this was just a ploy to get out of boot camp. By evening chow we got word that they weren't buying his bullshit and he is going back to training in a couple of days. What a shit bird.

This Scribe job is really starting to wear on me. In addition to the normal boot camp rigors, it is constantly, "Where you at

Scribe?" "Get my hot trays Scribe." "Hey Scribe where is my Alpha-roster." "Write this down Scribe." "Scribe give Recruit Schmukatelli two hours of Fire Watch." "Where is my laundry chit Scribe."

***

Guys kept falling asleep when the Senior was talking to us tonight. The Senior was pissed that guys were nodding off so he left us alone with Lucifer. Lucifer had us duck walking (walking while in a squatting position) around the squad bay for an hour and doing jumping jacks and squat thrusts along the way. Then he made us put on our Gortex rain coats and pants. PTing with that extra layer made it like 120 degrees in the squad bay. To ensure that nobody passed out, we each downed about four canteens which, I think, are a quart each. First my buddy Stewart puked from the combination of dinner followed by PT and ridiculous amounts of water. As the smell of vomit began to waft through the squad bay it became contagious and another guy puked, then another. To Lucifer it was a game to see how many victims he could claim. Every time another guy would puke, he would howl his evil laugh of satisfaction. The chain reaction of projectile vomit got at least ten guys to puke and in some cases re-puke. Then we did push-ups, the pukers splashing their chests into their own vomit. When we were done more guys went to the bathroom and puked. For the record, I stood my ground and found the whole thing pretty funny until I had to help clean it up.

I think that was Lucifer's way of telling us that Team Week is over and that we are in for a lot more hell before we walk across that parade deck. I think the fact that Guerra gained fifteen pounds during team week and is now eleven pounds overweight also helped precipitate Puke Fest 2000. Depending on how much he puked, Guerra has to lose about eleven pounds in eleven days to make weight. Guerra was one of the repeat pukers during the vomit barrage so maybe Lucifer has a method to his madness.

On the bright side, the puke session got us out of drill, which we already did for about three straight hours this afternoon.

Monday, September 4, 2000

Today sucked. We did six hours of drill. Lunch consisted of three bites of an orange through the peel and ten seconds to eat a sandwich. To make matters worse we got a fourth DI. In the two month since I've been here I have become very skilled at accounting for all three DIs if I had to smack a bug off my arm or wipe sweat from my brow. With a fourth DI in the mix, I have to start over.

The new DI, Drill Instructor Staff Sergeant Helmann is stereotypical DI. If you saw this guy in civvies, 500 miles from the nearest Marine Corps base, you'd know he was a Marine Corps Drill Instructor because his skin is like leather, his jaw is a right angle, he appears as though he gets a fresh regulation haircut three times per day and he is in perfect shape. I'm not sure what to make of him or why he is here or what. My guess is he is a new Drill Instructor learning the ropes.

***

Yesterday was Sunday so there was no mail. I was looking forward to mail all day today but at about 1600 realized that it was Labor Day and we would have to wait yet another day for a piece of mail.

***

I thought A-line was supposed to start this week but I guess not because today was a normal long boring day in the squad bay and on the drill field.

***

We found out today that Imish was finally discharged. I'm not sure if he got an honorable discharge or one of the lesser discharges like a general discharge.

***

We did a three mile PT run today and my time was 20:25 a far cry from the 18:00 I am working toward, but still pretty decent.

***

I don't think I ever mentioned the term BCDs, which stands for birth control devices. BCDs are just really unflattering, thick glasses with a "geek strap" that goes around your head that are issued to guys who during the initial physical the day we arrived on the island, are deemed to have vision problems. The birth control portion of the term derives from the assumption that a recruit wearing these glasses is so hideous that all opportunities to procreate are eliminated. Basically they make the wearer look like a really ugly Clark Kent.

Glasses are also called portholes and the term portholes doubles as the name of any recruit wearing glasses. Before the DIs learned our names, this was a convenient way to distinguish recruits a little. A DI would say something like, "Hey, you, portholes! Go in the big gear locker and get me a mop."

Tuesday, September 5, 2000

Drill Instructor Sergeant Willis told us this morning that he thinks the new DI, Drill Instructor Staff Sergeant Helmann, is a spy trying to determine if Willis is abusing recruits. I can't tell if this is a boot camp head game or if Drill Instructor Sergeant Willis is really serious. I guess he could be a spy. Willis does bend and, at times, break the rules. Willis reminded us that he has been with us from the beginning and asked us who we were loyal to. It's weird because I hate Willis, and he makes our lives a living hell, and made a bunch of us puke last night, but for some strange reason I do feel strongly loyal to him and think he has pushed us all to the limit and made us better Marines.

Later in the day during drill I distinctly noticed that Drill Instructor Staff Sergeant Helmann's makes unusually gentle corrections. Whereas Willis will smack that shit out of your hand if your thumb is not exactly on the seam of your trousers when you come to attention; Helmann softly places your hand where it belongs. It is so gentle that it is almost out of place, like he is going out of his way to show how rough Willis is. I'm trying to think if I've ever heard him curse. I don't think I have. The whole situation reminds me of a cop movie and Helmann is working for Internal Affairs and has infiltrated our precinct.

We had a class on cover and concealment today. Cover is the thing you hide behind to stop rounds from hitting you, like a pile of rocks or sand bags. Concealment is making yourself invisible to the enemy with camouflage and by dulling anything shiny that reflects light. We also had a class about how to get, and keep, your night vision so you can see what the hell you are doing on night operations. After the classes, we had a long day of drill and then we went on a night movement. At 2200 we cammied-up our faces with paint and went "snoop'n and poop'n" through the woods trying to avoid booby traps and trip flares. I stumbled across one of the trip flares and almost crapped my pants. A trip flare is basically a string that if you step on it, it releases a flare into the sky to let the enemy know where you are. I tripped it and for a few seconds I heard a sizzling sound but saw nothing. I thought the flare was going to fly right up my butt, but it didn't. After what seemed like a long time, it flew up in the air and gave away our position. With my nerves already frayed, all the hairs on my neck stood at attention when I heard Willis's creepy voice in my right ear whisper sarcastically, "Good job nasty. You just got us all killed."

After I got everybody killed, we low-crawled through the mud and completed some tactical obstacle courses. The trip flare fiasco notwithstanding, this exactly the kind of stuff I joined the Marine Corps to do.

Wednesday, September 6, 2000

We were very busy today doing a lot of combat-oriented training so the day flew by. We shot from tactical shooting positions rather than the sterile and somewhat unrealistic four positions we used to qualify on the range two weeks ago. We fired from a simulated rooftop, from inside a bunker and in the prone behind a pile of rocks. It was just great. Instead of just shooting at a still target we fired on moving targets and targets that popped up for just a few seconds. The best way to describe A-Line in relation to the rifle range is: The Range is like taking batting practice off of a pitching machine whereas A-line is like batting off of a an actual pitcher. This training was probably the most enjoyable I have had since I've been here. I don't know why other recruits I have spoken to warned that this is one of the hardest weeks.

We got a lot of mail tonight because we had not gotten any in while. I got like ten letters. My buddy Stewart even got a letter from his dad. He had not heard from his old man in three years so you could see the total excitement in Stewart's face.

***

Today is my brother Pat's 33rd birthday. You may recall from an early entry that he was the overzealous Sergeant Slaughter fan who jumped in the ring during Slaughter's 1985 bout with the dreaded Russian Nicolai Volkov.

***

In a few minutes we will head back out to the field for a night fire. I will report on it tomorrow.

Thursday, September 7, 2000

Last night we did a night fire. Basically we did all of the combat firing positions that we practiced during the day, and earlier this week, and applied them at night. Night firing is basically the same as firing during the day except that you use the bigger rear site on the M-16. It was fun because we were firing tracer rounds, which leave an orange-green streak as the rounds fly down range. While I was watching the guys ahead of me shoot, the sky filled with streaking tracers reminded me of a cross between *Star Wars* and CNN's coverage of the Gulf War. It was very exciting and, again, exactly the kind of stuff that made me and thousands of others want to join the Marines.

We packed up all of our gear into seabags except for the stuff we are going to need for Friday and Saturday. It made me nervous to haphazardly stuff my notes for this journal into a seabag and throw it on a truck but it had to be done and if you're reading this you know the journal didn't get lost.

We have been doing a lot of weapons maintenance lately and I have begun to notice myself getting more and more meticulous when it comes to cleaning. I even feel as though I am getting more and more mechanically inclined from assembling and disassembling this rifle over and over.

Other than what I mentioned above, we drilled endlessly, hour after hour all day. It was fucking brutal.

Friday, September 8, 2000 (3 Weeks Until Graduation)

Today kind of sucked because we didn't get any mail and because we drilled for I don't know how long. I am starting to hate the recruits who still have not mastered all of the drill movements. We have drilled probably for a couple hundred hours in the past two and a half months and if you are still making left faces when the command is right face I have to believe it is because of a lack of effort. There are only a handful of these "shit birds" but they are constantly causing us to go the pit. I think we are passed the point where no matter what our efforts won't be good enough. We can do a good job and be spared the pit because I think we have finished the tearing-down phase and are in the building-back-up phase. It is so frustrating because the DIs have ceased being the enemy and the non-hacker recruits are the enemy. Until we get them up to speed we are all going to pay the price.

I am on a strict self-imposed diet until the final weigh-in next week. For lunch I gave away the chips and Oreos that came in my bag nasty and just ate the bologna sandwich and apple. This was not easy to do but was a clear indication that all of the discipline of boot camp is having a positive effect on me. The Senior took us to evening chow and allowed us each to have a small piece of cake, or "pastry" as we say. I am proud to report that I declined.

It is hard to believe that we are going back to our old barracks at First Battalion at the end of the week. When we came out here four weeks ago we were not even half way done. Now we are returning to mainside for the home stretch. Next week is BWT (Basic Warrior Training), then the Crucible, and then transition week. Then it's goodbye Parris Island.

Saturday, September 9, 2000

We had a ten mile hump back to our regular barracks today. A lot of guys hate humps but they don't bother me that much. I just throw my pack on and, when possible, daydream and check out the scenery. Plus I have a policy of forcing myself to realize that anything physical is helping me get into better shape and I should therefore enjoy it.

The Senior Drill Instructor weighed me in right after the hump and, with nothing in my stomach and having sweated out all of my water weight. I weighed in at miniscule 184 pounds. This weight is artificially low and once I put some fluids in my body I'll weigh a few more pounds but I think that today was my final weigh-in so no more worries about weight. Since I got here weighing 230 pounds, I have lost forty-six pounds in sixty-four days. Let's see Doctor Atkins beat that!

I've lost so much weight that when my parents come down for graduation I might have to carry a sign that says "Lalor," like the limo driver's at the airport, so they'll recognize me.

There are a lot of milestone events coming up this week. Wednesday is a big inspection. At some point we have the final drill competition with the other platoons. Thursday is the final PFT. Monday we go for our high and tight haircuts, one of the final overt changes that distinguishes recruit from Marine. For so long these events seemed like they were years away but now here they are just a couple of days away.

I remember when I first got here I was thinking about what it would be like to be three weeks from graduation. It thought it would never come and now it's almost here. I still have to complete the PFT, BWT and the Crucible without getting injured but I have never been injury-prone and, if I did twist an ankle, I would figure out away to slog through everything and ultimately hobble off this island on time.

I'm so sick of this place it is amazing. It's the same thing every day, hurry up and wait, stand-by to stand-by to stand-by. This morning the DIs woke us up fifteen minutes early so we could beat the rush to chow and avoid the lines. Well, of course, every other platoon in First Battalion had the same idea, so we waited for fifteen minutes, standing "A to B." A to B is a colorful Parris Island term to describe standing in line at such close interval that your stomach touches the butt of the guy in front of you. A to B stands for "asshole to bellybutton." At VMI we had an equally colorful term to describe the same cramped formation, "nuts to butts."

Today when everyone else had square away time to prepare their fancy green Service Alpha's (Green dress uniform) for the inspection, I was bogged down doing Scribe stuff. We have to iron everything ourselves and I am the world's worse ironer so having less time than everyone else to prep my uniform is particularly inconvenient. We also have to IP (Irish pennant) the uniform. An Irish pennant is the little wisp of thread that sticks out of a piece of clothing. On planet Earth you barely notice such things. On Parris Island, IP's are a capital offense. That these little nuisances are attributed to my ancestral homeland, the Emerald Isle, is no doubt a result of the fact that much of our naval and maritime parlance comes from the British Royal Navy. Bad enough the Limeys held all of Ireland captive for eight centuries, using the word Irish in a term that means untidy adds insult to injury. Where are the political correctness police when you need them?

Drill Instructor Sergeant Willis was discussing current events today. He incorrectly mentioned that Dick Cheney was presently the Secretary of Defense and would resign if elected Vice President. Feeling my oats a little, but remembering to use the proper recruit-to-DI etiquette, I set him straight. I informed the uncharacteristically calm Willis that Cheney had not been at Defense in nearly eight years. He must have been in a good mood or worried that Helmann is spying on him because instead of dragging me onto the quarterdeck, he simply said quietly, "The Drill Instructor stands corrected." Correcting Willis was just a reflex that has been suppressed for the past two and a half months that reared its head today. It just sort of popped out of my mouth and before I could do anything about it I was just sitting there thinking holy crap what did I just do? Fortunately and surprisingly, it worked out.

Overall, I can't complain. The days have been moving pretty quickly and most of the big worries about whether I'll graduate on time, namely my weight and the rifle range, are behind me. I think the longest, most torturous day will be September 29, Graduation Day. Even though we graduate at 1000 it is going to be tough to see my parent's on Thursday night and eat lunch with them, feel semi-normal, and then have to go back in the barracks and be a recruit again for another sixteen hours. Plus I'll be so excited and filled with three months worth of intense anticipation, I doubt I'll be able to sleep. You can't stop time so, come hell or high water, graduation will come and I'll be getting off this island.

CHAPTER 7: Basic Warrior Training

Sunday, September 10, 2000

I saw a kid in church this morning who was a student in my Social Studies class just three months ago. It was at the very end of Mass and I spotted him a few pews away and I climbed over like ten guys to get to him. He was sitting while everyone was standing and looked pretty sad. His name is Ryan Tate, he was a great kid, respectful and positive, so it was hard to see him slumped down in his pew looking almost beaten. He seemed shocked to see me and I don't think he recognized me at first. He knew I was going to be down here this summer so it was not a total shock. He said in an uncharacteristically timid voice, "Hey, Mr. Lalor, how is it going?" He told me that he was terribly homesick. I told the eighteen-year-old that "I'm an old man" and I get unbearably homesick too and not to dwell on it. Hopefully this helped him out a little. Seeing him helped me because it made feel a little closer to home.

My Scribe job has been running me ragged again and I'm still not ready for inspection. This morning I had to run a bunch of errands for the DIs, plus do all of the accountability for who is going to church and to which church. I had to distribute gear to the guys who are missing it and pass out stencils so that the recruits can stencil their names inside their dress uniforms for the inspection. I'm also preparing all of the paperwork for the laundry for the upcoming week to save time during what I'm sure will be a busy week. As much as it sucks having my free time monopolized by the DIs, it was almost worth it today when Drill Instructor Sergeant Willis, sounding like Mr. T, who he sort of looks like said, "Damn boy, you better than that old Scribe. I'm glad his ass got fired." Positive feedback is so rare that I took that as a high compliment and for a while didn't mind all of the extra work.

Also, the other day I was assigned an A-Scribe to help me out. His name is Chan and he is a seventeen-year-old Asian kid from Manhattan. He is a really good sport and doesn't seem to mind when I pull him from square away time to help me out.

The guys who are "guaranteed PFCs" - which means they came into boot camp as a Private First Class because they had some college or were Eagle Scouts - plus the guys who "pick up" PFC in boot camp because they are good recruits, will graduate with one stripe on each shoulder. The PFC's uniforms are still at the tailor shop getting the stripes sewn on and we won't get them back until tomorrow. So we are going to have to stay up past Taps tomorrow night, fight each other for one of the few irons, and prep our uniforms when we could be sleeping.

Monday, September 11, 2000

We got normal Marine Corps high-and-tight haircuts today as opposed to the standard scalping we have been getting since we got here. I have what doctors call "a little bit of a hair loss problem," so my new hair-do isn't all that high. It's more like a tight and even tighter. Long ago I embraced my ever growing forehead but it was only about two years ago that I realized I was losing hair on top too. I still remember the date. It was Saturday, October 17, 1998. I remember because it was Game 1 of the Yankees versus Padres World Series. Tino and Knoblauch homered and the Yanks scored seven runs in the seventh inning to win 9-6 and I learned I had a big freaking bald spot on the top of my dome at the tender age of twenty-two.

At the time I was working as a bouncer at a bar called McGillicuddy's in New Paltz, New York. Because of my diverse jobs as a teacher and bouncer, I used to say I was shaping young minds by day and cracking skulls by night. I was in the backroom where they keep the booze and where the monitors are for the security cameras. On one of the grainy black-and-white screens I saw a direct, overhead shot of a guy with a round, bald spot right on the top of his head. I thought to myself, "Who is that?" then, for some reason, I reached up to touch my head and the guy on the screen was doing the same thing. It was then and there that I first saw what my friend Glover calls "the Irish Yarmulka." Receding hairline aside, this haircut is a nice milestone to finally have reached. Besides a regulation military haircut is among the best covers for male-pattern baldness.

***

I went to dental again today and they still couldn't get me numb. I was at dental so long that I missed PT, which I don't like to do because I never want to look like a weasel. After dental, we got time to prep our uniforms for the big inspection. We got our blouse with the PFC Chevrons sewn on this morning, which is even more exciting than the haircuts. I think I got every last Irish pennant off of that sucker and now have to iron the hell out of my gabardine trousers until they are absolutely perfect.

A relatively good day was ruined when MP's came and took my buddy Tobego out of the chow line. Apparently he got a "Dear John" letter from his girlfriend a while back and wrote her a nasty reply. The girl told her mother about it and the mother called somebody important and said that Tobego was sending threatening letters. I guess it's true what they say, "Hell hath no fury like a woman scorned." He might be charged with conduct unbecoming a Marine. I think the girl is just immature and knows enough about boot camp to know that she holds all the cards and that one accusatory phone call from her and she can make Tobego's life a living hell. I feel bad that Tobego has to have this on his mind when he should be thinking about getting through the next couple weeks and graduating.

We all marched over to medical this afternoon to get more shots. Being back in that building and seeing the faces of the same medical personnel from two and a half months ago, gave me *de ja vu* of my first day on the island. Today was more laid back only because I am used to getting yelled at and more familiar with the surroundings. Plus, back in early July, there was a tremendous fear of the unknown with regards to whether or not I would be able to handle boot camp. Today there is none of that because I've made it this far and I am confident, come September 29th, I'll be marching across the parade deck, my head held high.

***

Today, back in the real world, it is my little sister Meghan's 21st Birthday.

Tuesday, September 12, 2000

We had a "mote" run today. When I first heard that expression I thought it had something to do with the fact that we were all trapped on an island and the surrounding water was essentially a moat like you would see around a medieval castle. As it turns out, the term "mote" stems from the fact that the Marine Corps moves too fast to include the extra couple of syllables that make up the word "*motivational.*"

This was the last Platoon PT before the final PFT. In fact, since we will be out in the field for much of the next two weeks, this might be the last regular PT of boot camp, other than the Family Day four mile mote run. After PT we spent most of the day prepping for inspections, including a very, very thorough weapons maintenance session.

We finally had the inspection today in our olive-drab Green Service Alpha blouse and green pants, sharply contrasted by bright red chevrons on either shoulder. It is probably Marine Corps heresy to say so, but I think the Alphas are the sharpest looking uniform in the Marine Corps inventory, even better than the legendary Dress Blues.

Standing there in that perfectly pressed uniform I couldn't help but realize how close I was to my lifelong dream of claiming the title of United States Marine. At this point, the uniform is complete except for the black EGAs that normally adorn the lapels. Since we are not yet Marines we do not rate to wear it. We'll get our EGAs at the post-Crucible ceremony, when we officially become Marines.

After so much preparation, the inspection finally came and went and I have to say it was much ado about nothing. Most of the inspection was questions on knowledge and to see if the uniform fit properly. My uniform didn't fit because since the last tailoring in August I lost a lot of weight. They sent me directly from the inspection to the tailor shop. As it turns out, I went from a 44 Regular blouse to a 43 Regular and my waist went from thirty-eight inches to thirty-six. Thank God I don't have to pay for all of this tailoring.

Drill Instructor Staff Sergeant Helmann earned some points with the platoon by telling us that we were not so lacking as a platoon that we needed a fourth Drill Instructor as was believed by some of us. He gave us a pep talk explaining that he had been a San Diego Drill Instructor a few years ago but has since been back in the Fleet and is now learning the ropes to become a Parris Island DI.

If you live west of the Mississippi, you go to boot in San Diego. Recruits east of the Mississippi come here. Overall I think it is the same thing whether you are on the west coast or east but, of course, there are rivalries and the accusation that guys who do their boot in San Diego are less-than-Marines because they are "Hollywood Marines." My view is "boot camp is boot camp." However, my own pet theory is that Parris Island is a little tougher because it is in Beaufort, South Carolina, also known as the middle of nowhere. Since we are in a remote, small town the DIs have nothing to do but think of ways to make our lives miserable. On top of that, they are ornery because they are stuck in a tiny town. Based on nothing but my imagination, I assume San Diego DIs are at the beach and surfing in their free time. Thus, they are, in general, in a much better mood and, in turn, are easier on recruits. I have nothing at all to base this on but it's as good an analysis as any.

On Thursday we go into a real gas chamber with our gas masks on but we have to take them off briefly to learn how to properly don and clear the mask in a contaminated environment. I have heard that this is one of the worse parts of boot camp.

We have been getting bigger portions at chow lately. This sounds good but it really isn't because when you get a lot of chow you realize just how bad it tastes. When you're hungry you'll eat the apple, the core, and all the seeds inside even after you dropped the apple in the sand. When you are pretty content, and past the point of having enough food to survive, only then do you realize that the food is pretty crappy. I guess that is to be expected considering most of the chow preparation is done by recruits doing a one week Team Week tour-of-duty in the chow hall.

We have not gotten mail since Saturday and the next two nights are in the field so I can't expect any mail until Friday the earliest. That sucks.

Wednesday, September 13, 2000

Today we finally had Company Drill, which is the drill competition between the six platoons in our company. I think things went okay. We could have done better but the DIs seem happy, so I'm happy. Afterward, Drill Instructor Sergeant Willis said, "Good job…pieces of shit. You are pieces of shit but you are my pieces of shit." In a highly unusually moment of levity the Senior joked, "That's his way of saying, 'I love you.'"

Ironically, the world famous Marine Corps Silent Drill Team, which is based in Washington DC, was here on Parris Island today. These guys are Marines who drill for a living. I have heard that you have to be at least six foot tall to even be considered for the silent drill team, although I don't know why you would want to be on the Silent Drill Team. I think it's a little weird when guys want to be in the Marine Corps Band. These silent drill guys are even stranger because they are pretty much the same as band members, but they don't have instruments.

After we got packed for BWT, we went and watched the Silent Drill Team. I have to admit that they are pretty impressive because they are so precise and they throw their rifles up in the air and catch them effortlessly. They know exactly what to do and when to do it without any commands. Since there are no verbal commands all you can hear is the snap and pop of the Marines executing the rifle movements and the clap-clap of their shoes hitting the deck. They wear Dress Blues with white trousers, which is unusual but looks very sharp. The Silent Drill Team was accompanied by "The Commandant's Own" drum and bugle corps. I don't know anything about music, and this was the first music I've heard in two and a half months, but I thought they were pretty good.

As I have said before, there are six platoons in my company and four companies in our battalion. This week, my platoon, and the other platoons in our company that we routinely train with and compete against, became the senior recruits in the battalion. Thus, when we go to the chow hall or the parade deck, we see all of the out-of-shape, First Phase recruits with un-bloused boots who can barely drill, and look at them and ask ourselves if we were ever that nasty. I remember first being here and being very impressed by how quick and loud worlds exploded out of the mouths of Third Phase Recruits.

Even the Second Phase Recruits are pretty nasty compared to us salty recruits only a few weeks from claiming the title. At least the Second Phase guys blouse their boots and have a clue how to drill. Some of them are as sharp and crisp as Third Phase Recruits but they still have a lot of weak links. By Third Phase, the non-hackers have either been dropped or learned to hack. Being the saltiest recruits in the battalion is yet another milestone and sign of the times which helps motivate me down the home stretch.

Recruits who are going out to the active-duty Marine Corps and recruits who will go into the Reserves after boot camp and MOS training are treated the same and are for the most part indistinguishable from each other. This is good for training purposes, and for maintaining the reputation and proficiency of the reserves. Where it is not so good is when it comes to buying uniforms. Today I had to plunk down $120 via my smart card (Parris Island debit card) and buy two more sets of cammies for a total of eight. There is no way a reservist training once a month and two weeks during the summer needs to have the same amount of cammies as an active-duty guy. The odds of ever getting activated are slim to none. Besides, the last major activation of Marines was for Operation Desert Storm ten years ago and, in that case, they wore brown desert cammies and not the normal green ones that I just wasted my hard-earned money on. My plan is to avoid wearing these new cammies for the rest of boot camp and SOI and sell them to an Army-Navy store and hopefully get fifty cents on the dollar.

We finally started Basic Warrior Training (BWT) today. We bused out here to "the field" in the early evening, stored our gear, got organized, set up the Fire Watch roster, and then hit the rack. We set up shop in plywood Quonset huts, which are about a quarter of the size of the squad bay and, therefore, extremely cramped. A Quonset hut is somewhere between a tent like you would see on the show M.A.S.H. and a cabin without walls. It has a dirt floor and some limited electricity and is as hot and muggy as hell. We brought our PT gear out with us and will take the PFT out here somewhere tomorrow.

Thursday, September 14, 2000

We took the final PFT this morning. I banged out ten perfect pull ups, which I'm okay with. I had hoped for more, but ten is about what I expected. Things were going alright early on with the crunches and I was confident that I'd do a hundred, as I have been doing for about a month now. However, in the middle of the crunches, the Senior came and over and yelled that I wasn't doing them right because I was lifting my ass of the ground a little to gain momentum. He warned that he might have to deduct points. This made me become overly cautious and I began making sure my entire back hit the ground in between each crunch rather than my shoulder blades quickly touching the deck and then going back, which is both efficient and within the regulations. As a further precaution, I made sure that every inch of my forearms hit my thighs when I came up on each crunch even though you really just need to touch a portion of the forearm. These precautions slowed me down and despite routinely getting a hundred crunches I dropped to eighty-nine.

One of the last things my brother Patrick said to me before I left was, "Get an eighteen minute run time. That's an order!" Whereas I never thought I could get a perfect twenty pull ups, I believed that a perfect eighteen minute run was within my grasp and I was hell bent on doing in. I used everything from my brother's order, to humming to myself the music from the *Rocky* movies, which has always served to motivate me before an important sporting event in my youth. I also used my hatred of this teacher I worked with who used to try to bully me around because he had been at the school for decades.

In PT, and even before boot camp, I was always able to push myself to the brink for the last few hundred yards of a run. But today, I honest-to-God pushed myself the entire time. I used a trick that the Senior taught us whereby you start off at a good pace and pick a person ahead of you that you want to pass. Then run your ass off until you pass that guy. Immediately upon passing the target you pick out another guy to pass and so on. This sounded a little hokey to me at first but I have to say it worked.

I was feeling pretty good about things when my time at the 1.5 mile point was 10:05. I was not quite on pace for eighteen minutes but I was not so far off the pace as to make it impossible and I knew I would be able to summon some adrenaline for one last hard dash to the finish line. With about a half mile remaining I set my sites on the Guide from one of the other platoons in our company who was fifty yards ahead of me when I spotted him. This guy suffers from a common disorder whereby Guides and Squad Leaders think that they are quasi-DIs and begin to talk and act like they are DIs. Anyway, a couple of weeks ago, I was borrowing a mop from this guy's platoon. It is never fun going to another platoon's squad bay because it is like going behind enemy lines. As I walked across the other platoon's quarterdeck I heard what I thought was a DI's voice behind me say "stop nasty." Then he started to quarterdeck me and as I was dropping to do push-ups I saw that it was not a DI but rather this jackass Guide. I got up and told him "fuck off, pal" and we had a shoving match and his DIs came out of the DI hut and quarterdecked the both of us.

When I saw this same guy toward the end of the PFT run I vowed I would absolutely not let him beat me. I came up behind him and he saw it was me and we got into a sprinting match for a good 250 yards and, to my surprise, he began to fall back. Elated, I began to coast a tiny bit.

The course was on a windy, old landing strip that we had never run before and I couldn't see the finish line until there was only about fifty yards left. When I saw the finish line I poured it on and thought my heart was going pop. I beat that jackass Guide but I crossed the finish line with a time of 18:19.

I was happy with my time and shocked that I was able to really push myself the whole time, beat the asshole DI-wannabe and finish in the top twenty out of 250 or so recruits. Despite this, I can't help but think that if I would have known early where the finish line was, I could have broken into my sprint sooner and finished in eighteen minutes. What's done is done and, overall, I'm happy with my PFT performance.

A First Class PFT is 225 or better. I got 89 points for crunches, 50 points for pull ups (5 points each) and 98 points for the run, which is a total of 237. I'm happy but I could be happier.

After the PFT we went back to the Quonset huts and put on our boots and cammies and went over to the dreaded gas chamber. As always, we waited on a long line before we got to enter the chamber. Waiting on line we got see guys on their way out, puking, boogers streaming down their noses and their eyes red and teary. As our turn to enter approached I was filled with dread. When I first entered the chamber, for a few seconds I thought to myself, hey this is isn't so bad. Then my neck, completely exposed to the gas, began to burn a little. Then it burned a lot. Then the top of my head, exposed and a little light in the hair department, began to scorch.

The purpose of the gas chamber is to make sure that you can properly use your gas mask in a chemical environment and to give you confidence that it works. In boot camp it also serves as a test of discipline; a test several in my platoon failed. With the gas mask on and my eyes barely open I couldn't tell who was who but some recruits felt their neck starting to burn and began to panic, requiring a DI to forcefully restrain them and prevent them from running out the door. It is a bad idea to freak out in the chamber because when a recruit does try to bust out, they keep him inside and make him finish up in the chamber with his original group and then they make him come back in with a different group to see if he can do it without panicking.

While inside they made us shake our heads vigorously to ensure that the mask was on properly and that the seal made between the mask and our cheeks doesn't break upon moving. Next we had to break the seal and expose our eyes, mouth and nose to the gas. This was horrible. I squeezed my eyes as tight as I could and tried to hold my breath. The problem was I did exactly what they told us not to do, and instinctively took a big gulp of air before holding my breath. By gulping the air I pulled in a lot of CS gas which of course made me cough and allowed more gas into my mouth, lungs and nose. Finally, we had to take the mask completely off and hold it out in front of us. We were not allowed to put the mask back on until everyone had their mask out in front of them. I was terrified to open my eyes so I didn't but I could hear recruits struggling with the DI and later learned it was – big surprise - Recruit Bishop refusing to take his mask off.

As we stood there, eyes slammed shut and mouth sealed, I couldn't hold it anymore and reluctantly sipped a quick bit of air and burned the hell out of my lungs but managed to keep from having a coughing fit. Donning is simply putting the mask on our heads and faces and clearing is the act of blowing the bad air out of the mask and ensuring that you have a seal and are only drawing clean air. The five minutes or so of coughing and burning inside that gas chamber "seemed to last as long as six weeks on Parris Island," to quote Billy Joel's song, *Goodnight Saigon*. Finally, we were allowed to don and clear our masks. When it was over, we went out into the bright sun, hacked and blew our noses and spit and, in some cases, vomited. Then we had lunch.

Today was our introduction to Meals Ready to Eat or MREs. Maybe I was just really hungry or thankful that my taste buds still worked after the gas chamber, but the MRE was delicious. The food reminded me of what I imagine astronauts eat because it has some weird chemical in it to preserve it. To heat the "main meal" there is this little pouch that has in it what looks like a grey piece of sandpaper. You slide the sealed pouch containing the food into the heating bag and add water. Somehow the water reacts with that sandpaper-looking thing and the water gets hot - extremely hot - and heats the meal. In addition to a "main meal" and a dessert, like pound cake or Skittles, the MRE also comes with salt, pepper, a tiny jar of Tabasco and two pieces of Chicklet gum.

Next we set up tents in neat rows. The tents are extremely old-fashioned and I can't believe that we are using such a primitive system in the 21st Century. Basically, you carry half the tent and your buddy carries the other half. When you need the tent you snap the two shelter halves together and use these two sticks to prop it up. Then you tie the lanyards to the sticks and to spikes in the ground at either end of the tent. And there you have it, a dirt floor tent that is about three feet by five feet of floor space and two and a half feet high at its highest point. Luxurious.

Once the tents were set up, Drill Instructor Staff Sergeant Erickson gave out mail, joked a little, and answered some questions we had about the Marine Corps. Hell, we did everything but roast marshmallows. It was the first time Erickson didn't act like a prick. Finally we did field hygiene which basically consists of brushing your teeth and shaving. To shave you pour water into your steel WWI issue canteen cup to act as the sink normally does. Then you shave as you normally do, dipping the razor into the water to clean it off.

As I hit the rack in my half of the shelter under the stars, I couldn't help but feel like I was right where I wanted to be. In the Marine Corps, in the field, training to defend this great nation.

Friday, September 15, 2000 (2 Weeks Until Graduation)

This morning we were up at 0400 (known colloquially as "zero four") to break down the shelter halves and march off to the rappel tower. Of course we were very early to the tower and ate an MRE breakfast while awaiting the arrival of the instructors. I ate a room-temperature boneless pork chop with buttered noodles, which was not exactly IHOP.

Just the preparation to rappel is stressful because the DIs and the rappelling instructors are yelling at you to hurry up and grab a helmet, grab a rope, get in this line, and get in that line. The "black shirt" instructors at the tower were the biggest jerks I have encountered on Parris Island because they were not nearly as impressive as DIs or even PMIs but they are drunk on their own power over the powerless recruits and are unbearably arrogant. They are also low on my list because they tightened the rappel harness around my legs so tightly that my thighs went numb and my nuts were being crushed to the point where I began to wonder if I would be able to sire an heir.

I had, in my youth, a slight fear of heights. I was never crazy about going over bridges, but it was nothing too severe. Then, when I was thirteen years old, I went to a water park in New Jersey called Action Park with friends from my baseball team. One of the attractions was cliff diving off a man-made cliff into a pool. All of my buddies were doing cannon balls and jack knives off the ten or twelve foot high cliff, but my brain was simply unable to command my foot to take the necessary step forward off of the cliff. I stood up there looking down at the water paralyzed for about a half an hour and finally gave up and walked away with my tail snuggly tucked between my legs. It was the first time in my life I was unable to do something that other kids were doing with ease.

The situation repeated itself the next summer when I was perched up in a tree unable to swing down on the homemade "Tarzan swing" that had been erected by local kids at creek near my home. Same situation, except this time it was just me and one other buddy. After a good forty-five minutes my friend Mike was able to coax me into putting all of the fears and doubts out of my mind and literally take the plunge. It worked and I cleared my mind, grabbed the rope, and swung down into the water. Then I got out of the water toweled off and we left. I had conquered the fear for the moment but I knew in the back of my mind that my fear was not really of heights but rather of free-falling from heights and this fear is still far from vanquished.

I spent the next several years subconsciously avoiding similar confrontations with height and water but then, at VMI, I had to address this problem when we were doing a training exercise whereby we were to jump off of a ledge into a river. On that occasion, I applied the blank-mind, just-do-it approach and stepped off the ledge as soon as I got up to it. Instead of stealthily slicing through the air and smoothly into the water, my arms and legs flailed about and I hit the water not like a scalpel, as was the task but like a large, jagged boulder. We also rappelled once at VMI but the cliff was much smaller and therefore less daunting. Still I didn't do well. Instead of gracefully sliding down with a series of backwards leaps like we were supposed to, I sort of hobbled down with tiny jumps, hard landings, and a lot of derision from the instructors.

As I climbed the stairs to the top of the Parris Island rappel tower I could not help but worry about two things. Number one, would I become paralyzed at the top of the tower, my brain unable to make my legs move. And number two, assuming I did get out onto the rappel wall, would I screw it up and plunge down unto the ground, which obviously was far less forgiving than the water I had feared in my youth.

The rappel tower is 47 ½ feet tall which does not seem like that high until you walk up the stairs and realize that you are well above most of the trees. The instructors want to get all of the guys who are afraid of heights and think they are going to have trouble rappelling to the front of the line. Under normal circumstances I would never voluntarily join such a dubious group but my harness was tied so unbelievably tight and I was in such discomfort that I fibbed and claimed that I was worried about rappelling just so I could go to the head of the line, rappel and get this goddamn harness off sooner.

The guys who were really scared and who froze at the top of the wall eventually get a not-so-gentle nudge from the instructor. It sounds dangerous but it's not really because the rappeler is tied-in with his harness and, although the rappeler controls his own stopping and going with the rope behind his back, there is an instructor on the deck who controls the break by taking a few steps backwards while pulling on the rope. By simply taking a step back and pulling on the rope, the instructor on the deck can bring the rappeler to a complete stop. Even with this seemingly fool-proof safety precaution, I was still shitting bricks.

When, finally, it was my turn, I wasted no time to stave off the much-feared height paralysis. I nervously followed the instructor's commands. I had my butt hanging over the wall, my toes on the ledge, and my heels dangling off the wall as my black leather-gloved right hand tightly gripped the rope behind my back which would serve as my break. I released the break, took a step down with my left foot and immediately splatted my face and chest against the top of the wall. Now, pinned to the wall by a combination of the ropes and fear, I had to, as the instructors bitched at me, slowly walk my feet up the wall until the point where I was perpendicular to it. Cautiously but with a blank mind, I took the steps necessary to right the ship. After the sheer fright of that first tumble that landed me smack against the wall, I was relatively calm and completed the necessary jumps to rappel the rest of the wall without incident.

Nothing ever goes smoothly.

After rappelling we did fast roping which is basically the same idea as sliding down a fire pole. It simulates sliding down a rope out of an in-flight helicopter, or "helo" as we say. We started from a height of about thirty-five feet and, after rappelling, I was not nervous and felt more confident in my ability to accomplish this task. I slid down relatively slowly and in control, reached the bottom, and, like one of those fifty-pound Mary Lou Retton gymnasts, I stuck the landing.

All in all, rappelling was a positive event because it was a confidence booster. After rappelling we took a bus back to the rear and to the familiar First Battalion barracks.

***

Drill Instructor Helmann is becoming an impediment to our quality-of-life because his perspective is different from the other DIs. The three original DIs saw us when we were fat, couldn't march, didn't sound off, and couldn't PT well. Because the original three DIs see the marked improvement from then until now, we look pretty good. Drill Instructor Staff Sergeant Helmann first saw us when we were two-thirds of the way toward becoming Marines and after most of the overt improvements had been made. Thus, to him we have not improved much since we began and we are decidedly unimpressive. The platoon should be past the point where the DIs divide us and make us turn on one another but because Drill Instructor Staff Sergeant Helmann treats us like First Phase recruits we're going through that whole process again.

All that said, Hellman did have a bright moment this evening. Back at the chow hall a recruit from another platoon started choking so badly that Drill Instructor Staff Sergeant Helmann had to give him the Heimlich maneuver. Drill Instructor Staff Sergeant Helmann and eventually some EMTs were working on the guy for at least five minutes before they dislodged whatever was stuck in his throat. Despite all of the chaos of the choking, the Heimlich, the EMT's coming in, everything went on as normal. Guys ushered through the chow line, kept eating, kept emptying trays, kept exiting the chow hall. The well-oiled machine just kept chugging along. I took this as a positive development for all of us because it means that despite some unusual circumstances and chaos we were able to carry out our normal operations. In this case, it was just following through on our chow hall ritual but boot camp is preparation for combat so the fact that we were able to focus on the mission, albeit the relatively simple completion of evening chow, means that we have to some degree been prepared for what the DIs call the "fog of war."

***

It is 2130. Lights are out. Chan and I just finished the Fire Watch roster. I'm beat.

CHAPTER 8: The Crucible

Saturday, September 16, 2000

There was not much on the training schedule today, which is never good. As my mother says, "idle hands are the devil's workshop." When the schedule is light that devil's workshop phenomenon works in both directions. The recruits have time to mess around and as a result get in trouble. The DIs are without a specific training objective and, naturally, turn toward physical fitness achieved through "Incentive Training." The result is recruits face down in pit or doing mountain climbers on the quarterdeck.

I heard a rumor today that a hurricane might hit Parris Island. Last year Parris Island got evacuated because of a hurricane but I'm not sure where they went. Some guys think it would be good to get evacuated because we would get off the island. But my thought it is it would be an indefinite period of no training leaving the DIs all the time in the world to make our lives miserable.

The Senior took us to what he said was our last pit call during which he ordered us to hold sand in our hands and said, "This is where your discipline began." Right after the pit we went to the phones. Everyone is getting a quick call home to help their parents finalize plans for Family Day and Graduation. It pisses me off a little that everyone gets to call because those of us who got double 100's on the First Phase test were supposed to get a phone call home. Well we are getting that phone call today with everybody else so we would have gotten the call even without the perfect test scores.

As it turns out I couldn't get through to anyone, so the whole phone call turned out to be a big disappointment. It's probably for the best because most of the guys say since calling home they are more homesick than ever.

For the Crucible, the platoon will be divided into five teams of fifteen recruits and one DI. Recruits will either be with one of our four DIs or a DI from a different platoon. So long as I am with one of the original three DIs, I would be happy. I just don't want to climb the last hill of boot camp with Drill Instructor Staff Sergeant Helmann who doesn't respect us because he hasn't witnessed our transformation from the beginning. And I certainly didn't want to be with some DI I have never met. In a perfect world I would be with Drill Instructor Sergeant Willis because even though he is a mean SOB he has had the most positive effect on me and is my favorite DI.

As it turns out I am in a team with Drill Instructor Staff Sergeant Erickson, so I could have done better and gotten the Senior or Drill Instructor Sergeant Willis, but I could have done worse and gotten Helmann or a Drill Instructor to be named later. Stewart and Ryan are in my team, so I'll have some of my good buddies with me on the Crucible, which is great. Stewart will be fun to have around and Ryan is very bright and will be a big help with some of the obstacles, which from what I heard are both physically and mentally challenging.

Rumors spread late this afternoon that we were going to get to watch a movie in the squad bay tonight. I guess they want to motivate us for the Crucible. I have learned to always be cautiously optimistic to avoid disappointment so my optimism about watching a movie was guarded. As it turned out we did watch the movie, *Any Given Sunday,* which despite being about NFL football is a pretty crappy flick. Save for a cameo appearance by LT (Lawrence Taylor), one of my all time favorites, the movie stunk and I mostly wrote letters while only half paying attention to the film's weak plot.

Sunday, September 17, 2000

Remember that guy Kaye in our platoon who got dropped because he couldn't pass the mock-PFT? We saw him working in the chow hall today. He finally passed the PFT, got picked up by another platoon, and now is on Team Week. He was in good spirits and while he was washing dishes in the "pot shack" he wished us all good luck on the Crucible as we turned in our trays and dinnerware after morning chow.

After Mass we got the Crucible blessing from the chaplain who will be accompanying us as we attempt to achieve the last objective before graduation. The blessing at first seemed comforting but then I began to wonder how tough is this thing going to be that they hold us after Mass just to bless us? The chaplain is a good source of information because he goes on the Crucible every three weeks. One thing that only the chaplain would admit and which made me a little nervous was that the DIs struggle to finish the Crucible. He said they always finish because they have to maintain their reputation among the recruits and their fellow DIs but on the final hump back from the field to the EGA ceremony, the DIs are limping on blistered feet with red eyes and growling bellies just like the Recruits. The Chaplain said the Crucible is difficult

because of the blisters on your feet and sleep deprivation and all
the rest but that the overwhelming majority of those recruits who
start it finish it even if only on pure adrenaline and motivation.

***

I have to hand it to the DIs for always thinking ahead. Today
they had us iron and starch a pair of cammies for when we return
from the Crucible. As Drill Instructor Sergeant Willis put it we
"don't want to look like a bag of ass" on our first day as Marines.

***

Ever since I got off diet tray and got below my weight limit
Willis began to call me "Fat Bastard." Every five minutes it's
"Where you at fat bastard?" Obviously I am puzzled why he
waited for me to lose all of that weight to give me this moniker.
My guess is that constantly calling me "Fat Bastard" is his way
of reminding me that I used to be a fat bastard and he hasn't
forgotten it. Or maybe he is trying to tell me that I have to stay
fit, lest I become a fat bastard again. Who knows? Lucifer works
in mysterious ways.

***

Because I am now so adept at taking my notes for this journal,
I recently began keeping them in a spiral notebook with my notes
from the classes we take rather than on scraps of paper as I did
for the first two plus months. However, I won't be able to tote
the notebook on the Crucible so I bought two tiny camouflaged
covered notebooks during our last PX call; one for any notes I

may need to take as part of the Crucible and one for this journal. Hopefully I'll have a little down time each day to record what happens. Barring that, I'll work hard to remember everything the way I did for the first week of boot camp before we were issued pens and paper.

Monday, September 18, 2000

We got up this morning and had a very challenging but motivational indoor PT circuit course of push-ups, up-downs, side-straddle-hops, and mountain climbers. Then we were issued our two and a half MREs to be rationed-out over the fifty-six hours of the Crucible. Given my limited food supply, my goal is to hold off on eating anything until evening chow of the first day.

Because I am the Scribe, I have access to the DIs' records and I happened across the composite picture of our platoon. The composite picture is all of the individual head shots of Marines on one big page. That picture was taken a while ago so in it I am not nearly as in shape as I am now but still much slimmer than when I got here. I'm not thrilled with the picture but what am I going to do?

After noon chow we got our travel brief to finalize our transportation home after boot camp and, more importantly, to get us to SOI on time when our ten day leave is over. I helped Stewart with his travel plans and arranged for the two of us to be on the same flight from Newark Airport back down to SOI. This way, whoever drives me to the airport can drive him because he only lives thirty minutes from me.

The weather is stormy, which could make for a memorable but hellish Crucible. I don't care either way because in sixty plus hours I'll be a Marine. The Company First Sergeant, who is like the DI's DI, said that recruits have actually died on the Crucible. I'm not sure if this is an exaggeration or hype. Either way, I am more concerned about breaking my leg than I am dying.

One thing that is making me nervous is a story I heard from a guy in my platoon who went to sick call a while back and said there was a guy who broke his ankle on the Crucible's night hump and was put on medical hold and did not graduate on time. In my mind, I was already finished with boot camp, so this story brought me back to reality. As the DIs say when we start to get too big for our britches, "You ain't on the bus yet!" Staying safe on the Crucible is a delicate balance though because I know from playing and coaching football that being overly cautious in an effort not to get hurt often causes injury.

Of course there is also the infamous Ribbon Creek incident from the fifties where a Parris Island DI took a platoon of recruits out on a night movement through a swamp and six recruits drowned. The DI was court-martialed on manslaughter charges and the case became a battle over whether Marine Corps training was too brutal. Chesty Puller, the most decorated Marine in history, came and gave dramatic testimony on behalf of the DI and realistic training. The DI was acquitted of manslaughter but found guilty of the lesser offense of negligent homicide, and drinking on-duty, and busted down to private.

That I'm much more concerned about breaking an ankle and being on Parris Island any longer than I am about dying on the night hump kind of puts the boot camp experience in perspective.

I was hoping for some pre-Crucible mail tonight to keep me motivated but it didn't happen. This evening I ate my last chow hall meal as a recruit and every meal (other than my two and a half MREs) for the rest of my life will be as a United States Marine. We are hitting the rack at 2000 tonight and at 0200 tomorrow we'll get up and let the games begin. I'm trying hard not to get too excited because I don't want to be unable to sleep during our last real night of sleeping. I'd be lying if I said I wasn't really fired up about our final test, The Crucible. From what I have been told The Crucible is fifty-six hours with little sleep and less food. You complete a series of obstacles and, all told, we will hump more than fifty miles. When we arrive back on Thursday morning we will be handed an Eagle Globe and Anchor and finally claim the title of United States Marine. I absolutely cannot wait to be a Marine. Undoubtedly, becoming a United States Marine is the longest running goal of my life and I have taken an unusual, and long, route to achieve it but now I am only three grueling days away.

Tuesday, September 19, 2000

The six mile hump that launched the Crucible was not bad at all, likely because my veins were coursing with adrenaline brought on by the fact that soon I would be a Marine. The hitch of the morning was Stewart, who forgot the magazines for his M-16 and his chow. Some things never change. After some yelling and screaming by the DIs, we got Stewart everything he needed and we were off. In general, the DIs are noticeably more positive and supportive than usual, which I'm sure is the plan. I am certain that they will bust Stewart's chops for this but nothing like they would have done a few weeks ago for what is a pretty major infraction. They still scream and yell and mock guys a little but it is much less sinister than it was before the Crucible. I'm curious how we will be treated after we become Marines on Thursday.

A lot of guys ate some of their limited chow supply this morning but I'm sticking to my plan of not eating anything until tonight. When we get a second to eat and guys are grabbing a piece of pound cake or crackers out of their MRE I usually take the opportunity to add brief entries into this journal. It's a good system because it gives me something to do other than stare at guys who are stuffing their faces and helps ensure that I won't waste my food with boredom eating.

After the hump out to the field we were tasked with five or six Leadership Reaction Obstacles. The obstacles usually involve getting the entire team of recruits over a wall or across a body of water using ropes and the buddy system. So far the obstacles are not that physically demanding but I think ultimately the climbing will take its toll on us. At around 1000 we humped three miles to a firing range for a live-fire, combat-simulation exercise. I was a little hungry and sleepy when the hump started but I caught my second wind mid-way to the range. I was extremely worried about blisters on my feet because of all of the horror stories I have heard about the Crucible eating up guys' feet. In the back of my mind I can hear Lieutenant Dan Taylor from *Forrest Gump* telling Forrest and Bubba to take care of their feet. I have always had hard, calloused feet and never had the kind of blister problems guys used to get every summer when high school football started with double sessions. I wasn't going to take any chances though, so I put moleskin on all of the parts of my foot that had any redness or had ever gotten sore. So far, so good, and my feet feel fine while several other recruits are limping a little and have already sought minor treatment from the corpsman.

The unknown distance firing range was a lot of fun. It felt like being in a war movie. We were all hunkered down in the "tree line" (woods) and one of the instructors unleashed some kind of grenade that created a wall of green smoke. Using the smoke as our cover we ran about a hundred yards until we got to a bunker. From the bunker window we fired ten shots. Then we ran through the woods and into a simulated ambush where three of us, including me, became simulated casualties. The uninjured had to perform "buddy aid" and transport us to safety. I got dragged 500 yards by two guys pulling on my H-harness (also known as war gear, deuce gear or 782 gear) which is basically a vest that holds our magazine pouches and canteens. They were pulling me from the straps on my shoulders so my butt was dragging along the ground the whole way causing dirt and rocks and twigs to end up in my crack, a rather miserable occurrence considering I was not going to see a shower for another forty-eight hours.

This event was a lot of fun but it reminded me of my trip to Disneyland (or Disney World, whichever one is in California) in 1989 when the lines were so long that I only got to go on four rides the whole day. Today was hours of humping, and more hours of waiting, for a quick ten minutes of adrenaline pumping war games.

After the shooting, we humped another three miles and set up the hooches (tents) and then ate, or in my case wrote. I was tempted to eat all morning and afternoon but I stood my ground except for the two pieces of Chicklet gum I ate out of my MRE.

After setting up the hooches, we marched over to what is called the Belleau Wood Day Movement Course named for the WWI battle of Belleau Wood, France where the Germans gave the Marine Corps the nickname Teufelhunden, which loosely translates to Devil Dogs. The Marine Corps' performance in that battle really established the modern Corps as one the elite fighting forces in the world. See that, even though I was writing this journal I still paid attention to all of those classes.

I am a Fire Team Leader so I am responsible for three other recruits. The day movement course starts on a simulated helo (helicopter, sometimes referred to as a bird) to simulate landing in a hot LZ (landing zone). We got out of the helo and ran to the beginning of the course and laid in the prone behind a bunch of rocks for maximum cover and concealment. Our mission was to move tactically over, under and through hundreds of yards of obstacles carrying our weapons, gear, and ammo cans filled with concrete.

When I wanted to move my guys, I screamed as loud as I could to be heard over the simulated machine gun fire, "PREPARE TO RUSH!" This preparatory command puts the guys on notice that they are about to get up and move up. Then I'd give the command of execution, "RUSH!"

We were taught in A-Line to use a pretty goofy but effective technique to ensure that we don't run for too long because doing so dramatically increases the chance the enemy will be able to sight in on you and kill you. The technique simply requires the recruit to say to himself as he is running, "I'm up, they see me, I'm down." Once you get to "I'm down" you better by headed for some piece of "micro-terrain" to hide behind for cover and concealment or else the odds are pretty good that you are going to be shot. This is a good technique because diving into the mud sucks so there is a temptation to run in long bursts but doing so would be deadly in a combat situation.

The course involved a lot of bayoneting dummies, low-crawling under barbed wire, climbing over walls, fire team rushes like I described, and dragging members of the team who the course instructors determined to be casualties. My team slogged through the mud and through the obstacles but got sent back a few times because guys were running and not employing a proper "I'm up, they see me, I'm down." We were probably going at it non-stop and full speed for a good hour and half before we finally got to the end of the approximately half-mile course. Because of the crawling, and running, and diving, and mud, and carrying the ammo cans, and other recruits, this was the ass-kicker of ass-kickers and afterwards I was exhausted and wondered how I was going to summon the energy to make it to Thursday.

After the day movement course, we did a couple of Leadership reaction events which, compared to humping and low-crawling, are becoming a relaxing treat. I must have gotten my third wind at some point without noticing it because I got a compliment by one of the black shirt instructors who said, "Ooh-Rah Motivator!" when I finished the course still chugging along at a pretty good speed. Ironically, this was the same instructor I encountered last week at the rappel tower who tied my harness so tight he crushed my balls and imperiled my chance of procreating.

Most everything on the Crucible is named for some person or event in Marine Corps history. One of the first Leadership reaction obstacles we undertook was Cukela's Wall. From what I have learned, Cukela was a WWI Marine who earned the Medal of Honor for singled-handedly bayoneting a couple Germans, capturing a few more, blowing up others with their own grenades, and taking two of their machine guns. Not a bad day at the office.

Another event, Basilone's Challenge, is named for WWII Marine John Basilone whom General Douglas MacArthur called "a one-man army" and who is the only man in the history of the United States awarded the Medal of Honor, the Navy Cross, and the Purple Heart. He fought in the Philippines, Guadalcanal and eventually gave his life on Iwo Jima.

As a student of history and a lapsed Social Studies teacher, I love that the Marine Corps constantly incorporates its glorious past into the training of Marines in the present. It makes you say to yourself, "I'm going to wear the same uniform as this guy, I

better get my shit together and live up to the giants of the past."
Although obviously not a perfect parallel, it reminds me of how
the New York Yankees keep the past alive with Monument Park,
old-timers day, retiring numbers, and events to honor individual
Yankee greats of the past.

At around 2030 we formed up to begin the night hump. The
DIs have been really concerned about guys getting separated from
the platoon and getting lost in the dark woods. They have also
told us of recruits who fell and were subsequently trampled by the
column of recruits that followed causing injuries serious enough
that they couldn't graduate. With all of this swirling around in my
mind, I was concerned because I have been known to be a little on
the clumsy side. When I was twelve and worked for that former-
Marine landscaper, he used to jokingly call me "grace" because I
was such a klutz and constantly tripped over rakes and hoses and
just about anything a kid can tangle his feet around. It would be
unbearable to come this far only to literally trip and fall so close to
the end and prolong my stay on this God-awful, shitty island.

I didn't eat all day and it really wasn't a problem. Unlike in the
civilian world, or even back in the rear, on the Crucible there are
few reminders of food to make you hungry. In the civilian world
there are advertisements everywhere. The mere site of McDonalds'
golden arches sticking out above the trees on a highway makes my
mouth water for a Big Mac. In the rear, the smell from the chow
hall can make your stomach growl. It is not that the chow hall
food is so good, but the fact that there is only one place where all
your meals are consumed for months makes that smell a powerful
hunger trigger. Out here when guys eat all you smell is the nasty
MRE chemicals, so my fast has been surprisingly easy.

At around 2100, I decided not to eat anything for the rest of
the day because it would be great to wake up tomorrow morning

with a full complement of two and a half MREs. My thinking is, I'd rather suck it up now at the beginning of the Crucible than suffer at the end when I'm already run down. Some guys have already finished all of their chow for the rest of the Crucible. For them I have no sympathy. If they didn't learn anything about discipline in the past ten weeks maybe two days without food will teach them. If a guy lost his chow or somebody swiped his MRE I would give him a little of my chow but if they were just undisciplined idiots who couldn't control themselves, I'm not helping out.

It's about 2130 and it's off to the night hump on which I will report tomorrow.

Wednesday, September 20, 2000

Last night's hump was a combination of the *Blair Witch Project* and the Disneyland ride Space Mountain. We moved so fast and it was so dark I had to hold on to the pack strap of the guy in front of me. At a couple stages we held hands with the guy in front of and behind us to avoid getting separated or falling. I'm not sure if it was the darkness, fatigue, paranoia about getting injured, or a combination of all three, but my mind and eyes were playing tricks on me throughout the movement. It would appear as though we were about to go up a hill but then we'd actually be going down. This kind of thing happened to me dozens of times. I was stumbling over rocks and stumps sure that I was going to fall down, get trampled, and not graduate. I couldn't tell you if it lasted an hour or ten hours because there was no time to think about it. On more than one occasion I thought we were coming upon lights which I was certain meant the end of the hump but each time it turned out to be trick of the brain. Two guys near me fell and it sounded like DIs quickly scooped them up and put them back into the formation but I'm really not sure what happened to the guys who went down.

After I don't know how long, we finished the night hump and I was unscathed. Sometime after midnight or so we got back to the hooches, had a little mandatory hygiene time to shave and brush teeth and then settle in. Despite finishing in one piece, I have to say that the night hump was the absolute worse part of boot camp because of the way the paranoia over getting injured combined with the fatigue to make me crazy. I'm pretty sure that there weren't any serious injuries from my platoon because I haven't heard anything and I don't notice anyone missing.

Drill Instructor Staff Sergeant Erickson stepped on our hooch about fifteen minutes after we got into it so we had to get out and fix it. He pretended like it was an accident but I think he was just being his prick self and messing with us. Still, I got a solid three hours of rack time. Although a couple of times during the night, I was besieged by those horrible dehydration cramps which seize up your hamstrings. What a painful and helpless experience it is when your hammy tightens like an overstretched rubber band that is about to snap. I'll have to remember to drink a bunch of water before I hit the rack tonight. As always some poor bastards had their precious little bit of sleep interrupted by a Fire Watch shift, which were mercifully reduced from an hour down to fifteen minutes. I was lucky and didn't have to stand watch but I will likely pay the price and stand watch tonight when I am even more exhausted.

As the sun came up this morning, I ate a little bit of my MRE cheese and crackers, a main meal and two Fig Newtons. I checked on my feet and realized that despite all of the humping my feet felt fine and I was ready to take on day two of the Crucible. I was tired and despite eating, felt weak but still I was confident that my second wind would kick in when it was needed as it did several times yesterday.

This morning we did a bunch of those Leadership reaction courses with some pugil sticks mixed in. I'm proud to say I pummeled my first pugil sticks opponent with two knockdowns in thirty seconds. When we did pugil sticks during First Phase I was thirty pounds heavier and had to fight all of the big boys. Now I'm a buck ninety but stronger and quicker fighting other guys under two hundred pounds and I'm cleaning up.

At around 1000 this morning it hit me that in less than twenty-four hours I would realize a dream twenty-four years in the making. This revelation and my pugil stick victories gave me the burst of motivation I needed to get through the day. It was also during the late morning that I ate a little more chow. Once you eat a little chow it is hard to stop, which is how guys ate all of their chow on day one. I managed to limit myself to a snack because I heard a rumor that during today's hump we would get an apple.

At noon we had a half-mile rescue run race. Basically there are four-man teams and you have to carry one of the guys from start to finish. We only came in third because we wasted a lot of time making things more complicated than necessary. My brother Pat saw a documentary on the Crucible and I remembered him saying in a recent letter that using your belts was the key to one of the difficult events on the Crucible. Unfortunately, I couldn't remember which event and I was trying to use the belts for every event. Anyway, trying to use my belt slowed us down and we didn't do so well.

Unlike most of boot camp, where everything is done as a platoon, out here you really only see the guys in your fifteen man team during the day. When you live and train with guys all day, every day for nearly three months, it is strange not to have them all around for the grand finale. On the bright side, there are jugs of cold Gatorade stationed throughout the training area to replenish our electrolytes.

After the race, we were attempting to navigate the Marine Obstacle Course when the announcement came that there was lightening within five miles of Parris Island. Because of the lightening we had to sit for more than an hour under a Thunder Dome waiting out the storm. This sucked because it made me sleepy and despite the fact that we were mere hours from claiming the title, we were still being told to sit "right-hand-right-knee-left-hand-left-knee-backs-straight-eyes-front-aye-aye-sir."

It was under the Thunder Dome that I noticed that almost half the guys were out of food and I realized just how brilliant it was to stave off eating for the first twenty-four hours of the Crucible. I still have two main meals, pound cake and apple sauce warming up in the bullpen. One guy offered to give me $100 for a 3.8 ounce ham slice. Of course we have no money on us but he was promising to give it to me when we got Libo (liberty) on Sunday and had access to ATMs. I refused, in part because I had no pity on him for being so undisciplined, and also because I knew that he would be unlikely to pay the $100 debt for a piece of petrified ham three days after he had digested it.

By 1400 the lightening threat was gone and we were training, even though it was pouring out. As they say, "If it ain't raining, we ain't trainng" which doesn't make any sense but it is a nice rhyme. As the rain collected on the top of my camouflage cover, all I could think about was how miserable it was going to be sleeping in the mud in a sopping wet shelter half with a soaked poncho liner.

After the rain delay, we conducted the Inchon Individual Movement Course named for the daring amphibious landing of Marines at Inchon, Korea in 1950. The individual movement course was your standard Crucible fare. A lot of climbing, carrying heavy stuff over walls and through concrete tubes similar to what we did as Fire Teams yesterday, only harder because we would get fifty yards toward the objective and a DI or an instructor would send us back to the beginning. It started to make everyone turn on each other because we were expecting this to be an individual effort event but we were being punished for the weak links, which I have to admit does makes sense militarily. We made it through, although it took a lot out of us. By 1600 I had very little left in my tank.

After a quick break for evening chow we finished up a few more of the Leadership reaction events. The last event before we hit the rack is the night infiltration course which is basically the same sort of obstacles we did today, but in the dark. The scuttlebutt is that this is the hardest event of the Crucible. I learned in my time aboard Parris Island that nothing is ever as good or as bad as everyone says it is going to be so I had a wait-and-see attitude toward the event.

As it turned out the night movement was a pretty miserable affair. It was all flesh-tearing, low-crawling on knees and elbows and my recently rediscovered hip bones that were raw from the previous two days. But we were so close to the end that it really didn't bother me that much. After the night movement, we humped back to the hooches and packed for tomorrow. I drew a Fire Watch shift, but as almost everything the last few days, it really doesn't bother me because this is the last night of my life I'll go to bed as a non-Marine.

Thursday, September 21, 2000

It was a nasty, rainy night but the shelter half did the job and we are still pretty dry when we awoke this morning. Reveille was at 0430 but we didn't step off on the hump for a while after that, I think because there was lightning. For some reason, the DIs were more ornery and impatient than ever. I was however, relatively calm as we waited to start the final hump to the Eagle Glove and Anchor ceremony where finally I would become a Marine.

This morning, for the first time, we donned our "name tape cammies" which are the camouflage utilities that have our last names stitched above the right breast pocket and "U.S. Marines" stitched above the other pocket. The name tape cammies are symbolic because this is a regulation Marine Uniform and not the blank recruit uniform that we have been wearing all along.

Because of the lightning, the hump back was reduced from nine miles to six. At the three mile mark we got a break and were given a banana and Gatorade. The second half of the hump flew by because we were all so motivated and we were singing ditties the whole way. For the last 500 yards we could see the bronze Iwo Jima Memorial shooting up from its granite base with a glorious American flag unfurled above the immortal scene. We marched straight for that statue to claim the title United States Marines.

When finally we arrived at the memorial, all six platoons formed up around it and the Chaplain gave a prayer. Then the Company First Sergeant spoke to us about how the Iwo Jima flag raisers immortalized in that beautiful statue exemplified the Marine Corps' Core Values of Honor, Courage, and Commitment. He challenged us to live up to their legacy. Then over loud speakers Lee Greenwood's "Proud to be an American" began to play as the DIs came around and handed each Marine a black Eagle Globe and Anchor which symbolizes that we have grown from recruit to Marine. I was handed my EGA by Drill Instructor Staff Sergeant Helmann, which was less than ideal, but I was not going to let it ruin the moment.

For a lot of reasons the ceremony is highly emotional. First of all, you are physically exhausted, which tends to make people emotional. Plus, we each just achieved a goal we have been working day and night toward for nearly three months. Then, there is a strong sense of patriotism because of the music and the memorial. The result: as the DIs hand out the EGAs a lot of newly minted Marines have tears in their eyes. Not to sound like a hard-ass, but I wasn't one of them.

Once all of the EGAs were handed out, the six platoons that comprise our Company sang the Marine Corps hymn. Never has that song meant more to me than this morning with the Iwo Jima memorial smiling down on us and my life's longest running ambition finally realized.

Next the First Sergeant called us all to attention and commanded the Senior Drill Instructors of each of the platoons to "Take charge of your Marines and feed them a Warrior's Breakfast." This was the first time we were referred to as Marines. The Warrior's Breakfast consists of just about everything you could ever want; steak, eggs, bagels, ice cream, sausage, biscuits and gravy. It was like Denny's with a buffet table. As it turns out Krispy Kreme donuts were conspicuous by their absence, but how can I complain?

We sat with our teams from the Crucible, Drill Instructor included. It was very strange breaking bread with the guys who made our lives miserable for so long. Drill Instructor Staff Sergeant Erickson was magnanimous and even admitted that our team had a doubly hard time on the day infiltration course yesterday because he told the instructors to smoke us. Despite hearing that, Erickson was cool to us at breakfast and there was too much happiness and satisfaction in the air to hold grudges.

I guess the Senior figured out that I am interested in politics and he brought me over to debate a Senior Drill Instructor from another platoon. We lightly covered the presidential race and

Hillary Clinton's run for Senate in New York because Senior Drill Instructor Staff Sergeant Velázquez was from the Empire State also. I let him know I thought Hillary was a no good carpet-bagger and that we didn't need her or her draft-dodging husband in our home state. He agreed.

Despite being Marines we still stand at attention when we talk to a DI and we still refer to them as "Sir" even though all DIs are enlisted men and after boot camp, enlisted men are never referred to as Sir.

One of the things we will do this week is try to learn how to speak normally again. We no longer use the awkward preface "this recruit" that we long ago perfected. If we need to refer to ourselves we simply say "I" like normal people. Old habits die hard though and many of us say "This Marine requests permission" which is unnecessary and sounds pretty stupid.

Remember the guy Kaye who got dropped from our platoon? He was still working in the chow hall with his new platoon. I felt bad for him. We were celebrating becoming Marines and eating a feast and this poor guy who was with us for the first two months of it all was washing our dishes. Even Drill Instructor Sergeant Willis, as heartless a guy as ever there was, encouraged us to go give Kaye our support, which many of us did as we exited the chow hall and past the pot shack where Kaye was toiling.

After chow we were all expecting a few hours of bed rest to sleep off the huge breakfast and catch up on the sleep we missed during the Crucible. Unfortunately, Drill Instructor Staff Sergeant Helmann was the only DI left in the squad bay with us. We showered and had a hygiene inspection by Helmann and a corpsman to make sure no one had any nasty rashes or blisters. After the inspection Hellmann shocked the hell out of us by treating us like Forming recruits and not the Marines that we were. He made us tear the bedding off the racks and then make it up and tear it apart again. We were exhausted and in disbelief because we thought this kind of thing was behind us. We were Marines now. What was this guy trying to pull? We shouldn't be treated like this. Our real DIs were treating us like the Marines that we are but this DI-come-lately was treating us as if we just got off the bus. Frankly, I'd rather go to the pit or the quarterdeck and get smoked than make the racks over and over. At least the pit and quarterdeck gives you some PT and keeps you in shape.

After about an hour of these games, half delirious and completely exhausted we hit the rack except for the poor bastard who had to stand Fire Watch. I slept like I had been awake for ten years straight and enjoyed what was undoubtedly the best rack time I ever had. At about 1530 we awoke, put on the name tape cammies we pressed before the Crucible and went to evening chow. Afterward we were given our Core Value cards which are red plastic and the size of a credit card with the Core Values printed on them. The purpose of the card is to keep it in your wallet, whether on duty or off, as a reminder that we are charged with living up to the Core Values of Honor, Courage and Commitment.

***

After evening chow I got a bunch of mail, including a letter from my parents which miraculously was perfectly timed to say "Congratulations on completing the Crucible and for getting to the end of boot camp."

I'm not sure what the next six days of transition week will be like. I was always looking toward the Crucible as the end of the line and never gave much thought to the final post-Crucible week.

I guess we'll find out when I wake up tomorrow.

CHAPTER 9: Transition Week

Friday, September 22, 2000 (1 Week Until Graduation)

This afternoon we had a graduation parade practice. Basically it is still drill but unlike the drilling we did for the past eleven weeks, there are no rifles, there is considerably less yelling and there is a bright light at the end of the tunnel because graduation is only a week away.

Today we also got our official boot camp portraits back. I'm a little disappointed because they were taken twenty pounds ago so when I look back at this picture, decades from now it won't reflect the svelte Marine who marched across the parade deck on graduation day. Back when the pictures were taken in July or early August we ordered packages of pictures much the same way school kids order so many wallet sizes and 8 x 10s etc. I have noticed that the guys who hate boot camp the most got the biggest package. One guy Nathan, who once-upon-a-time asked a Marine giving a class how he could go about quitting the Marine Corps, got a portrait of himself that is at least 50% bigger than life-size. Drill Instructor Sergeant Willis called it the "I love me" picture.

Tonight and probably for the rest of the weekend we are cleaning our weapons to turn them back in. Drill Instructor Staff

Sergeant Erickson said that if your weapon is declared "unsat" by the armorer you have to clean it on Family Day. I think this might be an empty threat but I'm not taking any chances. I remember that my brother's boot camp platoon was ordered to clean the barracks after they graduated and some of the guys missed the bus off the island and subsequently missed their flights home. Needless to say I am cleaning the hell out of this thing because I don't want to miss one second of Family Day.

***

We now have our very own *Lord of the Flies* scenario unfolding in the platoon.

Unlike the past eighty or so nights, last night there were no Drill Instructor in the barracks after evening chow. The Guide and the Squad Leaders are in charge now when the DIs are not around. The new Marines are a little drunk on their own power and trying to act like Drill Instructors. One of the Squad Leaders, Kistemaker, the prior-service Army guy whose leadership abilities I normally respect, went around while we were hygiening and took all of the unlocked padlocks and linked them together into a big knot just as the DIs did back in the First Phase. Granted, footlockers are supposed to be locked when you are in the head but a DI-like stunt like that is only going to make the job of governing the platoon that much harder over the next week.

The Guide, who I have never been a big fan of, is threatening to take away our "Boot Libo" this Sunday if we do not obey him and the Squad Leaders. This kind of leadership by threat is not going to be effective. The Guide has likewise threatened to report to the Senior any unruly recruits. This really undermined him because leadership by tattle-tale is an admission of the limits of his power. He'll learn to be a better leader over the course of the next week and then when he goes into the bottom of the Marine Corps' barrel with an experienced unit. There he'll find out a little more and by the time the Guide is in a leadership billet he'll be ready. As frustrating as it is now to watch, in the long run it is a good system.

Saturday, September 23, 2000

This morning we had the first PT run as Marines. We were in formation going at a steady pace, in a good mood, singing loud ditties and looking sharp. This is the kind of stuff you see on recruiting videos and boot camp documentaries. Most PT runs are not so dignified because the DIs are trying to improve our PT and break the weak links. Typically guy's tongues are wagging, we are huffing and puffing and have torrential armpit stains. Plus on a normal PT run a guy or two will fall out on the side of the road and puke. I guess this is all part of the process of being broken down, purged of bad habits and weakness, and built back up as Marines. Anyway, we looked sharp this morning even if our not so crisp PT experiences of the past are still fresh in my memory.

In the late morning we were broken up into groups by MOS. As you might expect the biggest group was for "0300 Infantry." At least a quarter of the guys in the platoon are going to be grunts. Because I didn't know any better I always just assumed that all DIs were infantry. That's not true at all. In fact our Senior is motor T (motor transport), Willis is supply, and Erickson is a swim instructor although I think he may have had a different MOS originally. Having an experienced infantryman, like DI Sergeant Murphy from Platoon 1378, answer our questions and do a little mentoring was extremely enlightening. The active duty guys had questions about SOI (School of Infantry) and "floats" which is the term for the Marine Expeditionary Units which float around the high seas all over the world ready to act as "America's 911 Force."

***

When the platoon got back from a personal finance class at RTF, Drill Instructor Sergeant Willis was handing out mail, giving advice, cracking jokes, and telling "war stories" about his time in the Marine Corps. Willis is still calling me "fat bastard" even though I am a Marine now. When he has some clerical BS for me to do he continues to yell "Where you at fat bastard?" Now that I am a Marine and a little cocky and pretty certain Drill Instructor Sergeant Willis isn't going to kill me, I run over there and shout "Sir. Fat Bastard reporting as ordered. Sir." Because as the Scribe I have access to everyone's service record book (SRB), including my own, I know that Willis does not hate me and that he probably even respects me. This afternoon I saw that he wrote that I had "made a 180 degree turn around in fitness and appearance" and that I am now "one of the platoon's stronger PTers." This was motivating to read and is a big part of why I have no problem taking all of the "Fat Bastard" stuff in stride.

***

Willis was in good spirits and gave recruits-turned-new-Marines an opportunity to do impressions of him and the other DIs. Some of the guys did pretty dead-on impressions, particularly of Willis. Willis is easier than the other to caricature because he has a unique gravelly quality to his voice and a very apparent

Brooklyn accent with a touch of southern drawl from his time as a Marine in the South.

After Willis left the members of the platoon had sort of town hall meeting to discuss how best to get the squad bay squared away and get on our on-base liberty tomorrow without any hitches. Drill Instructor Staff Sergeant Helmann would be the only DI with us tomorrow and we all knew from that stunt with the racks after the Crucible he doesn't see us or treat us like Marines. We didn't want to give Helmann any excuse to keep us here cleaning the squad bay while all of the others platoons were eating pizza and making phone calls.

For the whole time we have been here the Sunday routine was for the Protestants to start field day when they got back from church while the Catholics were at Mass. To demonstrate our initiative and to get a jump on the clean up, the platoon decided to have the Catholics start clean up while the Protestants were at church. It was a good idea and even if Helmann wanted to be a prick we would have time to fix any discrepancies before liberty was sounded at 1300.

For the most part, today was as I envisioned post-Crucible boot camp would be because we were only semi-supervised, taking care of our uniforms, and cleaning up the squad bay. After evening chow we were on our own to hygiene and make sure the Fire Watch was established and the lights went out at exactly 2100. The Guide and Squad Leaders must have learned from the difficulty that resulted from their heavy-handed leadership tactics yesterday because they pretty much laid off today. It went smoothly and as my head hit the pillow at 2100 I couldn't help but think that in sixteen short hours I would be drinking a soda with a big fat piece of pepperoni pizza in my mouth.

Sunday, September 24, 2000

Remember a long time ago I mentioned guys in church who were about to graduate the following Friday wearing a dress uniform? Well today that is us. We put on our "Service Charlies" a uniform that consists of shiny black shoes, olive green gabardine trousers, and a khaki short-sleeved shirt with a rather big collar over a crisp white t-shirt. For a cover we wear the "piss cover." The shape of the piss cover resembles the paper hat a short-order cook might wear and is similar to the kind of hat you'd see American Legion or VFW guys wearing at parades. The piss cover is the same olive green material as our trousers. It comes up to a peak in the middle and has one black EGA on the right, front side. Why it is called a piss cover I don't know.

They don't want us setting a bad example for the newer recruits or to "look like ass" on Libo so we had an inspection beforehand. Save for one, well-hidden Irish pennant, I didn't have any problems with the inspection.

After church we had a formation and the company First Sergeant sounded liberty which set off a controlled dash to the phones, the on-base Pizza Hut, and the "seven day store," which is like a 7-11. After we were fallen out, it took about thirty seconds for Stewart to get lost. Everyone was striding off to the various hot spots and Stewart was wandering about, half-panicked yelling for me, still pronouncing my name wrong. "Lay-ler. Lay-ler." Stewart and I went against the grain and together we headed for the phones first, rather than Pizza Hut. When we got to the phone bank each of the ten phones had two or three new Marines queued up already. The wait was only about twenty-five minutes, which by boot camp standards wasn't that bad.

Boot Libo was four hours of eating pizza, making phone calls from pay phones, and buying magazines and newspapers. The term "liberty", like everything else on Parris Island, is a misnomer. Technically, we were supposed to march in step wherever we went with our "Libo buddies." Although from what I could see this rule was rarely obeyed and scantly enforced. We were also barred from walking while eating or drinking and from crossing anywhere but at designated cross walks. Ah, sweet liberty.

Much the same way we overdid it in the Weapons Battalion chow hall, when it was all-you-can-eat for us while working during Team Week, today was an orgy of gluttony. Guys who only weigh a buck twenty-five were ordering two and three meat-lovers pizzas and enough bread sticks to build a house. When the grease settled and the smoke cleared, there were semi-eaten pizzas throughout the cafeteria-style dining room and guys were trying in vain to give away their leftovers as they sat bloated and weary enjoying the air-conditioning. Like everybody else I overindulged, buying cookies, two medium pies, a steak sandwich and an extra large Coke.

After eating, we hit the Marine Exchange which is kind of like an on-base JC Penney, but about twenty-five percent cheaper and sans sales tax. I bought the requisite thirty-two ounce Gatorade bottle which we were mandated to buy because tomorrow we would turn in canteens and needed something to hold water to stay hydrated during the remaining three days of graduation practice and PT. Also at the exchange, I purchased some postcards and Twizzlers, which as you may know "make mouths happy."

Then it was off to the 7 Day Store which is a term I just can't understand. Obviously the name comes from the fact that it is open every day but you'd think they could be a little more creative. I was dying for some election news so I bought the only paper they had, Friday's *USA Today* to catch up on the presidential election. At this point, a forty-eight hour old newspaper is hot off the presses. *USA Today* is not known for its depth of coverage, so I looked around the 7 Day Store for a *Time* or *US News & World Report* but couldn't find them among the endless selection of gun magazines, hunting and fishing mags and Me-and-my-pick-up-truck Monthly. Okay, I made that last one up.

A couple of things that were difficult to get used to again were interacting with civilians, using money, and having to keep track of your wallet for the first time in three months. I managed fine but it took some getting used to and I am starting to understand why "transition week" is important to have before we are sent back into society.

1700 was the official end of Boot Libo, but Marines always arrive "fifteen minutes prior" to any assignment so we would all turn into pumpkins at 1645. Stewart and I made it back with three or four minutes to spare, which was perfect because I didn't want to have to make a mad dash for the squad bay but I also didn't want to squander a significant chunk of my Libo and get back ridiculously early as did many in our platoon.

I feel so reinvigorated after today's festivities that it's going to be hard to fall asleep.

Monday, September 25, 2000

We got our official orders for where and when to report next. I was hoping the orders would answer whether I would be done with SOI by Thanksgiving Day. Unfortunately the orders tell you when to get there but not when you're leaving. The orders say that SOI has thirty-six Training Days but that doesn't help because it doesn't say whether there is training on Saturday and Sunday. Also, from what I am told, SOI training doesn't always start on time.

The open contract guys found out what line of work they would be in for the next four years. As expected about three-quarters of the open contracts are going to become infantrymen and the others will be cooks.

Next we had a class on conduct during boot leave. The Marine Corps doesn't want bad publicity or injured or incarcerated Marines, so they give you a class on how to avoid getting into trouble while you are home. It is not rocket science; it's basically don't fight, don't drive fast, don't drink and drive, and don't do drugs.

Then we got a class called "Marriage and the First Term Marine" given by the Series Gunnery Sergeant. He made a diplomatic and strong case for not getting married during your first four year enlistment. His basic argument was that statistically marriages by young Marines don't work out because all of the things that make marriage difficult are compounded and exasperated by the realities of military life. This is an important class because there are so many eighteen and nineteen year olds looking to get married. As the Series Gunny put it, "It's easy to get married, but it's hard to get divorced."

Before evening chow we got our pictures taken for our Military IDs and we were issued our dog tags.

***

Just in case anyone forgets that we are still on Parris Island, Willis went on a classic Drill Instructor Sergeant Willis rampage after evening chow. He found a bunch of seabags unlocked and just like old times began dumping them out, running up and down the squad bay looking for other unlocked seabags, knocking recruits over along the way. In the aftermath of Willis's blitzkrieg the squad bay was littered with uniforms, hygiene items, and personal affects. It was no big deal though because everything is labeled and we quickly got the squad bay back to normal. This episode was just the latest reminder to us that according to Willis, we "ain't on the bus yet!" No, we certainly ain't.

Tuesday, September 26, 2000

I had dental this morning and I was over there for about three hours but only got to watch a little CNN FN. They say a bear market is coming but they have been predicting that for two years now. I know because I have been teaching a course in economics and followed this stuff closely.

After I got my teeth fixed, we went as a platoon to pay our final bills for all of the haircuts, uniforms, soap and such that we have been using since we got here. It literally pays to be a Private First Class (PFC) rather than simply a Private. A Private gets paid $380 twice per month but a PFC gets $455 per paycheck. I was getting paid PFC all along because I, as I explained in an earlier entry, "had college." You can also be a "guaranteed PFC" if you were an Eagle Scout or if you got one of your buddies to enlist. "Guaranteed PFC" means that when you graduate you are a PFC and you get paid as a PFC throughout boot camp.

Then there are those who get meritoriously promoted to PFC for being good recruits. They won't start getting paid as a PFC until the end of boot camp when the paperwork goes through indicating that they have been promoted.

Once all of my bills were paid, I was left with $1,004 plus I think I'll get another direct deposit of $455 minus taxes on Friday. This will allow me to live pretty high on the hog during my boot leave and will permit me to really live it up and make this an epic Notre Dame trip.

***

Today we got all of the various boot camp souvenirs we ordered a while back. I got a steel Marine Corps Ring although I am not really a ring guy. A huge part of the VMI experience was getting your class ring during the first semester of your junior year. I think subconsciously I bought this ring because it is symbolic of having completely expunged any regrets I had about leaving VMI after the first year.

I went pretty easy on the purchase of Marine Corps doo-dads buying just the ring. Other guys bought rings, heart lockets for their girlfriends to put their picture in, money clips, and almost anything else that you could attach to an EGA or the letters USMC.

Wednesday, September 27, 2000

Today was the Battalion Commanders inspection; supposedly the final hurdle before graduation. But I don't think it's a real hurdle at all because the DIs are not going to let you be inspected if your uniform is not perfect and, even if there is a discrepancy, I don't see the Battalion Commander preventing a guy from graduating because of an Irish pennant. The key to passing an inspection is in your words and voice not in your uniform or rifle. When the Battalion Commander or any inspector steps in front of you he is looking for a confident Marine who is not stressed out by the presence of someone of higher rank. Thus, if you answer loudly and confidently you won't have a problem. If you are timid and sound unsure of yourself you invite closer scrutiny and inevitably you are going to get dinged for some sort of a deficiency.

When the full-bird Colonel stepped in front of me, he said that my uniform looked good. He looked at my rifle and said he saw some dirt on it, which is impossible. Because I barked "Aye, aye Sir" when he informed me of the alleged dirt and quickly and forcefully snatched back my rifle when he was done inspecting, he saw I was confident and I passed.

Right after the inspections we marched over in our Alpha uniforms and turned in our weapons to the armory. While we were turning the rifles in, a new Company was being issued their rifles. After the armory we got back the paper bag of personal affects that we handed in the night we got here. I came on the island empty-handed, so the bag contained simply the clothes I had on my back and the shoes I had on my feet when I set foot on the yellow footprints, backwards, long ago.

***

Before I came here I was told that the sand fleas were worse than the heat. But other than being an annoyance, the sand fleas never bothered me that much until recently. Maybe it's because summer is turning into fall but lately they seem to be particularly vicious. In the past week it has become common to have ten or fifteen of those buggers eating away at your neck and arms at one time. I feel bad for the recruits just getting here who are going to have to contend with these angry bugs.

Late this afternoon we packed all of our stuff in our seabags and garment bag save what we would need for the next two days. It felt great to have my bags packed with my parents set to arrive tomorrow. The light at the end of the tunnel is so close it is blinding me. Tonight was our last dinner in the chow hall because tomorrow is Family Day and we'll eat with our family at Pizza Hut or some other restaurant on the island. Friday is graduation and we are out of here by 1000.

As usual, we hauled-ass to get over to the chow hall before any of the other platoons. We started going though the line but some jackass in our platoon knocked over a bunch of empty trays as he rushed into the chow hall and no one bothered to pick them up. As a result, Drill Instructor Sergeant Willis about-faced us and marched us out of the chow hall and parked us outside in the blazing Carolina sun and allowed three other platoons to go ahead of us. No, we are not on the bus yet.

Yesterday I began counting down hours and chows in addition to half days until we get off the island. I'm trying hard not to get too excited and make the waiting even more unbearable. The military has a custom of counting down the days and referring to the last day as "a wake up." For example, Family Day is Thursday September 28th. Under the "and a wake up" countdown method, on September 1st I would have said "27 and a wake up." But the problem with this is that although you wake up on the day you have been looking forward to, you don't actually get to leave or in this case meet with your family as soon as you wake up. Thus on the day you have been looking forward to you have nothing to count down and those are some of the most anxious and drawn out hours of the whole experience. Call me crazy, but I need to count the hours to keep my sanity.

CHAPTER 10: Graduation

Thursday, September 28, 2000

During this morning's mote run I got stuck being a road guard. I was tasked with the job because I'm a strong runner and the road guard has to sprint up ahead of the platoon at every intersection and halt the traffic so the platoon can run by unobstructed. After the platoon runs by the road guard has to catch up and repeat this process at every intersection and parking lot exit for four-miles. Despite the somewhat complimentary motivation for making me a road guard, I was disappointed that I didn't get to run with the platoon and share in all of the camaraderie of the final PT session of boot camp.

After the run I was even more disappointed when I learned that Drill Instructor Sergeant Willis, not realizing that I was on road guard duty, summoned me out to call the cadence for the platoon. Of course he referred to me not by name but with the familiar "Where you at Fat Bastard?" I've been around Willis long enough to know that the privilege of calling the cadence for the platoon was a high compliment.

After "PT Recovery," which constitutes a shower and changing into cammies, we had a final graduation practice. The Drill Master, a Gunnery Sergeant who oversees all of the drill competitions and, evidently, the graduation ceremony, was leading the practice session. He was not happy with our performance and even barked at the DIs. I think we did just fine but the Drill Master is just used to bitching at everyone.

Next we field day'd the squad bay because families will be touring the barracks later this afternoon. Then we put on our Charlie uniform. Family Day starts with us marching onto the parade deck and is followed by a ceremony explaining briefly our training and acknowledging any VIPs who are in the viewing area. During the ceremony I scanned and scanned the grand stand looking for my parents but couldn't find them. A letter was sent home to our families instructing them to wear red, the official color of First Battalion. This made finding my parents in the crowd of roughly 1500 to 2000 people very difficult, especially because I was at attention and unable to move anything but my eyeballs. Finally, with about five seconds left in the ceremony I spotted my parents and planned my line of march to them when we given permission to do so.

When the Senior Drill Instructor finally gave the command to "fall out" I marched right up to my parents, who hardly recognized me because I was forty pounds lighter than when they saw me off on the Fourth of July. My dad was on this island as a Third Battalion recruit back in the summer of 1962 and was also here for my brother's graduation in 1989 so it was very interesting to tour the island with him and to hear what had changed and what hadn't. My brother Pat would have come but he recently started a new job and was not able to take the time off.

A lot of guys wanted to introduce their parents to the Drill Instructors and get pictures taken with them but I wasn't really into that. Those bastards are so seared into my memory that no pictures will be needed to recall their ugly faces. But it was kind of interesting to see guys who for three months avoided so much as making eye contact with DIs, running up to them, wide-eyed and asking to take a picture with big shit-eating grins on their face.

My parents and I ate lunch, visited the Parris Island museum, the rifle range, and got caught up on what my many siblings were up to. Before I knew it Family Day was nearly over. At about 1715 we headed toward the barracks because although Family Day officially ended at 1800, the fifteen-minutes-prior rule applied and I really didn't want to cut it close and get bitched at in front of my parents. Plus this gave my parents an opportunity to see the squad bay and for my dad to compare the barracks of today with the barracks of thirty-eight years ago.

I changed into cammies, put my stuff in the car my parents rented for a quick getaway tomorrow, bid my folks farewell until the morning, and headed back into the squad bay. By 1845 everything was back to normal and was if we had just returned from a hump, not Family Day. We stood online in the squad bay and went through our accountability drill to see if we were all there. One jackass was actually late and got reamed pretty good.

During square away time the Senior Drill Instructor called me into his office. As the Scribe it was not at all uncommon and quite annoying to be summoned into the DI shack. Instead of tasking me with another last-minute project, he handed me his gold Senior Drill Instructor's Eagle Glove and Anchor belt buckle from his first cycle as a DI, shook my hand and said, "outstanding job." I didn't know if he meant outstanding job as the Scribe or as a recruit in general but I was flattered and glad to get some recognition. Then knowing that I could potentially become an officer because of my bachelor's degree and having discovered my passion for politics he said, "The next time I see you I expect you to be a General or a Senator." Lofty expectations indeed but I am a believer that high expectations lead to achievement.

Getting this reward and compliment from the Senior means that my hard work over the past three months did not go unnoticed. With a new spring in my step, the result of finally getting some individual praise, I happily made up the final Fire Watch roster of boot camp.

Tomorrow is going to be a busy day and I didn't want to miss saying goodbye to Stewart. A few minutes ago I went over to his rack let him know that I was proud of him and that I knew he would make an outstanding Marine. He thanked me for helping him get through boot camp. We shook hands and I wondered if I'd every see him again.

We have morning chow and then graduation practice early tomorrow and then at 0915 we form up for the 1000 graduation which takes less than ten minutes. I just can't wait to get off this island, move about freely, have no deadlines, take my time eating and getting dressed, feel clean after a shower, and to actually wear real clothes. It is 2130 and I'm about to lay my head down a mere fourteen hours from getting off this island.

Friday, September 29, 2000

This morning came pretty quickly and I had no problem springing out of my rack when, for the last time on Parris Island, I heard the last Fire Watch exclaim "Reveille!, Reveille! Reveille!" We ate our last meal in the First Battalion Chow Hall and then packed everything that was left into our dittie bags. I didn't get rid of enough stuff in my seabag yesterday so my dittie bag bulged with shower shoes, combat boots, and hygiene gear to the point that the zipper busted. Using a little Marine Corps ingenuity I took the humungous safety pin that for three months kept my laundry bag closed and fastened my dittie bag so that none of the contents would leak out.

After some typical Parris Island hurry-up-and-wait, we marched to the parade deck and a bigger crowd than I expected clad in bright red shirts cheered with thunderous applause. Never before have I marched so erect and with such text book precision as I did while taking my final strides aboard this God forsaken island. The band played the National Anthem and the Marine Corps Hymn followed by a few other John Phillip Souza marches and at long last the time came for the words I thought I would never hear. The narrator explained to the crowd over the loud speaker that the Senior Drill Instructors would now give "the last order of boot camp, and the most welcome."

Then Senior Drill Instructor Staff Sergeant Jefferson said, "Platoon 1377 .... Dismissed!" Upon that command as practiced, we took two steps back and in unison responded "Aye, aye Sir." Then we about-faced and barked the Marine Corps battle cry "Ooh-Rah!"

With that, boot camp was over and my dream fully realized.

EPILOGUE

After my ten days of boot leave, I went to SOI at Camp Geiger in Jacksonville, North Carolina to learn the finer points of being a Marine Corps grunt. We didn't think too much about it at the time, but during my first week at SOI the USS *Cole* was attacked by al Qaeda. This event foreshadowed the coming Global War on Terror.

After SOI, as planned, I transitioned to reserve status with Fox Company 2nd Battalion 25th Marine Regiment. My time on reserve duty, and as a law student for that matter, was brief because on September 11, 2001, two weeks into my first semester at Pace Law School, our nation was attacked by al Qaeda.

That day was especially trying for me and my family because my sister Suzanne worked on the 92nd Floor of the North Tower of the World Trade Center and it wasn't until that afternoon when we learned Suzanne was safe. She was a few minutes behind schedule that morning and, instead of being in her office when her building was attacked, she was at the foot of the towers. She was delayed because she was icing our sister Meghan's birthday cake to bring to a celebration at the Yankee game that evening.

Because of this experience, I have taken the War on Terror both seriously and personally.

My unit was called to active service beginning in January 2002. We thought we were going to be shipped off to fight the Taliban in Afghanistan and we even went to Mountain Warfare School in the Sierra Nevada Mountains to train for it. But as it turned out we spent 2002 based out of Camp Lejeune, North Carolina training and serving as a ready-reaction force during those uncertain months after 9/11.

My unit was activated a second time and deployed to Iraq in March 2003 at the start of Operation Iraqi Freedom. I served as a S.A.W gunner while conducting security and stabilization operations in the Shia city of Nasiriyah, located along the Euphrates River in southern Iraq. We patrolled the streets, established checkpoints and acted on intelligence to thwart enemy attacks and confiscate insurgent weapons.

My brother Pat got married on July Fourth 2003 while I was in Iraq. I managed to commandeer a satellite phone that day to call him to wish him the best. Then I called my brother Danny and read my Best Man speech to his voicemail so he could relay the toast at the reception.

When our tour of duty was up we were relieved by the Italian Army, who unlike the Marine Corps, subscribed to a reactive doctrine of remaining in the FOB (forward operating base) until an incident occurred and then responded. This flawed thinking cost them lives when they were hit by a suicide truck attack that killed nineteen soldiers two months after they took over the building formerly occupied by my unit. The lesson I learned from this tragedy informed my world view because the Italian allies had essentially a pre-9/11 reactionary policy that made the successful attack on their position inevitable. The incident convinced me that despite the controversy and the failure to find Weapons of Mass Destruction, the mission in Iraq was making the United States safer just as our constant presents in the streets of Nasiriyah kept us from suffering the same fate as the Italians.

When I got home I re-enrolled in law school and in the first weeks of starting over after a two year leave of absence, I met a lovely elementary-school-teacher-turned-law-student named Mary Jo Martin. We dated for eleven months before I popped the question. We got married in summer 2005, had our first child Katherine Mary in 2006 and graduated from law school together in May 2007. A few months later we had our daughter Riley Maireid and, in December 2008, our son Michael Glover entered the world.

***

In the years after Parris Island I managed to accomplish some of the goals I was inspired to set while in boot camp like, completing the 2001 Marine Corps Marathon in Washington DC. The Marine Corps taught me to think proactively and gave me the confidence to take on big challenges. So when Hurricane Katrina ravaged the Gulf Coast, motivated by the way the country rallied behind New York on 9/11, I drove with two other Marine reservists 1400 miles to the affected area. A New Orleans police officer, who was also a ranking member of a Marine Reserve unit in Louisiana, took notice of our efforts and put us up for the Navy and Marine Corps Achievement Medal for performing search and rescue missions in The Big Easy.

One of the Marines who went with me to New Orleans was Mike Glover, the same friend I hung out with in Albany my last night before boot camp. Glover was an usher in my wedding and a law school classmate who was also deeply impacted by the 9/11 attacks which killed a number friends who were firefighters and workers in the Twin Towers. Glover enlisted in 2004 and that summer I made my only trip back to Parris Island for his boot camp graduation. Eleven months after our trip to New Orleans, on 16 August 2006, Glover was the point man on a patrol just outside Fallujah, Iraq when he was killed by a sniper's bullet. I still can't believe he is gone.

That same year, Dave Mahoney, a friend of nearly three decades who was like a brother because at times over the years he lived with my family, enlisted in the Marine Corps at the ripe old age of thirty-two. You might recall that Dave was the guy who dropped me off at the recruiter's office in Poughkeepsie to begin the journey to boot camp. Dave completed a tour of duty in Iraq from 2008 to 2009 and, thank God, came back in one piece.

Because of my Marine Corps service and 9/11, I became very passionate about making sure our country maintained the political will to finish what we'd started in Iraq and the War on Terror generally. I wrote op-eds, organized rallies, and made television and radio appearances to support the notion that we must stay on offense against our terrorist enemies and support our troops and their mission.

One interesting episode that occurred as a result of this activism happened at an anti-war rally in White Plains, New York in 2005. After listening to speaker-after-speaker rail about "atrocities" our troops were committing in Iraq, I approached the ringleader to show him some pictures of me and my Marine buddies playfully interacting with the Iraqi children we had befriended. My goal was to challenge the ridiculous claims being made by the speakers. Instead of looking at what I was trying to show him the guy in charge mistook me for the next speaker and guided me to the podium to address the crowd. Standing there I gazed out at a sea of anti-military rabble and felt like Forrest Gump when he gave that speech on the steps of the Lincoln Memorial in his uniform in that iconic scene from the Academy Award-winning movie. Seizing the unique opportunity to rain on their parade and get my pro-troop side of the story out, I spoke for a minute and a half about the good work our troops were doing in Iraq and around the world. Faced with the facts from a first-hand perspective they cut the microphone just as I was hitting my stride.

On another occasion, I cut my evening class to stage a counter-demonstration to these same anti-military types who were trying to issue mock war crimes indictments to the local Marine recruiters. The next day a picture of me holding the Marine Corps flag and arguing with my anti-military adversaries appeared on the cover of the New York Journal News. The professor whose class I cut was overtly hostile to me the next class and for the rest of the semester. My grade probably suffered but he can kiss my star-spangled ass.

I took a crack at a Congressional seat in 2008 finding an innovative way for a middle class family man to mount a serious Congressional run. By working the midnight shift as a security officer charged with guarding cadavers in the gross anatomy laboratory at a local medical college from midnight to eight, I had my days and evenings free to campaign and help care for my children. I defied the odds and the political establishment to earn the nomination of the Republican Party and garnered 116,000 votes in the general election, the most for any challenger in the history of the District. I put up a good fight but it was not to be and I lost the election to incumbent Congressman John Hall, a liberal pop singer from the seventies' band Orleans.

Also in 2008, I cobbled together a coalition of Republican Iraq Veterans running for the U.S. House of Representatives. By coordinating press events, fundraising activities and providing logistical support for member campaigns, we helped thirteen of our Iraq Vet candidates earn the nomination and get on the general election ballot. Two Iraq Vet candidates won seats in the House of Representatives. In 2009 I formally established Iraq Vets for Congress as a federally recognized Political Action Committee to recruit, fund and elect federal office conservative Republican Veterans.

***

I've been a full time civilian for a few years and I'm a pretty conventional suburban dad. I have a mini-van, change a lot of diapers, frequent Chucky Cheese and take my daughters to ballet class on Saturday morning. Not a day goes by that I don't think about the hell we went through for three glorious months on Parris Island and I'm certain I'll always carry a profound sense of pride for having claimed the title United States Marine.

Once a Marine always a Marine isn't just a slogan. It is fact. Semper Fi!

GLOSSARY

300 PFT   a perfect Physical Fitness Test score; requires 20 dead hang pull-ups, 100 crunches in 2 minutes and a three mile run in 18 minutes or less.

A-line   the week of recruit training where recruits begin to learn tactical skills like rappelling, night fire and fire and maneuver tactics

ASVAB   Armed Services Vocational Aptitude Battery; a test given to prospective recruits prior to shipping to boot camp to determine if the recruit is intelligent enough to join a branch of the military; the test is also used to help determine the appropriate military occupational specialty for an individual recruit

Aye, aye, sir!   acknowledgement of a superior officer's command.

bag nasty   lunch served in a brown paper bag at the
                       rifle range; usually consists of a bologna
                       sandwich, mustard packet, orange, potato
                       chips and cookies

Barney Style   an oversimplified method of instruction;
                       name is derived from children's character
                       Barney

Big Gear   a locker in the squad bay where cleaning
Locker   supplies and other equipment are stored

Big Gear   recruit responsible for handing out and
Locker Recruit   collecting supplies from the Big Gear
                       Locker

black flag   a flag that goes up designating that it is too
                       hot to train outside

blouse   the unfortunate name for the long-sleeved
                       camouflage Marine Corps uniform shirt

blousing boots   tucking the cuff of camouflage trousers up
                       under a green rubber band

boot leave   ten days of leave after boot camp

bulkhead   wall

butts   large pile of earth behind the targets on a
                       firing range to stop stray bullets.

brown cow   chocolate milk

BWT   Basic Warrior Training; week of training
                       dedicated to learning how to operate
                       tactically in the field

by the numbers   step by step instructions given by DIs to accomplish a task

BZO   Battle Site Zero; also known as "doping" the weapon; the process of customizing a rifle sites to the individual shooter to ensure accurate shooting

cadence   rhythmic chants used to keep Marines in step while marching or running

cammies   term for the standard camouflage utility uniform worn by Marines

civies   civilian clothing

corpsman   Navy enlisted medic

cover   hat worn as part of a Marine uniform

cross legged   shooting position that is similar to sitting Indian style

Crucible   final test before a recruit becomes a Marine; consists of three days in the field with minimal food and sleep, approximately fifty miles of humps and a series of obstacles recruits must overcome by using teamwork and leadership skills

data book   record of a recruit's marksmanship and range conditions

deck   term for the floor or ground

DI   Drill Instructor; responsible for training
                        recruits; most boot camp platoons have
                        three DIs including a Senior Drill Instructor
                        who acts as the platoon commander

DI highway   the path in the middle of the squad bay
                        formed by the gauntlet of recruits standing
                        online in front of footlockers where Drill
                        Instructors walk when inspecting or
                        instructing recruits

DI hut   Drill Instructors office in the barracks;
                        serves as the sleeping quarters for the Drill
                        Instructor on duty at night

diet tray   term for meals eaten by those recruits on the
                        weight control program; recruits remain on
                        diet tray until they get under the maximum
                        weight for their height; meals usually
                        include relatively low fat selections such as
                        boiled chicken and rice

dittie bag   small green or camouflage duffle bag used
                        by Marines to carry uniform and hygiene
                        items

dive-bomber   A form of physical training that begins in a
push-up   modified push-up position with legs spread
                        and butt up in the air so the body resembles
                        a pyramid; to perform this exercise the
                        recruit swoops down and forward lowering
                        his butt until his back is arched and most
                        of his torso is in front of his hands; to
                        complete the exercise the recruit swings
                        backward and returns up to the original
                        position

double-time   run

double rations   increased food portions for those recruits who need to gain weight to be within weight standards; is the opposite of diet tray

drill   marching and rifle manual that simulates classic military formations and teaches recruits instant obedience to orders

eating duck   phrase used to describe when recruits are only in the chow hall long enough to *duck* down for a few seconds to eat before returning to training

evening chow   dinner

fat body   derisive term to describe those recruits who appear out of shape or who are formally participating in weight control and /or diet tray programs

field day   cleaning the barracks

Fire Watch   guard duty; at least two recruits stand Fire Watch in the squad bay at night to alert the Drill Instructors of any disturbances and to enforce the Drill Instructor's orders

FOB   forward operating base

footlocker   wooden trunk located at the foot of a Recruit's bed where clothing and toiletries are stored

Forming	initial administrative phase of boot camp when recruits arrive and are issued uniforms and equipment and given a battery of physical exams
fraudulent enlistment	when a recruit conceals some element of ineligibility for service such as past drug use or a medical condition
gear accountability	knowing where your uniform and equipment are at all times
GI can	garbage can
go-fasters	government issued athletic footwear
Grass Week	a week of formal rifle range instruction that involves learning the fundamentals of marksmanship and the basic shooting positions; the name comes from the fact that much of the week involves recruits in the grass getting into the shooting positions for long periods and aiming the rifle at small targets
Green Monster	camouflage covered binder that contains information a recruit is required to memorize such as rules, rank structure, chain of command, Marine Corps history, and first aid
Guide	the senior recruit in the platoon, carries the platoon guidon
Guidon	a red banner on a long flag pole that bears the platoon number

Hatch	door
Head	bathroom
head call	trip to the bathroom
hooch	tent
hot tray	meals taken out of the cafeteria in Styrofoam take-out boxes and brought back to the squad bay for sick or punished recruits
hump	a long forced march usually completed while carrying full packs, supplies and rifles; designed to build endurance and strength
hygiene	a verb that means to wash, shave, brush teeth or perform any other routine grooming activities
ink stick	pen
infiltration course	advance through obstacles under simulated fire
Irish pennant	small piece of thread that dangles from the uniform
ISMT	Indoor Simulated Marksmanship Trainer; a very realistic video game that simulates shooting the M-16

IST	Initial Strength Test, consists of a 1.5 mile run, pull-ups and crunches; to Pass a recruit must complete the 1.5 mile run in 13:30, complete two proper dead hang pull ups and thirty five crunches in two minutes; recruits must pass this minimum standard to begin training; recruits who fail are sent to Physical Conditioning Platoon until they can pass the IST and begin training
jungle boots	light weight combat boots made for warmer climates
K D course	known distance course of fire used for rifle qualifications; shooters fire from the 200, 300 and 500-yard-lines
Knowledge	General term for all of the information a recruit has to memorize such as rules, rank structure, chain of command, Marine Corps history and first aid; information is contained in a camouflage covered binder known as the Green Monster
ladder well	stairway
Lance Corporal	third enlisted rank; E-3
Leave	extended absence from duty; earned similar to vacation time in civilian employment
Liberty	short absence from duty, is granted by commanding officer
LZ	landing zone

M-16 A2 Service Rifle	primary weapon used by Marines
Main-side	the main part of the base; as opposed to the rifle ranges and other training areas that are in remote locations; also known as the rear
MCT	Marine Combat Training, attended by non-infantry Marines after boot camp in lieu of School of Infantry; where non-infantry Marines learn basic infantry tactics prior to attending school for their particular military occupational specialty
MEPS	Military Entrance Processing Station; usually located in federal buildings, it is where recruits go to determine if they meet the physical and mental requirements to enlist in the Armed Forces
Moment of Truth	Term to describe the final line of defense against fraudulent enlistments; when recruits arrive, Marines have a chance to disclose any potentially disqualifying information such as past drug use, injury or illness
moonbeam	flashlight
morning chow	breakfast
MOS	Military Occupational Specialty
mote table	short for motivational table; a table in the squad bay that showcases pictures of things that recruits find motivating such as photos of girlfriends, pin ups, motorcycles, cars, and Marines in action

mote run   short hand for motivational run, designed to increase morale rather than for punishment or as part of regular physical training

MRE   Meals Ready to Eat

Mustang   an officer who was previously an enlisted Marine

NCO   non-commissioned officer; Corporal and above

noon chow   lunch

OCS   Officer Candidate School; basic training for officers, takes place in Quantico, Virginia.

off-hand   shooting from the standing position.

on-line   when recruits stand at attention in front of their footlocker with their heels on a black line that surrounds the squad bay; simulates the basic combat formation

PCP   Physical Conditioning Platoon; a special platoon for recruits who fail the Initial Strength Test; once a recruit passes the Initial Strength Test, he leaves PCP and joins a platoon about to start training; derisively called Pork Chop Platoon as a means of degrading member recruits for their lack of physical fitness

PFC   Private First Class; E-2; second enlisted rank

PFT   Physical Fitness Test; consists of a three
                         mile run, pull-ups and crunches; a recruit
                         must pass it to graduate boot camp, to
                         pass a recruit needs to run 3 miles in less
                         than 28:00, complete 3 dead hang pull ups
                         and 50 crunches in two minutes; a perfect
                         score is an 18:00 run, 20 pull ups and 100
                         crunches in two minutes

pick up   when a platoon is assigned Drill Instructors
                         and begins training, occurs after the
                         Forming phase

Pit   large sand pit located outside each barracks
                         where platoons do intense calisthenics as
                         punishment

pit call   punishment exercise conducted in a large
                         sand pit located outside each barracks;
                         usually involves push-ups, sit-ups, and
                         similar calisthenics activity

PMI   Primary Marksmanship Instructor; Marine
                         who teaches recruits how to accurately fire a
                         rifle and qualify with the M-16 rifle.

police sergeant   NCO charged with cleaning details and
                         materials

pot shack   area in the chow hall where dishes and pots
                         are cleaned

prac-ap   short-hand for practical application; term
                         describes actually performing a task such
                         as first aid as opposed to simply classroom
                         learning on the activity

Private	first enlisted rank; E-1
Pro / Con Marks	Proficiency and Conduct Marks; two-tiered system of rating Marines based on how well they perform their job and how well they behave; scores significantly impact promotions
PT	physical training, can be running, push-ups, or other calisthenics
PT recovery	the period after PT where recruits shower and change into cammies; in theory it is a rest period but in reality it is not
PT shower	brief shower after formal Physical Training is completed
pugil stick	a heavily padded training weapon that simulates close combat with a rifle and bayonet
PX	Post Exchange
quarterdeck	area of the squad bay in front of the Drill Instructor's office where recruits get smoked; can also be used as a verb as in "Recruit Schmukatelli lost his canteen and got quaterdecked for a half hour."
qual	short for qualify; as in qualify with a rifle
Qual Day	the day on the rifle range when recruits shoot for a score to qualify with the M-16
rappel	to descend from a wall or helicopter by rope

Recruit Schmukatelli	the boot camp equivalent of John Doe; refers to the generic recruit; often used by DIs or other personnel to explain how to do something
Rock Recruits	term used to describe recruits who are perceived as being intellectually deficient
Reveille	wake up time
road guards	recruits assigned to stop traffic while platoon crosses the road
RTF	Recruit Training Facility; location of classes on first-aid, Marine Corps history and the like; classrooms are modern and include a large video screen, stadium seating and air-conditioning
sand fleas	nasty little flies common on Parris Island that bite and pester recruits during drill and field training exercises
S.A.W. Gunner	Squad Automatic Rifleman; Marine who carries the M-249 light machine gun
Scribble	the assistant scribe
scuttlebutt	rumors
SDI	Senior Drill Instructor
Scribe	term used to describe a recruit designated to do administrative work for Drill Instructors

scuzz	a technique for cleaning the floor that requires recruits to lean over in a pyramid position and run up and down the squad bay on all fours pushing a rag on the deck
scuz rag	rag for cleaning squad bay
seabag	large green canvas bag used for storing gear and uniform items
secure	to lock up or put away
series	four platoons that train together
Senior Drill Instructor square away time	a term used to describe periods of time usually on Sunday morning or in the evenings before lights out, when recruits can polish their boots, organize their footlockers and prepare for the upcoming day
shelter half	half of a two-man tent
side-straddle-hops	military term for jumping jacks
Smoke	a term used to describe when the DIs personally and closely oversee an intense workout of one, some, or all of the recruits because of an infraction
snap in	taking a shooting position for long periods of time; designed to develop a consistent shooting position through muscle memory so that when you go to fire your weapon, your body instinctively knows where all its parts should be and you fire an accurate shot

SOI	School of Infantry, where Marines who have chosen to be infantryman go after boot camp to learn infantry tactics and skills
sound off	to yell loudly
squad bay	large room where all recruits in a platoon live; approximately one hundred feet long and thirty feet wide with approximately twenty bunk beds on each side of the squad bay
Squad Leaders	Recruits who march first in formation and who are responsible for making sure other recruits perform tasks correctly and quickly
square away	organize
SRB	Service Record Book, Marine Corps version of a personnel file
tactical re-load	reloading by changing magazines while moving from one shooting position to another
Taps	lights out; end of the day
Teufelhunden	German word which loosely translates to Devil Dog; was used to describe Marines at the Battle of Bellaeu Wood in WWI; genesis of the nickname Devil Dog to describe Marines
the rear	mainside; out of the field and back at main part of the base

tree line	any wooded area; the forest
UA	unauthorized absence; Marine Corps version of AWOL
unk	shorthand for unqualified; means that a recruit failed a test such as swim qualification of the rifle range
unsat	unsatisfactory
unsecure	unlocked or not properly stored
warrior's stance	the ready position in close combat training, similar to the position a boxer takes when preparing to punch
white cow	regular milk
Yellow Footprints	Four columns of footprints painted on the ground in a marching formation; when recruits get off the bus and arrive at boot camp they are immediately ordered to stand on a set of yellow footprints; doing so instantly organizes the new recruits into a platoon formation